Frederick County Virginia

DEED BOOK SERIES, VOLUME 7

Deed Books 19 and 20 1780-1785

Abstracted

Amelia C. Gilreath

HERITAGE BOOKS
2008

HERITAGE BOOKS
AN IMPRINT OF HERITAGE BOOKS, INC.

Books, CDs, and more—Worldwide

For our listing of thousands of titles see our website
at
www.HeritageBooks.com

Published 2008 by
HERITAGE BOOKS, INC.
Publishing Division
100 Railroad Ave. #104
Westminster, Maryland 21157

Copyright © 1995 Amelia C. Gilreath

All rights reserved. No part of this book may be reproduced or transmitted in any form or by any means, electronic or mechanical, including photocopying, recording or by any information storage and retrieval system without written permission from the author, except for the inclusion of brief quotations in a review.

International Standard Book Numbers
Paperbound: 978-1-58549-727-0
Clothbound: 978-0-7884-7182-7

FREDERICK COUNTY, VIRGINIA

DEED BOOK 19 [1780 - 1783]

(Abstracted)

Bk 19, p. 1 - 7 March 1780
    [Lease] Between Abraham Sovain of the Town of Winchester in County of Frederick [to] Elias Holding, Goaler of the County aforesaid ... consideration of five Shillings ... one moiety or half part of a certain Lott of Land in the Town of Winchester known by No. 44 on the east side of Cameron Street ... the whole being purchased by James Hog Jun. of James Wood dec'd. who obtained a Deed for the same from the Proprietor of Northern Neck and by the said James Hog conveyed to Joseph Jones who conveyed the same to Abraham Sovain ... Yielding and paying rent of one pepper corn on Lady day next ...
Wit: J. Peyton Jun.   Abraham Sovain
    Jno. Milton   Lidie (X) Sovain
    Will Kinkead
Recorded: 8 March 1780

Bk 19, p. 3 - 8 March 1780
    [Release] Between Abraham Sovain & Lydia his wife of Town of Winchester in County of Frederick [to] Elias Holding, Goaler of the County aforesaid ... consideration of eight hundred pounds ... Lot of Land in Town of Winchester (same as above) ...
Wit: same as above   Abraham Sovain
Recorded: 8 March 1780   Lidia (X) Sovain

Bk 19, p. 6 - 6 March 1780
    [Lease] Between Christopher Fry of Frederick County [to] John Duffield of the same place ... consideration of five shillings ... one Lott of Land in the addition to the Town of Winchester as laid out by James Wood Gent. dec'd. ... known by No. 3 ... Braddock Street on the west side ... which said Lott was conveyed by deeds of L & R from Mrs. Mary Wood widow of the above mentioned James Wood the 4th & 5th March 1773 to Abraham Bailey and by said Abraham Bailey conveyed to said Christopher Fry by deeds of L & R the 15th & 16th March 1776 ... Yielding and paying rent of one pepper corn on Lady day next ...
Wit: Thos. Wood   Christopher Fry
    Philip Woolwine
    Philip Helphinstin
Recorded: 8 March 1780

Bk 19, p. 8 - 7 March 1780
   [Release] Between Christopher Fry and Mary his wife of County of Frederick [to] John Duffield of the same place ... consideration of fifty pounds ... Lott in Town of Winchester ... No. 3 (same as above) ...
Wit: same as above   Christopher Fry
Recorded: 8 March 1780   Mary (X) Fry

Bk 19, p. 11 - 8 March 1780
   Between Mordicai Yarnall of Frederick County and Phebe his wife [to] Thomas Ferrel of the same place ... consideration of one hundred pounds ... a certain plantation or tract of land situate on the drains of Babbs Creek ... near the top of Babbs Mountain ... Containing two hundred and fifty five acres ...
Wit: none   Mordicai Yarnall
Recorded: 8 March 1780   Phebe Yarnall

Bk 19, p. 14 - 9 March 1780
   Between Alexander White of Frederick County and Elizabeth his wife [to] Robert White of County aforesaid ... consideration of four hundred pounds ... Tract of Land ... that is to say one plantation or tract of Land situate on both sides of Hoge Creek ... corner to John Lawrences land ... crossing Hoop Petticoat Gap Run ... Containing two hundred and sixty five acres ...
Wit: none   Alex. White
Recorded: 9 March 1780

Bk 19, p. 17 - 8 March 1780
   GREETINGS - I the said Thomas Hampton of Frederick County for and in consideration of the love good Will & affection which I have towards my step sons and daughters William Pollard Challen Dozzed Pollard Joseph Pollard Elisha Pollard and Nanny Pollard children of Frances Pollard who is now my wife have give and granted the following named negroes viz: one negro wench by name of Fanny & her five children Betty and Gerrad & her increase to be equally divided amongst them after the decease of their mother Frances my present wife ...
Wit: John (X) Nut   Thomas Hamton
   Swanson Lunsford
   Daniel Anderson
Recorded: 8 March 1780

Bk 19, p. 18 - 3 April 1780
   Between Joseph Wilkenson of County of Frederick and Mary his wife [to] Robert Lockart of the sd. County ... consideration of five thousand pounds ... tract of Land situate on both sides of back Creek ... in the whole four hundred acres after deducting there out one hundred acres which sd. Wilkenson sold and conveyed to Harrison Taylor ... Containing three hundred acres ...
Wit: J. Peyton Jun.   Joseph Wilkenson

Alex. White   Mary (X) Wilkenson
Robt. White
J. Gaml. Dowdall
Recorded: 4 April 1780

Bk 19, p. 21 - 3 April 1780
    Mary, apart from her husband, released Dower right to above land ...
                                                          Robt. White
                                                          J. Gaml. Dowdall

Bk 19, p. 21 - 1 April 1780
    Between Collumbus McDonald of County of Frederick [to] John Cunningham of County aforesaid ... consideration of one hundred & sixty pounds ... all the Right and title he the said Columbus McDonald hath by virtue of a Lease agreement to Edw. & Jost White by Lewis Neil for the term of ninety nine years bearing date 1st May 1770 ... corner to Abraham Neils lane ... corner joining Meredith Helm line ... Yielding and paying yearly one ear of Indian corn to said Columbus McDonald ...
Wit: John Kunhall (X)   Columb. (X) McDonald
  James Kunhall (X)   John (J) Cunningham
Recorded: 4 April 1780

Bk 19, p. 23 - 30 April 1780
    GREETINGS - Whereas Jacob Seabert and Mary Ann his wife by their (deed) in 1779 have sold and conveyed unto Alexander Drumgoole the fee simple Estate of and in one moiety part of a Certain Lott of Land situate in the borough of Winchester on the Westerly side of Cameron Street and known y the No. 31 together with one half part of the Out Lott in the commons of said Borough ... known by No. 30 ... Mary Ann the wife of within named Jacob Seabert now released dower right to said lotts.
                                                          Robt. White
                                                          Edw.d McGuire
Recorded: 2 March 1780   J. Gamal Dowdall

Bk 19, p. 25 - 3 March 1780
    Between John Varley and Catharine his wife of County of Chester and Colony of Pennsylvania [to] Jacob Varley son to said John Varley of the same place ... consideration of thirty seven pounds ... Tract of Land the same which was surveyed to John Lewis Beard and by him Assigned to Lewis Stephens and by him the said Lewis Stephens Transferred by Deed to sd John Varley and Catharine his wife situate lying and being on hogs Creek in the County of Frederick and Colony of Virginia ... survey thereof made (by) John Mauzy ... in George Rubles line ... containing two hundred and seventy six acres ...
Wit: Frederick Foose   John Varley
  Philip Rearly   Catharine (V) Varly
  Susanna Varly

Recorded: 2 May 1780

Bk 19, p. 28 - 6 March 1780
    [Lease] Between Henry Bower of Frederick County [to] Mordicai White of the County aforesaid ... consideration of five shillings ... Tract of Land containing four hundred and fifteen Acres be the same more or less situate lying and being on a drain of Cedar Creek ... survey thereof made by Peter Stephens ... was granted by Patent to the said Henry Bower the 18th March 1779 ... Yielding and paying rent of one pepper corn on Lady day next ...
Wit: Wm Womack   Henry (HB) Bower
   John Kean
Recorded: 2 May 1780

Bk 19, p. 30 - 7 March 1780
    [Release] Between Henry Bower and Dorothy his wife of Frederick County [to] Mordicai White of County aforesaid ... consideration of fifteen hundred pounds ... 415 Acres (same as above) ...
Wit: same as above   Henry (HB) Bower
Recorded: 2 May 1780   Dorothy (+) Bower

Bk 19, p. 33 - 12 April 1780
    [Lease] Between Mary Wood Executrix and Devisee of Col. James Wood late of Frederick County [to] Isaac Zane of Marlbro Iron works in County aforesaid ... consideration of five shillings ... three Lotts of Land situate lying and being on the southerly side of Boscowen Street in an addition to the Town of Winchester ... known by No. 7, 8 & 9 bounded by the East side of Stewart Street on the south side of Wolfe Street and on the west by the Land the sd Isaac Zane lately purchased of William Holliday including the water course which runs through the Town of Winchester ... Yielding and paying rent of one pepper corn on Lady day next ...
Wit: John Littler   Mary Wood
   Benj. Williams
   Robert Wood
   Alex. White
Recorded: 2 May 1780

Bk 19, p 35 - 13 April 1780
    [Release] Between Mary Wood Executrix and Devisee of Col. James Wood late of Frederick County [to] Isaac Zane Esq. of Marlbro Iron Works in County aforesaid ... consideration of three hundred pounds ... Three Lotts of Land (same as above) ...
Wit: same as above   Mary Wood
Recorded: 3 May 1780

Bk 19, p. 37 - 2 May 1780
    Between William Baylis Eldest Son and Heir at Law of John Baylis late of

County of Prince William Gentleman dec'd. [to] Abraham Sovain of the Borough of Winchester ... consideration of One thousand three hundred pounds ... a certain Lot or half acre of Land situate lying and being in an Addition to the Town of Winchester and numbered 203 ... which said Lot of Land was bequeathed to said William Baylis by the Last Will and Testament of said John Baylis dec'd. and recorded in the County of Prince William ...
Wit: J. Peyton Jr.   Will Baylis
    George Helm
    John Ritter
Recorded: 3 May 1780

Bk 19, p. 39 - 2 May 1780
    [Lease] Between Catharine Helphenstine relict of Peter Helphenstine late of County of Frederick dec'd. and Philip Helphenstine eldest son and Heir at Law of said Peter Helphenstine dec'd. they being acting Exors. of the last Will and Testament of said Decedent [to] Samuel May of County aforesaid ... consideration of five shillings ... Tract of land situate lying and being on the drains of Back Creek and known by the name of Brush Creek ... Containing one hundred and twenty seven Acres which said Tract of Land was granted to Joseph Trowbridge by Deed under the Hand and seal of the Right Honorable Thomas Lord Fairfax the 4th August 1764 and conveyed by said Trowbridge to John Leverison who conveyed same to David Heaton & said Heaton conveyed to Dennis Onan who conveyed same to Peter Helphenstine dec'd. ... Also one other tract of Land situate at the Fork of Brush Creek adjoining to the tract above mentioned ... in Joseph Watson's line ... corner to Dennis Onan ... containing four hundred and ninety eight acres which was granted to said Peter Helphenstine dec'd. by Deed from Rt. Hon.ble Thomas Lord Fairfax the 5th October 1778 ... Yielding and paying rent of one pepper corn on Lady day next ...
Wit: David Deadwick   Catharine (X) Helphenstine
    1 wit. signed in German   Philip Helphenstine
Recorded: 4 May 1780

Bk 19, p 40 - 3 May 1780
    [Release] Between Catharine Helphenstine Relict and Executrix of Peter Helphenstine late of County of Frederick and Philip Helphenstine Eldest son and Heir at Law and also Executor of said Peter Helphenstine dec'd. and Rebecca his wife [to] Samuel May of the said County ... consideration of Eleven hundred and twenty five pounds ... 127 Acre tract and 498 acre tract (same as above) ...
Wit: same as above   Catharine (X) Helphenstine
                                                            Philip Helphenstine
Recorded: 4 May 1780   Rebecca Helphenstine

Bk 19, p. 43 - 3 May 1780
    [Lease] Between James Keith of the Borough of Alexandria [to] John McDonald Eldest son and Heir at Law of Angus McDonald late of County of

Frederick ... consideration of five shillings ... all that Tract of land situate lying and being in County of Frederick ... corner to Col. Fairfax and near Hollingsworth's line ... containing Seventy acres it being part of a larger Tract Granted to William McMachen by Deed from the Proprietor of Northern Neck the 29th October 1753 and by said William McMachen conveyed to said James Keith by Deeds of L & R the 1st & 2nd Feb. 1770 ... Yielding and paying rent of one pepper corn on Lady day next.
Wit: none   Jas. Keith
Recorded: 4 May 1780

Bk 19, p. 45 - 4 May 1780
    [Release] Between James Keith of the Borough of Alexandria Esquire and ___ his wife [to] John McDonald eldest son and Heir at Law of Angus McDonald late of Frederick County ... consideration of One hundred pounds ... tract of Land containing 70 acres (same as above) ...
Wit: none   Jas. Keith
Recorded: 4 May 1780

Bk 19, p. 47 - 5 June 1780
    [Lease] Between Mary and Christian Nisewanger of County of Frederick [to] John Donaldson of the Town of Winchester ... consideration of five Shillings ... Part of a Tract of Land situate lying and being on the drains of Crooked run the said piece of Land is part of a larger Tract Containing 323 acres which was granted to said Mary and Christian Nisewanger by Deed under the hand and seal of the Right Honorable Thomas Lord Fairfax the 29th Sept. 1753 ... in the line of Henry Stephens ... corner to Peter Stephens patent near Lewis Stephens waggon road ... in the line of Edward Whitehead ... Containing one hundred and sixty one acres and a half ... Yielding and paying rent of one pepper corn on Lady day next ...
Wit: none   Mary (+) Nisewanger
Recorded: 6 June 1780   Christian Nisewanger

Bk 19, p. 48 - 6 June 1780
    [Release] Between Mary & Christian Nisewanger & Barbara his wife of County of Frederick [to] John Donaldson of the Town of Winchester ... consideration of one hundred & fifty pounds ... 164 1/2 acres (same as above) ...
Wit: none   Mary (+) Nisewanger
                                                                                                                        Christian Nisewanger
Recorded: 6 June 1780   Barbary (+) Nisewanger
    [Note: Lease shows 161 1/2 acres - Release shows 164 1/2 acres]

Bk 19, p. 50 - 1 May 1780
    [Lease] Between David Houseman of County of Berkeley in State of Virginia [to] George and Martin Houseman of County of Frederick ... consideration of five shillings ... all that part of a tract of Land lying on the drains of Opeckon and is part of a larger Tract containing 460 acres which was granted to William Cochran by Deed

from the Proprietor of Northern Neck ... the said Cochran conveyed to the said David Houseman by Deeds of L & R the 3rd and 4th August 1767 ... line of Col. Benjamin Grayson and corner to Nicholas Devolt ... corner to Grayson & Meridith Helm dec'd. ... containing two hundred & thirty acres ... Yielding and paying rent of one pepper corn on Lady day next ...
Wit: Wilson Stultz   David Houseman
    Philip (O) Stultz
    Joseph Day
Recorded: 6 June 1780

Bk 19, p. 51 - 2 May 1780
    [Release] Between David Houseman and Mary his wife of County of Berkeley in State of Virginia [to] George Houseman & Martin Houseman of County of Frederick ... consideration of fifty pounds ... 230 acres (same as above) ...
Wit: same as above   David Houseman
Recorded: 6 June 1780   Mary Houseman

Bk 19, p. 53 - 6 June 1780
    Between John Wolfe of County of Frederick and Elizabeth his wife [to] Charles Mynn Thruston Esq. of County aforesaid ... consideration of three thousand six hundred pounds ... a certain plantation situate on the western side of Shenandoah river containing Six hundred acres being part of forty thousand acres purchased by Jost Hite of Isaac and John Vanmetre and the same that was granted to Peter Wolfe by patent the 3rd October 1734 ... in a line of land belonging to the Honorable Robert Carter dec'd. ... the lands of Benjamin Burden ...
Wit: A. White   John Wolfe
Recorded: 6 June 1780   Elizabeth (X) Wolfe

Bk 19, p. 54 - 25 May 1780
    [Lease] Between William Glascock of County of Frederick [to] John Emmet of County aforesaid ... consideration of five shillings ... granted to farm let ... all that Lot of five acres of land Commonly called out Lotts known by No. 109 ... Yielding and paying rent of one grain of Indian Corn on the last day of the said term ...
Wit: Corn. Livingston   Wm Glascock
    Pat.k Shannon
    Dennis Bush
    John (#) Driver
Recorded: 6 June 1780

Bk 19, p. 55 - 26 May 1780
    [Release] Between William Glascock & Elizabeth Glascock of County of Frederick [to] John Emmet of County aforesaid ... consideration of two hundred pounds ... Lot of five acres (same as above) ...
Wit: same as above   Wm Glascock

Recorded: 6 June 1780   Elizabeth Glascock

Bk 19, p. 57 - 25 May 1780
    [Lease] Between William Glascock of County of Frederick [to] George Marker of County aforesaid ... consideration of five shillings ... granted to farm Lett ... all that Lot of five acres of land adjoining the Town of Stephensburg commonly called out Lott & known by No. 64 ... Yielding and paying rent of a grain of indian Corn on the last day of the said term ...
Wit: Corn. Livingston   Wm Glascock
    Patk. Shannon
    Dennis Bush
    John (#) Driver
Recorded: 6 June 1780

Bk 19, p. 58 - 26 May 1780
    [Release] Between Wm & Eliz. Glascock of County of Frederick [to] George Marker of County aforesaid ... consideration of two hundred pounds ... Lot of five acres of Land (same as above) ...
Wit: same as above   Wm Glascock
Recorded: 6 June 1780   Elizabeth Glascock

Bk 19, p. 59 - 25 May 1780
    [Lease] Between John Emit of County of Frederick [to] William Glascock of County aforesaid ... consideration of five shillings ... all that Lot or half acre of Land in the Town of Stephensburg known by No. 60 ... Yielding and paying rent of one grain of indian Corn on the last day of said term ...
Wit: Corn. Livingston   John Emitt
    Patk. Shannon
    George Marker
    Isaac Stephens
    John (#) Driver
Recorded: 6 June 1780

Bk 19, p. 61 - 26 May 1780
    [Release] Between John Emett and Mary his wife of County of Frederick [to] William Glascock of County aforesaid ... consideration of two hundred pounds ... Lot of one half acre (same as above) ...
Wit: same as above   John Emett
Recorded: 6 June 1780   Mary (M) Emett

Bk 19, p. 62 - 25 May 1780
    [Lease] Between George Marker of County of Frederick [to] John Emmet of County aforesaid ... consideration of five shillings ... all that Lot of five acres of Land commonly called out Lotts ... on the East side of Rabbit Lane ... known by Lot No.

110 containing five acres ... Yielding and paying one grain of indian Corn on the last day of said term ...
Wit: Wm Glascock George Marker
   Patk. Shannon
   John (#) Driver
   Isaac Stephens
Recorded: 6 June 1780

Bk 19, p. 63 - 26 May 1780
   [Release] Between George Marker & Ann his wife of County of Frederick [to] John Emmett of County aforesaid ... consideration of two hundred pounds ... Lott of five acres (same as above) ...
Wit: same as above George Marker
Recorded: 6 June 1780 Ann (X) Marker

Bk 19, p. 65 - 5 May 1780
   [Lease] Between John Neill Jr of County of Frederick [to] Henry Sims of County aforesaid ... consideration of five shillings ... all that part of a tract of land lying on the drains of Opeckon and is the part of the tract whereon said Neill now dwells ... Containing one hundred acres ... Yielding and paying rent of one pepper corn on lady day next ...
Wit: none John Neill
Recorded: 6 June 1780

Bk 19, p. 66 - 6 May 1780
   [Release] Between John Neill Jun. and Lydia his wife of County of Frederick [to] Henry Sims of County aforesaid ... consideration of two hundred and fifty pounds ... 100 acres (same as above) ...
Wit: none John Neill
Recorded: 6 June 1780 Lydia (X) Neill

Bk 19, p. 68 - 5 June 1780
   [Lease] Between John Stonebridge of County of Frederick [to] Casper Rinker of the same place ... consideration of five shillings ... a certain tract of about two hundred and twenty four acres & a half of Land lying on both sides of back Creek ... being part of a greater tract granted to said John Stonebridge assignee of George Julian son and Heir at Law of John Julian dec'd. by virtue of a patent from out of his Lordships Office the 7th Dec. 1779 ... two hundred and twenty four acres and a half ... in James Odells line ... in John McCools line ... Yielding and paying rent of one pepper corn on Lady day next ...
Wit: John McCoole John (X) Stonebridge
   Saml. Lewis
   Jacob Rinker
Recorded: 6 June 1780

Bk 19, p. 69 - 6 June 1780

[Release] Between John Stonebridge and Mary his wife of County of Frederick [to] Casper Rinker of the same place ... consideration of one hundred and twenty pounds ... 224 acres (same as above) ...

Wit: same as above
Recorded: 6 June 1780

John (X) Stonebridge
Mary Stonebridge

Bk 19, p. 71 - 10 Oct. 1779

Between William Gowdy and Magdalena his wife of County of Frederick [to] Robert Gamble of the same place ... Whereas said William Gowdy and Magdaline his wife by Deeds of L & R the 11th & 12th June 1778 did grant bargain and sell unto said Robert Gamble for the consideration in the said Deed of Release mentioned two hundred and Seventy two Acres of land ... being the plantation where the said William Gowdy then lived ... And whereas the said Court of the said County failed to sit several months ... which means the same were not recorded in the time limited by Law ... NOW this Indenture in consideration of five shillings ... the said plantation or Tract of Land in the Deeds of L & R above mentioned ...

Wit: Corns. Livingston
  John Emmett
  Lewis Stephens
Recorded: 6 June 1780

William Gowdy
Mary Magdaline (X) Gowdy

Bk 19, p. 73 - 5 June 1780

[Lease] Between Bryan Bruin of Winchester [to] Isaac Zane of Marlbro Iron Works Esquire of the other part ... consideration of five shillings ... a certain plantation Tract of Land situate on Turkey run a drain of Cedar Creek in County of Frederick ... in Lewis Stephens line ... containing two hundred and seventy nine acres ... Yielding and paying rent of one pepper corn on Lady day next ...

Wit: none
Recorded: 6 June 1780

Bryan Bruin

Bk 19, p. 74 - 6 June 1780

[Release] Between Bryan Bruin of Winchester [to] Isaac Zane of Marlbro Iron Works Esquire ... consideration of two hundred pounds ... 279 acres (same as above) being the same that was Granted to said Bryan Bruin by deed from the proprietors Office the 21st May 1763 ...

Wit: none
Recorded: 6 June 1780

Bryan Bruin

Bk 19, p. 76 - 7 Dec. 1779

GREETINGS - Whereas Isaac Foster and Margaret his wife by their certain Indentures of L & R the 5th & 6th April 1779 conveyed unto Robert Aldridge the fee simple estate of a certain Tract of Land situate in said County containing two hundred and three acres ... Margaret Foster now releases right of Dower ...

Recorded: 6 June 1780

Edward McGuire
Joseph Longacre

Bk 19, p. 77 - 3 July 1780
    Between Bryan Bruin of the Town of Winchester County of Frederick [to] Leanard Hingle of Berkeley County ... consideration of twelve hundred pounds ... a certain plantation situate on Timber Ridge ... containing four hundred acres being the same that was granted unto said Bryan Bruin from the Proprietors Office the 21st August 1779 ...
Wit: none   Bryan Bruin
Recorded: 4 July 1780

Bk 19, p. 79 - 9 Feb 1780
    [Lease] Between William Harill and Susannah his wife of County of Frederick [to] Allen Wiley of County of Spotsylvania ... consideration of five shillings ... Tract of Land lying and being on the South River of Shanandoe ... in which bounds there is contained 83 acres of land it being part of a tract of 416 acres granted to Thomas Chestor ... Thomas Chestor being possessed with said land did in his last Will and Testament authorize and apoint (sic) Charles Buck and James McKay his Exors. to grant and convey 416 acres to Thomas David Edward Martin and Nathan Smith by their deed the 14th Sept. 1756 said Smiths conveyed the above said 83 acres to said William Harrell by their deed the 2nd March 1776 said William Harrell doth convey unto said Allen Wiley ... Yielding and paying rent of one pepper corn on Lady day next ...
Wit: John Harrell   William (X) Harrell
    David (X) Smith
    John (X) Featheringal
    David Harrell
Recorded: 4 July 1780

Bk 19, p. 80 - 9 Feb. 1780
    [Release] Between William Harrell and Susannah his wife of County of Frederick [to] Allen Wiley of County of Spotsylvania ... consideration of three thousand pounds ... 83 acres (same as above) ...
Wit: same   William (X) Harrell
Recorded: 4 July 1780

Bk 19, p. 83 - 9 Feb. 1780
    [Lease] Between William Harrell & Susannah his wife of County of Frederick [to] Allen Wiley of County of Spotsylvania ... consideration of five shillings ... tract of Land lying and being on the South river Shando (sic) ... corner to Nathan Smith Lot ... corner to David Smith ... in which bounds there is contained 84 acres being part of a Tract of 416 acres granted to Thomas Chester ... said Chester did by his last Will and Testament authorize Charles Buck and James McKay his Exors. to convey

416 acres thereof to Thomas David Edward Martin and Nathan Smith by their deed of L & R the 14th & 15th Sept. 1756 said Smiths conveyed the above mentioned 84 acres to said William Harrell ... Yielding and paying rent of one pepper corn on lady day next ...
Wit: John (X) Featheringal   William (X) Harrell
     John Harrell
     David (X) Smith
     David Harrell
Recorded: 4 July 1780

Bk 19, p. 84 - 9 Feb. 1780
     [Release] Between William Harill & Susannah his wife of County of Frederick [to] Allen Wily of County of Spotsylvania ... consideration of 3000 pounds ... 84 acres (same as above) ... in Henry Clouds line ...
Wit: same as above   William (X) Harrell
Recorded: 4 July 1780

Bk 19, p. 86 - 18 May 1780
     [Lease] Between John Seyeant of County of Frederick [to] James Ross of County aforesaid ... consideration of five shillings ... all that part of a tract of land lying on the Spring head of Sleepy Creek ... containing one hundred and Eighty four acres ... Yielding and paying rent of one pepper corn on Lady day next ...
Wit: Lewis (L) Will   John (X) Seyeant
     Joseph Day
     William Goiney
Recorded: 1 August 1780

Bk 19, p. 88 - 19 May 1780
     [Release] Between John Seyeant and Rachel his wife of County of Frederick [to] James Ross of County of Frederick ... consideration of fourteen hundred pounds ... Tract of Land being part of a larger tract containing three hundred and eighty five acres granted to said John Seyeant by deed under the hand and Seal of the Right Honorable Thomas Lord Fairfax the 3rd Feb. 1778 ... 184 acres (same as above) ...
Wit: same as above   John (X) Seyeant
Recorded: 1 Aug. 1780   Rachel (R) Seyeant

Bk 19, p. 90 - 1 Aug. 1780
     Between Thomas Foley and Rachel his wife of County of Frederick [to] Jacob Baker of County aforesaid ... consideration of four thousand pounds ... Tract of Land containing ninety eight acres situate lying and being on the South side of the North River of Shannando ... line of Abraham Kendrick ...
Wit: Robert Allen   Thos. (T) Foley
     John Nisewanger   Rachel (R) Foley
     John Allen

Recorded: 1 Aug. 1780

Bk 19, p. 92 - 16 June 1780
  Between Robert Wilson and Mary his wife late Mary Calvert Relict of Robert Calvert dec'd., Isaiah Calvert Eldest son and heir at Law of said Robert, and Margaret his wife of County of Frederick [to] Nicholas Airheart late of Lancaster County in State of Pennsylvania ... consideration of eight Thousand pounds ... all their residue in a tract of Land which was granted to John Calvert dec'd. by Patent form the Crown Situate in County of Frederick and containing eight hundred and fifty acres after deducting 215 acres which was taken and conveyed to William Glover and 206 acres which was conveyed to Samuel Calvert ... there remains 429 acres ... by a survey made by Richard Rigg there appears to be but 327 acres ...

Wit: Edward McGuire	Robert Wilson
David Kennedy	Mary (X) Wilson
John Thomas	Isaiah Calvert
J. Peyton Jr.	Margaret Calvert

Recorded: 1 Aug. 1780

Bk 19, p. 94 - 16 June 1780
  Mary & Margaret wives of within named Robert & Isaiah release Dower right to above land ...
                Edward McGuire
                David Kennedy

Bk 19, p. 95 - 23 July 1780
  [Lease] Between Thomas Wright of County of Frederick [to] Asa Clevinger of said County ... consideration of five shillings ... all that part of a tract of Land Containing one hundred and sixty one acres and appears by deed from under the hand and Seal of the Right Honorable Thomas Lord Fairfax the 7th Nov. 1754 ... corner of a division between said Thomas Wright and Jonathan Wright ... corner to Richard Haines ... containing seventy one acres ... Yielding and paying rent of one pepper corn on Lady day next ...
Wit: Simeon Haines   Thomas Wright
 Wm Bendles (?)
 Jos. Day
Recorded: 1 Aug. 1780

Bk 19, p. 96 - 24 July 1780
  [Release] Between Thomas Wright of County of Frederick [to] Asa Clevinger of the said County ... consideration of one hundred and sixty pounds ... 71 acres (same as above) ...
Wit: same as above   Thomas Wright
Recorded: 1 Aug. 1780

Bk 19, p. 98 - 23 July 1780
    [Lease] Between Isaac Sutherland of County of Frederick [to] George Hutt of the County aforesaid ... consideration of five shillings ... all that part of a tract of Land ... which was granted unto said Isaac Sutherland by deed the 2nd July 1777 ... containing ten acres ... Yielding and paying rent of one pepper corn on Lady day next.
Wit: James Abernathy   Isaac (X) Sutherland
   Ruth Sutherland
   Jos. Day
Recorded: 1 Aug. 1780

Bk 19, p. 100 - 24 July 1780
    [Release] Between Isaac Sutherland and Sarah his wife of County of Frederick [to] George Hutt of County aforesaid ... consideration of twenty pounds ... 10 acres (same as above) ...
Wit: same as above   Isaac (X) Sutherland
Recorded: 1 Aug. 1780   Sarah (X) Sutherland

Bk 19, p. 102 - 24 July 1780
    [Lease] Between John Seyeant of County of Frederick [to] Lewis Wills of County aforesaid ... consideration of five shillings ... all that part of a Tract of Land lying on the waters of Sleepy Creek and is part of a larger Tract Granted to said John Seyeant by Deed the 3rd Feb. 1778 ... corner to James Ross ... containing two hundred and one acres ... Yielding and paying rent one pepper corn on Lady day next.
Wit: George Houseman   John (X) Seyeant
   Ruth Sutherland
   Joseph Day
Recorded: 1 Aug. 1780

Bk 19, p. 103 - 23 July 1780
    [Release] Between John Seyeant and Rachael his wife of County of Frederick [to] Lewis Wills of County aforesaid ... consideration of one hundred pounds ... 201 acres (same as above) ...
Wit: same as above   John (#) Seyeant
Recorded: 1 Aug. 1780   Rachel (R) Seyeant

Bk 19, p. 105 - 27 July 1780
    Between William Hankins and Jane his wife of County of Frederick [to] John Sharpe of County aforesaid ... consideration of five hundred pounds ... Tract of land Containing one hundred and forty six acres being part of a greater tract containing three hundred and fifty nine acres whereon said William Hankins lives ... corner to Thomas Churchman ...
Wit: Thomas Churchman   William (T) Hankins
   Patrick Quinn   Jane (|) Hankins
Recorded: 1 Aug. 1780

Bk 19, p. 107 - 23 July 1780

    [Lease] Between James Boys of County of Youghagania in State of Pennsylvania [to] William Frost of County of Frederick ... consideration of five shillings ... Tract of Land lying and being in County of Frederick on both sides of Babbs Creek which said tract was granted to said James Boys by Deed under the hand and Seal of the Right Honorable Thomas Lord Fairfax the 5th Jan. 1771 ... corner to William Frost and Thomas Province ... containing fifty five acres ... Yielding and paying rent of one pepper corn on lady day next ...

Wit: Waltr. Moffett   James Boys
   Jos. Day
   Geo. J. Troutwick
Recorded: 1 Aug. 1780

Bk 19, p. 109 - 24 July 1780

    [Release] Between James Boys and Mary his wife of County of Youghagana (sic) in State of Pennsylvania [to] William Frost of County of Frederick ... consideration of fifty pounds ... 55 acres (same as above) ...

Wit: same as above   James Boys
Recorded: 1 Aug. 1780   Mary (O) Boys

Bk 19, p. 111 - 19 July 1780

    [Lease] Between James Boys of County of Yohagana in Commonwealth of Virginia [to] George Bond of Berkeley County in the said Commonwealth ... consideration of five shillings ... all that tract of land containing three hundred and twenty seven acres lying and being on both sides of Babbs run a branch of Buck Creek in Frederick County ... granted to said James Boys by deed under the hand and Seal of the Right Honorable Thomas Lord Fairfax the 14th June 1780 ... Yielding and paying rent of one pepper corn on Lady day next ...

Wit: Waltr. Moffett   James Boys
   Peter Blackford
   Geo. J. Troutwick
Recorded: 1 Aug. 1780

Bk 19, p. 113 - 20 July 1780

    [Release] Between James Boys and Mary his wife of Yohagana County in Commonwealth of Virginia [to] George Bond of County of Berkeley in said Commonwealth ... consideration of Seven Thousand two hundred pounds ... 327 acres (same as above) ... corner to Azeriah Pugh ... in Mordicai Walkers Line ...

Wit: same as above   James Boys
Recorded: 1 Aug. 1780   Mary (O) Boys

Bk 19, p. 116 - 31 July 1780

    [Lease] Between James Boys of County of Youghagana in State of Pennsylvania [to] Robert Powell of County of Frederick ... consideration of five

shillings ... all that tract of land lying near back Creek which was granted to said Boys by deed the 13th June 1780 ... containing two hundred and Sixty five acres ... Yielding and paying rent of one pepper corn on Lady day next ...
Wit: none
Recorded: 1 Aug. 1780
James Boys

Bk 19, p. 117 - 1 Aug. 1780
[Release] Between James Boys and Mary his wife of County of Youghagana in State of Pennsylvania [to] Robert Powell of County of Frederick ... consideration of fifty pounds ... 265 acres (same as above) ...
Wit: none
Recorded: 1 Aug. 1780
James Boys
Mary (O) Boys

Bk 19, p. 119 - 9 Jan. 1778
[Lease] Between William Gilkeson of County of Lancaster in Province of Pennsylvania [to] John Gilkeson of County of Frederick ... consideration of five shillings ... a certain plantation situate lying and being in said County of Frederick ... corner to Stephen Hotzenpiler ... corner to James Vance & David Vance ... containing two hundred and twenty acres of which said plantation was conveyed to James Wilson dec'd. by deeds of L & R from Robert Wilson and Ganala his wife the 3rd & 4th June (illegible roman numerals) and twenty acres thereof being part of a tract of five hundred and forty three acres since conveyed to said James Wilson by said Robert Wilson and the whole as above was conveyed by said James Wilson and Margery his wife to said William Gilkeson by deeds of L & R the 5th & 6th Dec. 1769 ... Yielding and paying rent of one pepper corn on Lady day next ...
Wit: Thos. Wood
   Archd. McDonald
   Samuel Calvert
Recorded: 1 Aug. 1780
William Gilkeson

Bk 19, p. 121 - 10 Jan. 1780
[Release] Between William Gilkeson and Margaret his wife of County of Lancaster in Province of Pennsylvania [to] John Gilkeson of County of Frederick ... consideration of four hundred pounds ... 220 acres (same as above) ...
Wit: same as above
Recorded: 1 Aug. 1780
William Gilkeson

Bk 19, p. 124 - 18 July 1780
Between Henry Redman and Sarah his wife [to] Charles Mynn Thruston all of County of Frederick ... WHEREAS Peter Wolfe late of Wolfes Marsh in said County dec'd. by his last Will and Testament bequeathed unto said Sarah Redman his daughter all that tract of land whereon the said Henry Redman and said Sarah his wife now live during her natural life containing one hundred and eighty acres ... situate lying and being on Wolfes Marsh aforesaid ... NOW THIS INDENTURE for

and in consideration of two thousand eight hundred pounds ... all that above mentioned tract of land ...
Wit: Geo. Seaborn
    Saml. (X) Romine
    Jos. Delany
Recorded: 1 Aug. 1780

Henry (R) Redman
Sarah (S) Redman

Bk 19, p. 126 - 7 Dec. 1779
    Between James Carter and Ann his wife of Frederick County [to] Jacob Sowers of said County ... consideration of one thousand six hundred pounds ... Tract of Land ... containing two hundred and forty two acres ... corner to Heirs of John Calvert dec'd. in the line of Isaac Hollingsworth ... corner to Isaac & George Hollingsworth.
Wit: Joseph Holmes
    Robert Throckmorton
    David Kennedy
    J. Peyton Jr.
Recorded: 1 Aug. 1780

James Carter
Ann (A) Carter

Bk 19, p. 127 - 7 Dec. 1779
    The within mentioned Ann privily and apart from said James her husband released Dower right to said Land ...
Robert Throckmorton
Joseph Holmes

Bk 19, p. 128 - 5 June 1780
    [Lease] Between Francis Tygart of County of Hampshire and State of Virginia [to] Joshua Poiles (Pyles) of the town of Winchester ... consideration of five shillings ... one certain Lot or half acre of Land situate lying & being in a new Addition to the town of Winchester in County of Frederick (No. 155) as survey made by Mr. John Bailey ... granted to Jacob Castleman by Patent from the Proprietors Office the 15th May 1753 ... said Jacob Castleman by Deeds of L & R in 1770 conveyed to said Francis Tazzior (sic) ... Yielding and paying rent of one ear of Indian Corn on the Last day of said term ...
Wit: none
Recorded: 2 Aug. 1780

Francis Taggart

Bk 19, p. 129 - 6 June 1780
    [Release] Between Francis Taggeor of County of Hampshire and State of Virginia [to] Joshua Poiles (Pyles) of the Town of Winchester ... consideration of two thousand Pounds ... Lot of Land containing one half acre (same as above) ...
Wit: none
Recorded: 2 Aug. 1780

Francis Taggart

Bk 19, p. 132 - 11 Nov. 1774
    [Lease] Between Abraham Ferree of Lancaster County in the Province of

Pennsylvania [to] Benjamin Fry of County of Frederick ... consideration of five shillings ... three several Tracts of land situate lying and being on both sides of Cedar Creek in Counties of Frederick & Dunmore (late Frederick) ... the whole containing five hundred & seventy four acres being the same Tracts of Land that were conveyed by Paul Froman to said Abraham Ferree by Deeds of L & R the 2nd & 3rd Nov. 1767 ... Viz: Three hundred acres thereof being part of John Bransons patent for one thousand acres ... two hundred and fourteen acres thereof joining the Little North Mountain on drains of the (Cedar) Creek ... Corner to Paul Fromans patented Lands ... in the line of Joseph Fawcet ... sixty acres the remaining part of the above 574 acres being part of a larger tract of 353 acres lying on Fromans run one of the drains of Cedar Creek ... opposite Fromans Mill ... Yielding and paying rent of one pepper corn on Lady day next ...

Wit: Isaac Zane Abraham Ferree
　Richd. Rigg
　Jno. Croudson
　Jacob Fry
　William Carthrae
　Benj. Williams
Recorded: 3 Aug. 1780

Bk 19, p. 134 - 12 Nov. 1774
　[Release] Between Abraham Ferree and Elizabeth his wife of Lancaster County in Province of Pennsylvania [to] Benjamin Fry of County of Frederick ... consideration of nine hundred and seventy five pounds ... 574 acres (same as above).
Wit: same as above Abraham Ferree
Recorded: 3 Aug. 1780

Bk 19, p. 137 - 3 Aug. 1780
　KNOW all men by these present that we Benjamin Rutherford Robert Wood and Joseph Richardson are held and firmly bound unto John Smith Benjamin Seowick George Noble and James Barnell Genlm. Justices for County of Frederick in the full sum of five thousand pounds ... The Condition of the above obligation is such that the above bound Benjamin Rutherford is appointed vendue Master for said County ...
Wit: none Ben Rutherford
　　Robt. Wood
Recorded: 3 Aug. 1780 Jos. Richardson

Bk 19, p. 138 - 12 May 1780
　ARTICLES of agreement - Between Isaac Zane Esq. of Frederick County and Captain Samuel Gilkeson of Winchester of County aforesaid ... WHEREAS said Isaac Zane is about to erect a Water Grist Mill on his Land adjacent to the Burgh of Winchester which will rinder it necessary to cary the water from said Mill through the Lots of said Samuel Gilkeson ... NOW THIS INDENTURE Witnesseth that said

Samuel Gilkeson in Order to promote the above undertaking for the consideration hereafter mentioned doth agree to permit said Isaac Zane to dig on the northerly side of the present water course from Stewart to Washington Street through the lots of said Gilkeson ... In consideration said Isaac Zane to obligate himself to convey to the dairy of said Gilkeson a perpetual stream of water ... to be conveyed in troughs underground which are to be kept in repair by said Isaac Zane ...

Wit: Edward McGuire   Saml. Gilkeson
   Alexander White   Isaac Zane
   William Campbell
   William McGuire
Recorded: 3 Aug. 1780

Bk 19, p. 139 - 4 Sept. 1780

[Lease] Between James Jackson of County of Frederick [to] George Beamer of County aforesaid ... consideration of five shillings ... Tract of land situate lying and being on the drains of Buffaloe lick run a drain of Opeckon ... corner to Samuel Sample and on John Curlets line ... corner to Robert Glass ... containing ninety five acres & a half which said tract of land was granted to said James Jackson by deed the 26th Aug. 1771 from the Proprietor of Northern Neck ... Yielding and paying rent of one pepper corn on Lady day next ...

Wit: none   James (X) Jackson
Recorded: 5 Sept. 1780

Bk 19, p. 140 - 5 Sept. 1780

[Release] Between James Jackson and Eleanor his wife of County of Frederick [to] George Beamer of the County aforesaid ... consideration of two thousand one hundred and twenty five pounds ... one James Wilson's line ... 95 1/2 acres (same as above) ...

Wit: none   James (X) Jackson
Recorded: 5 Sept. 1780   Eleanor (X) Jackson

Bk 19, p. 143 - 4 Sept. 1780

KNOW all men by these presents that I Samuel Bishop for and in consideration of thirteen hundred pounds paid by Solomon Bishop do hereby relinquish unto said Solomon Bishop all my estate right title interest whatsoever in the tract of Land within mentioned under the rent restrictions covenants in the Lease mentioned ... for and during the remainder of the term and time therein mentioned from this estate ...

Wit: J. Peyton Jr.   Samuel Bishop
   Columbus (X) McDonald
   Thomas Rootes
   Jno. Thomas
Recorded: 5 Sept. 1780

Bk 19, p. 144 - 5 Sept. 1780

    Between George Goos and Mary his wife of County of Frederick [to] Michael Gardner Jacob Bickster /Bixter and John Smith of County aforesaid Trustees for a dutch Church and Schoolhouse on the land of this Indenture ... consideration of five shillings ... three acres of Land for the above purpose of a Dutch Church and Schoolhouse Jointly for the use of both the Lutheran and Calvinists Sects ... survey make by Mr. Thomas Rutherford ... which said three acres are part of a larger Tract of Land containing three hundred and ten acres granted to said George Goos by Thomas Lord Fairfax the 12th Oct. 1767 ...

Wit: none   George Goose

Recorded: 5 Sept. 1780

Bk 19, p. 146 - 23 Oct. 1780

    [Lease] Between John Gaddis Son and Heir at Law and Executor of William Gaddis dec'd. and Priscilla widow and relict and executrix of said William Gaddis dec'd. of County of Yohogania and Commonwealth of Virginia [to] William Hunshaw of Berkeley in Commonwealth aforesaid ... consideration of five shillings ... all that Tract of Land situate lying and being in County of Frederick ... Granted to the said William Gaddis dec'd. by the Right Hon.ble Thomas Lord Fairfax the 9th March 1752 ... also one other tract of Land adjoining the former Granted to said William Gaddis dec'd. by deed of Gift from Henry Bowen the 12th June 1750 ... in the line of Nicholas Henshaw ... in George Hobsons line ... corner to Henry Bowen ... containing one hundred and thirty nine acres ... Yielding and paying rent of one pepper corn on lady day next ...

Wit: James Wilson   John Gaddis
      George Cunningham   Priscilla Gaddis
      James Cowdon
      Edward Chapman

Recorded: 7 Nov. 1780

Bk 19, p. 148 - 24 Oct. 1780

    [Release] Between John Gaddis son and Heir at Law and Executor of William Gaddis dec'd. and Parcilla (sic) Gaddis widow and relict and Executrix of said William Gaddis dec'd. of County of Yohogania and Commonwealth of Virginia [to] William Henshaw of Berkeley County in Commonwealth aforesaid ... consideration of two hundred pounds ... 139 acres (same as above) ...

Wit: same as above   John Gaddis

Recorded: 7 Nov. 1780   Priscilla Gaddis

Bk 19, p. 150 - 6 Nov. 1780

    [Lease] Between Steven Myers of County of Frederick [to] Leonard Myers of County aforesaid ... consideration of five hundred pounds ... tract of Land containing ninety & half acres ... line of Stephen Myers deeded land ... Yielding and paying one grain of Indian Corn on the last day of said term ...

Wit: Wm Glascock Jr.　　　　　　　　　　　　Stephen Miers
　Jacob Miers
Recorded: 7 Nov. 1780

Bk 19, p. 151 - 7 Nov. 1780
　　[Release] Between Steven Myers and Elizabeth his wife of County of Frederick [to] Leonard Myers of County aforesaid ... consideration of five hundred pounds ... 90 1/2 acres (same as above) ...
Wit: same as above　　　　　　　　　　　　Stephen Myers
Recorded: 7 Nov. 1780　　　　　　　　　　　Elizabeth Myers

Bk 19, p. 153 - 7 Nov. 1780
　　Between Robert Glass and Sarah his wife of Parish of Frederick and County of Frederick [to] Peter Moore of the same Parish and County ... consideration of two Thousand seven hundred and Fifty pounds ... parcel of Land containing one hundred and eleven acres ... being part of a tract of two hundred and twenty three acres granted by the Lord Proprietor of Northern Neck to Thomas Wilson by deed the 4th Nov. (illegible roman numerals) ... Thomas Wilson conveyed to said Robert Glass by deeds of L & R the 5th & 6th April 1762 ...
Wit: none　　　　　　　　　　　　　　　　Robert Glass
Recorded: 7 Nov. 1780　　　　　　　　　　　Sarah Glass

Bk 19, p. 155 - 7 Nov. 1780
　　Between Robert Glass and Sarah his wife of Parish of Frederick and County of Frederick [to] Benedick Leadey of the same Parish and County ... consideration of two Thousand Seven hundred and Fifty pounds ... Tract of Land containing one hundred and twelve acres situate lying and being in Parish and County aforesaid being part of a tract of two hundred and twenty three acres granted by the Lord Proprietor of the Northern Neck to Thomas Wilson by deed the 4th Nov. (illegible roman numerals) ... and by said Thomas Wilson sold and conveyed to said Robert Glass by deeds of L & R the 5th & 6th April 1762 ...
Wit: none　　　　　　　　　　　　　　　　Robert Glass
Recorded: 7 Nov. 1780　　　　　　　　　　　Sarah Glass

Bk 19, p. 157 - 5 Sept. 1780
　　Between John Tharp and Priscilla his wife and Andrew Tharp of the Parish of Frederick and County of Frederick [to] Andrew Redd of the same Parish and County ... consideration of seven hundred pounds ... Tract of Land whereon the said Andrew Redd now lives ... containing three hundred acres it being part of two Tracts of Land granted by the Right Honorable Thomas Lord Fairfax proprietor of the Northern Neck to Zebulon Tharp by deeds the 2nd March & the 21st Oct. 1756 and by said Zebulon Tharp sold and conveyed to said John Tharp by Deed the 4th Dec. 1778 ... in William Evans line ... corner to George Wright ...
Wit: none　　　　　　　　　　　　　　　　John Tharp

Recorded: 7 Nov. 1780   Priscilla Tharp

Bk 19, p. 159 - 1 Nov. 1780
    [Lease] Between John Hite of County of Frederick [to] William Glascock of County aforesaid ... consideration of five shillings ... all that Lot or half acre of Land in the Town of Stephensburg ... known by No. 62 ... Yielding and paying rent of a grain of Indian Corn on the last day of said term ...
Wit: Micajah Hughes   Jno. Hite
   John Barrow
   Asa Clevinger
Recorded: 7 Nov. 1780

Bk 19, p. 160 - 2 Nov. 1780
    [Release] Between John Hite of County of Frederick [to] William Glascock Jun. of County aforesaid ... consideration of forty five pounds ... Lot No. 62 in the Town of Stephensburg (same as above) ...
Wit: same as above   Jno. Hite
Recorded: 7 Nov. 1780

Bk 19, p. 162 - __ day of __ 1780
    [Lease] Between Col. John Hite of Frederick County [to] Micajah Hughes of the same place ... consideration of five shillings ... a certain Lot of half an acre of Land situate in the Town of Stephensburg together with an out Lot of five acres in the Common of the said Town ... Lot of half acre known by No. 27 and said out Lot of the said Commons known by No. 125 ... which said Lots were conveyed to said John Hite by deed from Lewis Stephens proprietor of the said Town ... Yielding and paying rent of one pepper corn on Lady day next ...
Wit: Wm Glascock Jr.   Jno. Hite
   Asa Clevinger
   John Barrow
Recorded: 7 Nov. 1780

Bk 19, p. 163 - __ day of __ 1780
    [Release] Between Col. John Hite of Frederick County [to] Micajah Hughes of the same place ... consideration of Seven hundred and twenty pounds ... Half acre Lot No. 27 and out Lot No. 125 in the Town of Stephensburg (same as above) ...
Wit: same as above   Jno. Hite
Recorded: 7 Nov. 1780

Bk 19, p. 165 - 24 June 1780
    Between John Moxley and Ann his wife and Bartholomew Johnston and Abigail his wife all of the State of Maryland and County of Montgomery [to] Zepheniah Wood of the same State and County aforesaid ... consideration of three hundred and seventy five pounds ... part of a tract of Land situate in Frederick

County in Virginia on the drains of Sleepy Creek & Isaacs Creek ... containing two hundred acres of Land ...
Wit: Ens. Campbell
   Cha Hungerford
   William Taylor
Recorded: 7 Nov. 1780

Jno. Moxley
Anna (X) Moxley
Bartholomew Johnson
Abigail (X) Johnson

Bk 19, p. 167 - 14 June 1780

Between John Moxley and Ann his wife and Bartholomew Johnson and Abigail his wife of State of Maryland and County of Montgomery [to] Robert McCrea and Robert Mease of Fairfax County in Virginia ... consideration of two thousand pounds ... part of a Tract of Land situate in Frederick County on the drains of Sleepy Creek and Isaacs Creek ... in John Luptons line ... corner to Lupton and Robert Murphy ... containing four hundred and eighty seven Acres of Land ...
Wit: Ens. Campbell
   Chas. Hungerford
   William Taylor
Recorded: 8 Nov. 1780

Jno. Moxley
Ann Moxley
Bartho. Johnston
Abigail (X) Johnston

Bk 19, p. 170 - 2 Jan. 1781

KNOW all men by these present that we Robert Throckmorton Thomas Throckmorton Gabriel Throckmorton William Throckmorton & Robert Throckmorton (of Berkeley) are held firmly bound unto Robert White Edward McGuire David Kennedy Elisha Williams and George Noble Gent. Justices of Frederick County in the sum of Five hundred pounds ... The Condition of the above obligation is such that the above named Robert Throckmorton is appointed Sheriff for the County of Frederick ...
Wit: J. Peyton Jr.

Robert Throckmorton
Thos. Throckmorton
Gabriel Throckmorton
William Throckmorton
Robert Throckmorton

Recorded: 2 Jan. 1781

Bk 19, p. 172 - 2 Jan. 1781

KNOW all men by these presents that we Robert Throckmorton Thomas Throckmorton Gabriel Throckmorton and William Throckmorton and Robert Throckmorton (of Berkeley) are held and firmly bound unto Robert White, Edward McGuire, David Kennedy, Elisha Williams and George Noble Gent. Justices in the sum of one hundred thousand pounds ... the Condition of the above obligation is such that the above bound Robert Throckmorton is appointed Collector of the Taxes imposed by an Act of the General Assembly ...
Wit: J. Peyton Jr.

Robert Throckmorton
Thos. Throckmorton
Gabriel Throckmorton

Recorded: 2 Jan. 1781

William Throckmorton
Robert Throckmorton

Bk 19, p. 173 - 13 April 1779
    Between George Meade of the City of Philadelphia in the State of Pennsylvania Merchant Esq. and Henrietta Constantia his wife [to] John Hamilton of County of Augusta Yeoman ... consideration of one thousand pounds ... all that tract of Land situate lying and being on the drains of Opeckon Creek ... formerly granted unto Jonathan Lupton of sd County by the Proprietor of Northern Neck by deed the 14th March 1763 & for one hundred and eighty one acres ... and by said Jonathan Lupton afterward sold and conveyed to Joseph Watson of the Town of Alexandria in the County of Fairfax ... in John Luptons Patent line corner to Robert Hodgson ... corner to Hodgson & Samuel Merryfield ... corner to Merryfield and John Carey Dows late survey ... as by deeds of L & R from said Jonathan Lupton and Sarah his wife (to Joseph Watson) the 7th & 8th Feb. 1765 ... with other Lands put in Mortgage by said Joseph Watson to Garrett Meade of said City of Philadelphia Merchant ... AND Whereas said Joseph Watson failed to pay the money ... Charles Smith Gent. Sheriff of said County of Frederick sold by way of Publick Auction and aforesaid George Meade Esq. being highest bidder for the same ...

Wit: Thos. McKean
    Thos. Stritch
    James B. Nichols
Recorded: 6 Feb. 1781

George Meade
Henrietta Constantia Meade

Bk 19, p. 177 - 26 Sept. 1780
    [Lease] Between David Vance and Sarah his wife of County of Yohogania and Commonwealth of Virginia [to] David Brown of County of Frederick ... consideration of five shillings ... Tract of Land situate in the said County of Frederick ... containing four hundred and seven acres and also another tract of Land joining the tract of Land aforesaid ... containing 119 1/4 acres being part of Jost Hite's patent land conveyed to David Vance in May 1742 ... Yielding and paying rent of one pepper corn on Lady day next ...

Wit: Isaac Hite
    Jeremiah Cooper
    William Keyes
    Isaac England
Recorded: 6 Feb. 1781

David Vance

Bk 19, p. 178 - 27 Sept. 1780
    [Release] Between David Vance and Sarah his wife of County of Yohagania Commonwealth of Virginia [to] David Brown of County of Frederick ... consideration of Five hundred and fifty pounds ... 407 acres and 119 1/4 acres (same as above) ...

Wit: same as above
Recorded: 6 Feb. 1781

David Vance

[Page numbering went from 179 to 190 - no pages missing]

Bk 19, p. 191 - 7 Nov. 1780

[Lease] Between Robert Becket of Frederick County [to] John Gilkeson and Samuel Gilkeson of the same place ... consideration of five shillings ... two certain Tracts of land situate on the head of Opeckon Creek and contiguous to each other one of which said tracts ... corner to Nathaniel Cartmill and John Becket ... in the line of John Snapp ... containing two hundred and eighty five acres and being the same which said Robert Becket purchased of Samuel Becket ... the other tract containing one hundred and fifty acres which said tract of Land is part of a large tract of Land granted to Jost Hite by patent and by him conveyed to Samuel Glass by Deeds of L & R recorded in Orange County Court and by him conveyed to John Becket who by his last Will and Testament bequeath the same to said Robert Becket ... Yielding and paying rent of one pepper corn on Lady day next ...

Wit: Willm. Vance
    James Sinvall (?)
    Elisha Williams
    Joseph Holmes
    Robt. Allen
Recorded: 6 Feb. 1781

Robert Beckett
Jane Beckett

Bk 19, p. 193 - 7 Nov. 1780

[Release] Between Robert Becket and Jane his wife of Frederick County [to] John Gilkeson and Samuel Gilkeson of the same place ... consideration of twenty thousand Pounds ... two tracts of land ... 285 acres and 150 acres (same as above) ...

Wit: same as above
Recorded: 6 Feb. 1781

Robert Beckett
Jane Beckett

Bk 19, p. 196 - 8 Nov. 1780

Jane Becket released Dower right to above land ...

Joseph Holmes
Elisha Williams

Bk 19, p. 197 - 22 Dec. 1780

[Lease] Between Philip Woolwine of County of Frederick [to] Elizabeth Myers of the said County ... consideration of Five Shillings ... Tract of Land lying and being on the drains of Opeckon Creek and is part of the Tract whereon said Philip Woolwine now lives dwells ... corner to Henry Fink ... containing Fifty one acres ...

Wit: Jos. Richardson
    Joseph Day
    John Duffield
    Henry Baker Sen.
Recorded: 6 March 1781

Philip Woolvine

Bk 19, p. 198 - 23 Dec. 1781
    [Release] Between Philip Woolwine & Elizabeth his wife of County of Frederick [to] Elizabeth Myers of the said County ... consideration of Two thousand two hundred & 50 Pounds ... 51 Acres (same as above) ...
Wit: same as above   Philip Woolvine
Recorded: 6 March 1781   Elizabeth Woolvine

Bk 19, p. 200 - 22 Dec. 1780
    [Lease] Between Philip Woolvine of County of Frederick [to] Henry Fink of the said County ... consideration of five Shillings ... Tract of Land lying and being on the drains of Opeckon Creek and is part of the Tract whereon the said Philip Woolvine now dwelleth ... Containing one hundred Acres ... Yielding and paying rent of one Ear of Indian Corn on Lady day next ...
Wit: Joseph Day   Philip Woolvine
     Jos. Richardson
     John Duffield
     Henry Baker Sen.
Recorded: 6 March 1781

Bk 19, p. 201 - 23 Dec. 1781
    [Release] Between Philip Woolvine & Elizabeth his wife of County of Frederick [to] Henry Fink of the said County ... consideration of Five thousand Pounds ... 100 Acres (same as above) ...
Wit: same as above   Philip Woolvine
Recorded: 6 March 1781   Elizabeth Woolvine

Bk 19, p. 204 - 6 Feb. 1781
    Between Abraham Bowman and George Brinker Executors of the last Will and Testament of George Bowman Jr. dec'd. who was on of the Executors of George Bowman Sen. dec'd. Father of the said Abraham first mentioned George Bowman [to] Solomon Philips of County of ___ ... WHEREAS the right Honorable Thomas Lord Fairfax by Deed the 1st July 1754 did grant to said George Bowman Sen. a certain Tract of Land situate on Crook run in County of Frederick Containing three hundred and Seventy Acres ... Corner to the Land surveyed for John Duckworth in the line of Casper Mire ... and WHEREAS said George Bowman Sen. by his last Will and Testament directed the said land be sold which was done and purchased by said George Bowman Jun. who by his last Will and Testament likewise directed the same to be sold NOW THIS INDENTURE for and in consideration of Fifty Pounds ... Confirm to said Solomon Philips the Land above mentioned ...
Wit: none   Abram. Bowman
Recorded: 6 March 1781   George Brinker

Bk 19, p. 206 - 23 Feb. 1781
    Agreeable to the last Will and Testament of Joseph Bowman dec'd. We the

Subscribers being appointed by Order of Court have valued the Land of sd Bowman dec'd. at Five hundred & Forty five pounds in specie ...

              Elisha Williams
              Lewis Stephens Jun.
              Stephen Miers
              Nicholas Spery Jun.
              George Worth
              Thos. Bush
              John Nisewanger
              Edward Cartmill
              James Wilson
              David Nisewanger
              George Larrick
Recorded: 6 March 1781   James Hoge

Bk 19, p. 207 - 14 Oct. 1780

 KNOW all men by these presents that I Jacob Kendrick of County of Frederick for and in consideration of Thirty pounds Seventeen shillings and Six pence to me paid by Benjamin Kendrick of County aforesaid ... do bargain and deliver unto said Benjamin Kendrick one young Black mare about five years old ... two young cows and five heifers ...

Wit: Thos. Allen   Jacob Kendrick
  Mary (X) Kendrick
Recorded: 6 March 1781

Bk 19, p. 208 - 10 June 1779

 Between Mordicai Lewis of City of Philadelphia Merchant and Hanna his wife [to] Jacob Harman of the same City Merchant ... WHEREAS Robert Rutherford of Berkeley County in Virginia Esquire and Mary his wife by their Indenture the 13th Sept. 1777 made between them and John Reynoll and said Jacob Harman & Mordicai Lewis of the other part for the consideration therein mentioned did grant to said John Reynoll, Jacob Harman and Mordicai Lewis several Tracts of Land situate on & near Opeckon Creek in the County of Frederick ... one of them containing one hundred and fifty acres which was granted by the Right Honorable Thomas Lord Fairfax to Ralph Thompson ... one other of them containing four hundred acres which was granted by said Lord Fairfax to Edward Cirden ... one other of them containing two hundred and sixty five acres which was granted by said Lord Fairfax to Regen Reagan and the other of them Containing Eighty nine acres which was granted to John Abrill ... one moiety or half part of the same to said Jacob Harman & Mordicai Lewis in Common the other Moiety subject to the payment of Certain Sum of Money secured by Mortgage in said Indenture ... WHEREAS said Robert Rutherford & Mary his wife by Indenture the 13th Sept. 1777 for Consideration therein mentioned confirm to said John Reynoll Jacob Harman & Mordicai Lewis pieces of Land situate on both sides of Hogs Creek in said County of Frederick

containing Seven hundred & eighty four Acres ...
Wit: John Bringhurst Mordicai Lewis
    Mires Fisher Hannah Lewis
    John H. Huston
Recorded: 3 March 1781

Bk 19, p. 213 - 26 March 1781
    Between Bryan Bruin of Borough of Winchester in County of Frederick [to] Edward Smith of Borough & County aforesaid ... consideration of two Thousand Pounds ... a certain Lot or half acre of Land in the Borough of Winchester known by Number 19 and being the same whereon said Edward Smith now dwells together with a Lot of five Acres of Land in the Common of the said Borough known by Number 14.
Wit: none Bryan Bruin
Recorded: 3 April 1781

Bk 19, p. 215 - 30 March 1781
    [Lease] Between Allen McDonald (Lease of Stephen Jones) of County of Frederick [to] Peter Peterson of County aforesaid ... consideration of Twenty three Pounds ... for the rent Covenants hath granted to farm let ... a certain Tract of Land formerly the property of Lewis Neill dec'd. and was by said Lewis Neill devised to Edward and Jost White in the Year 1770 ... and was by said Edward and Jost White devised to ___ ... and was by said ___ devised to Stephen Jones and was by said Stephen Jones devised to above named Allen McDonald ... corner to said Lewis Neill ... Corner to Meredith Helm ... Containing seventy Acres ... term of Ninety nine years. ...
Wit: Ben. Rutherford Allen McDonald
    Meredith Helm
    Abraham Neill
Recorded: 3 April 1781

Bk 19, p. 217 - 3 Oct. 1780
    GREETINGS - Know all ye that I said Jacob Stearly for and in Consideration of the Natural Love and Affection which I have and bear unto Mary Mauck and also for other good causes and considerations have granted unto said Mary Mauck the one third part of my Goods Chattles Leases Debts Jewels and all my other Substance Moveables and Immoveable ... to have and to hold ...
Wit: Jos. Carter Jacob Stearly
    Benjamin Carter
Recorded: 3 April 1781

Bk 19, p. 218 - 3 Oct. 1780
    Between Jacob Stearly of Frederick County [to] Mary Mauck of the same place ... consideration of Natural Love and Affection ... parcel of Land lying and being on Sittlers run adjoining the Lands of Joseph Horner Containing Two hundred Acres

being a part of the Tract of Land the said Jacob Stearly purchased from Richard Carter in the Tenure and occupation of Phillip Kulee and John Smith ...
Wit: Jos. Carter   Jacob Stearly
    Benjamin Carter
Recorded: 3 April 1781

Bk 19, p. 220 - 5 Jan. 1781
    [Lease] Between Jacob Stearly of County of Frederick [to] Michael Mauck of County aforesaid ... consideration of five Shillings ... Tract of Land lying on Sitlers run a Branch of Opeckon ... granted unto Joseph Carter by Deed from under the hand and Seal of the Right Honorable Thomas Lord Fairfax the 27th March 1760 and by him conveyed to Richard Carter and by Richard Carter conveyed to said Jacob Stearly by Deed of L & R the 20th & 21st August 1773 ... in Robert Stewarts Line ... containing two hundred and Seventy acres ... Yielding and paying rent of one pepper corn on Lady day next ...
Wit: Joseph Carter   Jacob Stearly
    Benjamin Carter
    John Smith
Recorded: 3 April 1781

Bk 19, p. 222 - 4 Jan. 1781
    [Release] Between Jacob Stearly and Mary his wife of County of Frederick [to] Michael Mauck of County aforesaid ... consideration of two hundred and fifty pounds ... 270 Acres (same as above) ...
Wit: same as above   Jacob Stearly
Recorded: 3 April 1781   Mary ( ) Stearly

Bk 19, p. 225 - 18 May 1781
    [Lease] Between Peter Luke of County of Frederick [to] James Abernathy of County aforesaid ... consideration of Five Shillings ... all that Tract of Land on the drains of Opecon (sic) ... which said Tract was Granted to said Luke by Deed under the hand and Seal of the Right Honorable Thomas Lord Fairfax the 29th Oct. 1768 ... in Line of Heirs of John Neill dec'd. ... corner to William Beaslys Survey ... Corner to Beasly & Thomas Helm ... corner to Helm and Lewis Neill ... corner to said Neill & Meredith Helm ... corner to Cuthbert Bullit's late survey ... containing Five hundred and Sixty four Acres ... Yielding and paying rent of one pepper corn on Lady day next ...
Wit: Joseph Day   Peter Luke
    Nathl. Pitney
    Meredith Helm
Recorded: 7 Aug. 1781

Bk 19, p. 226 - 19 May 1781
    [Release] Between Peter Luke and Elizabeth his wife of County of Frederick

[to] James Abernathy of County aforesaid ... consideration of One thousand Pounds ... 564 Acres (same as above) ...
Wit: same as above
Recorded: 7 Aug. 1781

Peter Luke
Elizabeth (E) Luke

Bk 19, p. 229 - 20 May 1781
    [Lease] Between James Abernathy of County of Frederick [to] John Lock of County aforesaid ... consideration of five Shillings ... all that part of a Tract of Land lying on the drains of Opecon (sic) and is part of a Larger Tract Containing 564 Acres which was Granted to Peter Luke by Deed under the hand and Seal of the Right Honorable Thomas Lord Fairfax the 29th Oct. 1768 by said Luke conveyed to said Abernathy ... Line of Cuthbert Bullitt ... Containing Two hundred & Fifty seven Acres ... Yielding and paying Rent of one pepper Corn on Lady day next ...
Wit: Joseph Day
    Meredith Helm
    Thomas Campbell
Recorded: 7 Aug. 1781

Jas. Abernathy

Bk 19, p. 230 - 21 May 1781
    [Release] Between James Abernathy and Anne his wife of County of Frederick [to] John Lock of County aforesaid ... consideration of Two hundred and fifty Pounds ... 257 Acres (same as above) ...
Wit: same as above
Recorded: 7 Aug. 1781

Jas. Abernathy
Ann Abernathy

Bk 19, p. 233 - 17 Sept. 1781
    Between Martin Baker and Elizabeth his wife of County of Hanover & State of Virginia [to] William Frost of County of Frederick ... consideration of Seven thousand four hundred & Twenty Pounds ... Tract of Land situate lying and being upon Long Marsh containing by Estimation Two hundred & Eighty Seven Acres & three quarters more or less being the same Land which the sd Martin Baker purchased of Edward Snicker by Deed the 5th April 1773 and which sd Edwd. Snicker of Thomas Lofton Sen. by Deed ... which sd Thomas Lofton obtained by Patent of the Right Honorable Thomas Ld. Fairfax the 12th Oct. 1750 ... corner to Philips who purchased of Warner Washington Sen. who purchased of Geo. W. Fairfax ... near sd Frost now Dwelling house ...
Wit: Hugh Fergison
    Thomas Smith
    Nehemiah Garison
    Jesper Ball
Recorded: 2 Oct. 1781

Martin Baker
Elizabeth Baker

Bk 19, p. 235 - 25 Sept. 1781
    Hanover County - Elizabeth Baker the wife of the within named Martin Baker

released Dower right to said Land ...	John Lawrence
	Thos. Travilian
	John Thornton

Bk 19, p. 236 - 5 Nov. 1781

[Lease] Between Bryan Bruin of Winchester in Frederick County [to] John Donaldson of the same place ... consideration of five shillings ... two full equal third parts of Lott No. 19 situate in the said Borough of Winchester ... corner to Philip Hoover ... in the Line of Col. Holmes ... thro the said Window including about one third of the Chimmey in the middle of the said house to the back part ... containing about two third part of half an Acre of Land ... Also a proportional part of Lot No. 45 situate in the Common of the said Borough containing in the whole five Acres ... which said Lott No. 19 & 45 were granted to John Humphreys by Deed from Lord Fairfax the 15th May 1753 and the said John Humphreys conveyed to Ralph Humphreys who conveyed the same to said Bryan Bruin ... the said Bryan Bruin divided the said Lot No. 19 into tow parts and the remainder one third conveyed to sd. Col. Holmes ... Yielding and paying rent of one pepper corn on Lady day next ...
Wit: none	Bryan Bruin
Recorded: 4 Dec. 1781

Bk 19, p. 237 - 6 Nov. 1781

[Release] Between Bryan Bruin of Winchester in County of Frederick [to] John Donaldson of the same place ... consideration of One thousand Pounds ... two equal third parts of Lot of half and acre (Lot No. 19) and part of Lot No. 45 (same as above) ...
Wit: none	Bryan Bruin
Recorded: 4 Dec. 1781

Bk 19, p. 240 - 7 Aug. 1781

Between Nicholas Sperry Senior and Elizabeth his wife of County of Frederick [to] Nicholas Sperry Junior of County aforesaid ... consideration of one hundred and Fifty Pounds ... Tract of Land containing Four hundred and thirty Acres situate lying and being on the drains of the North River of Shannando ... at the line of George Bowman ... Lawrence Stephens corner ... at Casper Mires Line ...
Wit: George Keller	Nicholas (NSP) Sperry Senior
　Jacob Sperry	Elizabeth (O) Sperry
　John Sperry
Recorded: 7 Aug. 1781

Bk 19, p. 243 - 6 March 1781

Between Lewis Smalltzehaffin of County of Frederick [to] George Keller of County of Shanando ... consideration of Three Hundred pounds ... Tract of Land containing One hundred and Twenty nine Acres situate lying and being in the County of Frederick and hath been granted by Deeds of L & R from Jacob Gibson the 20th

and 21st Jan. MDCCLIII from a greater Tract to said Lewis Smallzehaffen ...
Wit: Jacob Sperry   Lewis (X) Smaltzehaffin
   John Sperry
Recorded: 7 Aug. 1781

Bk 19, p. 246 - 7 Sept. 1780
    KNOW all men by these present that I John Plank of County of Montgomery a Farmer for divers Considerations and Good Causes ... have made ordain Constituted and appoint my trusty friend Reuben Rowzie of County of Frederick my true and Lawful Attorney for me and in my name ...
Wit: Thos. Buck   John (J) Plank
   John Lee
Recorded: 7 Aug. 1781

Bk 19, p. 247 - 2 Aug. 1781
    Between Benjamin Shreve and Hannah his wife of Winchester in Frederick County [to] Philip Woolwine of County aforesaid ... consideration of one hundred and fifty pounds specie ... the following proportion of Lot No. 15 or the East side of Loudoun Street in the Borough of Winchester ... Lot next (to) John Haymaker ... to the line of Martin Rielley ... Also two Acres and a half of Land Situate in the Common of the said Town ... adjoining Henry Bakers Lot the same being one moiety of Lot No. 22 ...
Wit: J. Peyton Jun.   Benjamin Shreve
   John Reynolds   Hannah Shreve
   Jacob Kiger
   James Lownes
Recorded: 2 Oct. 1781

Bk 19, p. 249 - 1 Sept. 1781
    Between Edmund Taylor & Sarah his wife of County of Frederick [to] John Wayman of sd County ... consideration of Nine hundred Pounds eight Shillings ... all that Tract of Land situate lying and being in County aforesaid ... by the side of the Road mentioned in Barth Andersons Will ... Containing Three hundred & Seventy Acres more or less ... the said Tract of Land being composed of a Tract of Land containing One hundred & ninety one Acres whereof Twenty six Acres were patented by the Proprietors of Northern Neck to Danl. Johnson the 21 Jan. 1767 and the remaining 165 acres devised Ann Johnson by Barth Anderson her Father & afterwards sd 191 acres were sold to Edmund Taylor by sd Danl. Johnson & wife by Deeds of L & R the 6th & 7th Nov. 1769 ... also one other Tract of 39 acres sold to sd Edmund Taylor by Abraham Anderson by Deed of Sale the 5th Aug. 1770 ... one other Tract sold the sd Edmund Taylor by Cornelius Merschon by Deed the 5th May 1772 ...
Wit: Edward McGuire   Edmund Taylor
   Rob. Wood

F. Stribling
Recorded: 2 Oct. 1781

Bk 19, p. 251 - 5 Nov. 1781
[Lease] Between Bryan Bruin of Winchester in County of Frederick [to] Col. Joseph Holmes of the Borough and County aforesaid ... consideration of five shillings ... one full equal third part of a certain Lot of half an acre of Land Situate in the Borough of Winchester and known by number 19 fronting on Loudoun Street and adjoining the Publick Lots ... Corner to said Holmes house ... which said Lot No. 19 was granted to John Humphreys by Deed from Lord Fairfax the 15th May 1753 and by said John Humphreys conveyed to Ralph Humphreys who conveyed the same to said Bryan Bruin ... the other two thirds conveyed to John Donaldson ... Yielding and paying rent of one pepper corn on Lady day next ...
Wit: none   Bryan Bruin
Recorded: 4 Dec. 1781

Bk 19, p. 252 - 6 Nov. 1781
[Release] Between Bryan Bruin of Winchester in County of Frederick [to] Col. Joseph Holmes of the same place ... consideration of One thousand two hundred pounds ... third part of Lot 19 (same as above) ...
Wit: none   Bryan Bruin
Recorded: 4 Dec. 1781

Bk 19, p. 255 - 5 Nov. 1781
[Lease for 99 years] Between Bryan Bruin of Winchester of County of Frederick [to] John Donaldson of the same place ... consideration of annual rent ... granted to farm let ... one full equal third part of Lot Number 45 Situate in the Common of the said Borough of Winchester and containing in the whole five acres ... the other two thirds being conveyed in fee to said John Donaldson ... term of ninety and nine years ... Yielding and paying unto said Bryan Bruin the annual rent of one Ear of Indian Corn if the same shall be demanded ...
Wit: none   Bryan Bruin
Recorded: 4 Dec. 1781

Bk 19, p. 256 - 3 Dec. 1781
[Lease] Between Philip Woolwine of Borough of Winchester in Frederick County [to] Samuel May Merchant of the same place ... consideration of five shillings ... a certain Tract of Land ... corner to Henry Fink ... corner to Widow Moyers ... Containing 242 acres the same being part of a larger tract of Land that was conveyed to said Philip Woolwine by Deed from Samuel Sample ... Yielding and Paying rent of one pepper corn on Lady day next ...
Wit: J. Peyton Jr.   Philip Woolwine
   David Deadwick
   John Sowers

Recorded: 4 Dec. 1781

Bk 19, p. 258 - 4 Dec. 1781
[Release] Between Philip Woolwine & Elizabeth his wife of the Borough of Winchester County of Frederick [to] Samuel May of the same place ... consideration of one hundred & fifty five pounds ... 242 acres (same as above) ...
Wit: same as above
Recorded: 4 Dec. 1781
Philip Woolwine
Elizabeth Woolwine

Bk 19, p. 261 - 25 Nov. 1781
Between Samuel Gilkeson of the town of Winchester in County of Frederick and Susanna his wife [to] Philip Bush of the said Town of Winchester and David Pancoast of said County of Frederick ... consideration of Four hundred Pounds ... six Lots of Land each containing Nineteen thousand Seven hundred and forty square feet situated in an addition made to the Town of Winchester by Colonel James Wood dec'd. ... which said six Lots of Land form and compleat (sic) Square bounded by Boscowin Street on the North Stewart Street on the west Wolfe Street on the South Washington Street ... which Lots were conveyed to Robert Rutherford by two Deeds of L & R from Mary Wood widow and Executrix of said Colonel James Wood/ one set of two Lots the 28th & 29th August MDCCLX the other Likewise for two Lots the 1st & 2nd Oct. MDCCLXI by the said Robert Rutherford and Mary his wife to said Samuel Gilkeson by Deed the 7th Oct. MDCCLXXVII the other two Lots of Land conveyed to said Samuel Gilkeson by Deed the 7th Oct. MDCCLXXII from said Mary Wood widow and Executrix of said Col. James Wood ...
Wit: none
Recorded: 5 Feb. 1782
Saml. Gilkeson
Susannah Gilkeson

Bk 19, p. 264 - 31 Dec. 1781
Between John Kay of County of Hampshire [to] Benjamin Berry of County of Fredk. ... consideration of Sixty nine Pounds ... doth grant bargain and sell unto said Benj. Berry two Negroes one a man about Forty years old named Charles the other a Woman named Sook sixteen years old has a scar on her face occasioned by a burn ... said negroes and their increase ...
Wit: J. Milton
  Jno. Smith
  Wm Hickman Jun.
  Rich. Eastin
Recorded: 5 Feb. 1782
John Kay

Bk 19, p. 266 - 29 Dec. 1781
Between Joseph Self & Abigail his wife of County of Frederick [to] James McCool of County aforesaid ... consideration of Sixty pounds ... Tract of Land being Situate and lying on both sides of hunting Ridge on the drains of Hogg Creek in County of Frederick ... corner to Heirs of John Mauzey dec'd. ... Containing by

Estimation Three hundred & forty five Acres all which was granted by an original Survey by the Rt. Hon.ble Thomas Lord Fairfax by Deed the 5th June 1779 ...

Wit: Robt. Denny
    Saml. Denny
    Rachel Denny

Joseph Self
Abigail (X) Self

Recorded: 5 March 1782

Bk 19, p. 269 - 6 Feb. 1782

[Lease] Between Jacob Fortney [to] Alexander Drumgoold of County of Frederick ... consideration of five shillings ... one certain Lot of Land situate lying & being in an addition to the Town of Winchester ... it being the Lot No. 161 ... Survey and Plot thereof made by Mr. John Baylis the 1st Jan. 1758 which said Lot was granted to said Jacob Forney by Deed under the hand and Seal of the Right Hon.ble Thomas Lord Fairfax the 15th May 1753 ... Yielding and paying rent of one pepper corn on Lady day next ...

Wit: John Kerchival
    Philip Sperry
    John Hamilton
    Lewis Wolf

Jacob Fortney

Recorded: 5 March 1782

Bk 19, p. 270 - 6 Feb. 1782

[Release] Between Jacob Fortney [to] Alexander Drumgoole of the other part ... consideration of Four pounds ... Lot No. 161 in the town of Winchester (same as above) ...

Wit: same as above   Jacob Forney

Recorded: 5 March 1782

Bk 19, p. 272 - 24 Dec. 1781

[Lease] Between William Glascock of Frederick County [to] Jacob Leanard of County aforesaid ... consideration of Five Shillings ... a certain Lot of half acre of Land situate & lying in the Town of Stevensburgh known by No. 15 ... Yielding and paying rent of one grain of Corn on Lady day next ...

Wit: Stephen Miers   Wm Glascock
    Patrick Shannon
    William McLeor
    Jacob Miers

Recorded: 5 March 1782

Bk 19, p. 273 - 25 Dec. 1781

[Release] Between William Glascock & Elizabeth his wife of Frederick County [to] Jacob Leanord of County aforesaid ... consideration of Sixty Pounds ... Lot No. 15 in the Town of Stevensburgh (same as above) ...

Wit: same as above   Wm Glascock

Recorded: 5 March 1782   Elizabeth Glascock

Bk 19, p. 276 - 13 Feb. 1782
　　　[Lease] Between William Glascock of County of Frederick [to] William McCloud of County aforesaid ... consideration of five shillings ... a certain Lot of half acre of Land situate lying and being in the Town of Stevensburgh known by No. 24 ... Yielding and paying rent of one grain of Corn on Lady day next ...
Wit: Stephen Myers   Wm Glascock
　　Patrick Shannon
　　Jacob Myers
　　Jacob Lenard
Recorded: 5 March 1782

Bk 19, p. 277 - 14 Feb. 1782
　　　[Release] Between William Glascock & Elizabeth his wife of Frederick County [to] William McCloud of County aforesaid ... consideration of twelve pounds ... Lot No. 24 in the Town of Stephensburg (same as above) ...
Wit: same as above   Wm Glascock
Recorded: 5 March 1782   Elizabeth Glascock

Bk 19, p. 279 - 13 Dec. 1781
　　　Between John Ashby of County of Fauquier [to] Lewis Ashby son of said John Ashby of County of Frederick ... for and in consideration of natural love and affection which he hath and beareth to said Lewis Ashby and consideration of five shillings ... tract of Land situate in the County of Frederick (now in the possession of said Lewis Ashby) containing seven hundred & fifty Six acres ... corner to Robert Ashby ... corner to Joseph Berrys land ...
Wit: Jeremiah Darnall   John Ashby
　　James Wright
　　Susannah (X) Miller
　　Wm Smith
Recorded: 2 April 1782

Bk 19, p. 281 - 16 March 1782
　　　KNOW all men by these present that I Jacob Trout of Frederick County ... for and in consideration of eighty pounds paid in gold and silver by Philip Trout of the same County ... do bargain and sell unto said Philip Trout all the goods and household stuf and emplements (sic) being in the possession of Jacob Trout ... a Distill a Brew Kettle and two Mares two Cows four sheep etc ... etc ...
Wit: John Grove   Jacob Trout
　　Anthony Kline
Recorded: 2 April 1782

Bk 19, p. 281 - 23 March 1782

    Between Jacob Trout of County of Frederick [to] Philip Trout of the same County ... consideration of Forty Pounds in gold and silver ... that Lot or half acre of Land in the Town of Stephensburg ... known by No. 25 ... also one other Lott of five acres commonly called out Lot joining to the part of said Town known by number 63 ... Again another out Lott containing five acres and known by No. 108 ...

Wit: none   Jacob Trout

Recorded: 2 April 1782

Bk 19, p. 284 - 6 May 1782

    Between Lewis Stephens and Mary his wife of County of Frederick [to] Leonard Boyers of County aforesaid ... consideration of five Pounds ... all that lott or half acre of Land in the Town of Stephensburg ... known by No. 35 ... which said Lott of half an acre is part of a larger tract of Land containing 424 acres conveyed by deed of L & R the 2nd & 3rd May 1755 from Peter Stephens to Lewis Stephens ... said 424 acres is part of a greater Tract of 674 acres granted by patent to said Peter Stephens the 3rd Oct. 1734 ...

Wit: Jno. Taylor   Lewis Stephens
   Jacob Varley   Mary (M) Stephens
   Andrew Witman

Recorded: 7 May 1782

Bk 19, p. 287 - 7 May 1782

    GREETINGS - Know ye that I Mary Chrisman of County of Frederick for diver good causes & considerations do make ordain constitute appoint John Nisewanger & James Wilson of County aforesaid my true and lawful Attorney for me and in my name ...

Wit: Wm Glascock   Mary Chrisman
   John Brady

Recorded: 7 May 1782

Bk 19, p. 287 - 4 May 1782

    [Lease] Between Andrew Woolverton of County of Henry in State of Virginia [to] Christian Crum of Frederick County ... consideration of five Shillings ... Tract of Land situate in the said County of Frederick on the drains of Opeckon Creek containing two hundred and thirty nine acres after deducting thirty one acres therefrom which the said Andrew Woolverton conveyed to Isaac ___ which is taken off the lower side ... corner to John McMachen and Ralph Thompson ... corner to said Thompson and David Gilkeys survey ... corner to George Bruce ... corner to said Bruce and Bryan Bruin ... corner to said Bruin and Joseph Carter ... the aforesaid Lands was granted to Mary Litler by deed from the proprietor and by her conveyed to Nathl. Redd who conveyed same to said Andrew Wolverton ...

Wit: none   Andrew Woolverton

Recorded: 7 May 1782

Bk 19, p. 289 - 5 May 1782
  [Release] Between Andrew Woolverton and Sarah his wife of Henry County [to] Christian Crum of County of Frederick ... consideration of one hundred and thirty pounds ... 208 Acres (same as above) ...
Wit: none
Recorded: 7 May 1782
Andrew Woolverton
Sarah Woolverton

Bk 19, p. 291 - 8 Jan. 1782
  Between Samuel Glass of County of Ohio and Joseph Glass of County of Monongalia in State of Virginia [to] Samuel Gilkeson of Borough of Winchester in County of Frederick ... WHEREAS David Glass late of the County of Frederick dec'd. did by his last Will and Testament direct all his estate in lands to be sold by his exors. & appointed his two sons the above named Samuel Glass & Joseph Glass sole Exors. ... Now this Indenture for and in consideration of seven hundred & sixty five pounds ... Tract of land situate lying and being on Opeckon Creek ... corner to Benjamin Smith ... corner in Robert Glass' line ... in Joseph Glass' line ... containing four hundred and twenty nine Acres ...
Wit: Jno. Magill
  Robt. Allen
  Joseph Glass
Recorded: 7 May 1782
Samuel Glass
Joseph Glass

Bk 19, p. 294 - 7 May 1782
  KNOW all men by these present that we Robert Throckmorton high Sheriff of Frederick County and Robert Throckmorton (of Berkeley) Thomas Throckmorton & William Throckmorton are held and firmly bound unto the Treasurer for the Commonwealth in the full sum of ten thousand pounds ... The Condition of the above obligation is such that the above bound Robert Throckmorton shall truly and faithfully collect pay and account for all taxes imposed by an Act of General Assembly ...
Wit: J. Peyton Jr.

Recorded: 7 May 1782
Robert Throckmorton
Robert Throckmorton
Thos. Throckmorton
Wm. Throckmorton

Bk 19, p. 294 - 23 March 1782
  [Lease] Between Henry Anderson and Margaret his wife late Margaret Aldred relict and devisee of Christopher dec'd. of the Town of Winchester in County of Frederick [to] Henry Aldred of the same place ... consideration of five shillings ... one equal half part of the moiety of a Lott of land situate in an addition to the Town of Winchester made by James Wood Gent. now dec'd. ... known by the No. 7 ... conveyed by Mrs. Mary Wood Executrix of said James Wood dec'd. to Robert Pearis and by his Attorney in fact conveyed to sd Christopher Aldred dec'd. who by his last Will & Testament devised the same to his widow the said Margaret Anderson ...

Yielding and paying rent of one pepper corn on Lady day next ...
Wit: J. Peyton Jr.   Henry Anderson
     Michael Miller   Margt. (X) Anderson
     Christopher Hetherling
Recorded: 7 May 1782

Bk 19, p. 296 - 24 March 1782
  [Release] Between Henry Anderson and Margaret his wife late Margaret Aldred relict of Christopher Aldred dec'd. of Winchester in County of Frederick [to] Henry Aldred of the same (place) ... consideration of ten pounds ... one equal half part of their moiety of a lott of Land situate in Col. Woods addition to the Town of Winchester ... known by No. 7 (same as above) ...
Wit: same as above   Henry Anderson
Recorded: 7 May 1782   Margt. (X) Anderson

Bk 19, p. 298 - 30 April 1782
  [Lease] Between John Lemly of Winchester in Frederick County [to] John Brady of the same place ... consideration of five shillings ... part of a certain Lot or half acre of land situate in Winchester and known by No. 207 ... Yielding and paying rent of one pepper corn on Lady day next ...
Wit: Wm Alexander   John Lemly
     Christopher Wetzell
     Frederick Kurtz
Recorded: 7 May 1782

Bk 19, p. 300 - 1 May 1782
  [Release] Between John Lemly and (Catharine) his wife of Winchester in Frederick County [to] John Brady of the same place ... consideration of one hundred pounds ... part of Lot 207 situate in the east side of Loudoun Street in the said Borough of Winchester (same as above) ...
Wit: same as above   John Lemly
Recorded: 7 May 1782

Bk 19, p. 302 - 1 April 1782
  [Lease] Between Isaac Zane of County of Frederick [to] Gabriel Jones of County of Rockingham ... consideration of five shillings ... tract of land situate on the waters of Cedar Creek ... containing seven hundred and seventy five acres ... division between Joseph McDowell and James Colvill ... corner to Lawrence Stephens ... which tract of land is part of a tract of six hundred acres sold by Jost Hite to Charles McDowell and by said Charles McDowell & Rachael his wife by Deed of L & R conveyed to Casper Mesner and by said Mesner to Joseph McDowell by Deeds of L & R the 12th & 13th Aug. MDCCL also part of anther tract of two hundred & seventy five acres granted by deed from Thomas Lord Fairfax the 20th Sept. MDCCL to Joseph McDowell also one other tract conveyed by Lord Fairfax aforesaid to said

Joseph McDowell the 20th June MDCCLIV containing two hundred and fifty acres which said last mentioned tract and part of sd two first mentioned tracts the said Joseph McDowell and Margaret his wife conveyed to Lewis Stephens by Deeds of L & R the 3rd & 4th Sept. MDCCLXV ... the said deeds expressed said to contain seven hundred & sixty eight acres more or less ... by deed from said Lewis Stephens and Mary his wife to sd Isaac Zane the 3rd Sept. 1778 is said to contain 775 acres as above mentioned in several deeds (except that from Jost Hite to Charles McDowell) ... Yielding and paying rent of one pepper corn on Lady day next ...
Wit: Benjamin Fry   Isaac Zane
    Joseph Connard
    William Douglass Jun.
    Jno. Croudson
Recorded: 7 May 1782

Bk 19, p. 304 - 2 April 1782
    [Release] Between Isaac Zane of County of Frederick [to] Gabriel Jones of County of Rockingham ... consideration of one thousand pounds ... 775 acres (same as above) ...
Wit: same as above   Isaac Zane
Recorded: 7 May 1782

Bk 19, p. 307 - 6 May 1782
    [Lease] Between William Holliday of Winchester in Frederick County [to] James Walker of the same place ... consideration of Five shillings ... a certain Lot or half acre of Land situate in an addition made to the said Town of Winchester by James Wood Gent. dec'd. known by No. 7 and being the same which said James Wood conveyed to John Greenfield now dec'd. and by said Greenfield to Philip Bush who conveyed same to said William Holliday ... Yielding and paying rent of one pepper corn on Lady day next ...
Wit: none   William Holliday
Recorded: 9 May 1782

Bk 19, p. 308 - 7 May 1782
    [Release] Between William Holliday and Jane his wife of Winchester in Frederick County [to] James Walker of the same place ... consideration of Eighty pounds ... Lot No. 7 in the addition to the Town of Winchester (same as above) ...
Wit: same as above   William Holliday
Recorded: 9 May 1782

[Note: Lot No. 7 in Winchester was sold by Henry Anderson and Margaret his wife [to] Henry Aldred on 24 March 1782. Both Deeds sold Lot No. 7 ?]

Bk 19, p. 309 - __ day of __ 1781
    Between Philip Woolwine & Elizabeth his wife of Town of Winchester in

County of Frederick [to] William Pyle of the Town and County aforesaid ... consideration of One hundred & fifteen Pounds ... One half of a Lot or Quarter of an Acre of Land in The Town of Winchester on the west side of Cameron Street and known by No. 31 the same being the southern side of said Lott ... also one half of a Lott of Land in the Common of the said Town containing five Acres known by No. 30 ... which said two half Lotts were granted to Col. John Hite by Deed under the hand and Seal of the Rt. Hon.ble Thomas Lord Fairfax the 15th May 1753 and by said John Hite conveyed to Jacob Seabert, who conveyed the same to Daniel Bush and by him conveyed to Philip Bush and by said Philip Bush conveyed to Geo. Helm dec'd. Who in his last Will and Testament bequeathed same to his Son George Helm of whom the said Philip Woolwine purchased the same ...
Wit: Henry Prince   Philip Woolwine
     John Neill   Elizabeth Woolwine
Recorded: 4 June 1782

Bk 19, p. 310 - 3 June 1782
    Between Jacob Anderson & Christina his wife of the Town of Winchester [to] Michael (Miller) of Town & County aforesaid ... consideration of Eight Pounds ... all that Lott No. 133 situate & being in the Town of Winchester ... Containing in full one half Acres ... All of Lott No. 133 was granted to said Jacob Anderson by Deed the 15th May 1753 ...
Wit: George Helm   Jacob Anderson
     Jacob Harmen   Christina (+) Anderson
     John Flue (?)
Recorded: 4 June 1782

Bk 19, p. 312 - 13 May 1782
    GREETINGS - Whereas William Glascock and Elizabeth his wife by their certain Indenture of L & R the 24th & 25th Dec. 1781 have sold unto Jacob Leanard the fee simple estate of and in a certain Lot of half an Acre of Land known by No. 15 situate in Stephensburg ... Elizabeth Glascock now releases Dower right to said Land
...   Elisha Williams
Recorded: 4 June 1782   Joseph Longacre

Bk 19, p. 312 - 13 May 1782
    GREETINGS - Whereas William Glascock and Elizabeth his wife by their certain Indenture of L & R the 13th & 15th Feb. 1782 have sold and conveyed unto William McCloud the fee simple estate of and in Lot No. 24 situate in Stephensburg containing half an acre ... Elizabeth Glascock now releases Dower right to above land ...   Elisha Williams
Recorded: 4 June 1782   Joseph Longacre

Bk 19, p. 313 - 2 July 1782
    Between Alexander Drumgoold and Margaret Elizabeth his wife of County and

Parish of Frederick and Borough of Winchester [to] Miriam Calmes of the Parish and County aforesaid Spinster ... Consideration of Three Hundred pounds ... all that dividend or half part of the two Lots No. 31 in the Town of Winchester and whereon said Alexander Drumgoold now lives and No. 30 in the Common of the said Town ... The whole of the two Lots was granted by the Right Honorable Thomas Lord Fairfax to Col. John Hite by Deed the 15th May 1753 and by said John Hite and Sarah his wife sold and conveyed to Jacob Seabert by Deed of L & R the 1st & 2nd Aug. 1757 ... and by said Jacob Seabert and Mary his wife sold and conveyed to said Alexander Drumgoold by L & R the 6th & 7th Sept. 1779 ...
Wit: Jno. Magill
   Peter Catlett
   Ham.t Dowdall
   David Kennedy

Alexander Drumgoole
Margaret Elizabeth Drumgoole

Recorded: 6 Aug. 1782

Bk 19, p. 315 - 2 July 1782
   Between Miriam Calmes of County & Parish of Frederick Spinster [to] Alexander Drumgoold of the Borough of Winchester in County aforesaid ... for and in consideration of Three Hundred & Thirty pounds ... All that Lot or half acre of Land situate lying and being in the Town of Winchester No. 16 on the main Street ... survey & plott of said Town made by Mr. John Baylis ... also one other Lot or Tract of Land containing five Acres No. 15 being part of and included in a Tract of 439 Acres laid off as a Common for the benefit of the Inhabitants of the Town aforesaid ... which said two Lots was granted by the Right Honorable Thomas Lord Fairfax to Marquis Calmes late of said County by Deed the 15th May 1753 and by said Marquis Calmes having departed this life Intestate the two Lots aforesaid descended to William Calmes his Eldest son and Heir at Law and said William Calmes having also departed this life having first made his last Will and Testament the 8th Sept. 1773 devised the same to his daughter Miriam Calmes ...
Wit: John Magill
   Ham.l Dowdall
   David Kennedy
   William Taylor
   John S. Woodcock
   Peter Catlett

Miriam Calmes

Recorded: 6 July 1782

Bk 19, p. 316 -
   KNOW ye that we John Thomas and Else his wife of County of Gilford in the State of North Carolina ... That Whereas Captain Evan Thomas dec'd. did in his Life time obtain a Patent, One thousand and fourteen acres of Land under the Hand and Seal of William Gooch Esq. Governor of the Commonwealth the 12th Nov. 1735 ... in the County of Orange but now the County of Frederick and on the Norward (sic) side of Opeckon Creed and on a Branch known by Name of Thomas Marsh and being

part of one hundred Thousand Acres granted by order of the Council of Virginia to Morgan Bryan ... And whereas said Evan Thomas by his last Will and Testament the 18th June 1753 bequeathed unto his son John Thomas his then dwelling Plantation with about four hundred acres of Land ... Whereas said John Thomas having heretofore sold and conveyed all that part of the said Devise in the said Will to him made laying and being on the West side of the Great Road leading from Winchester to Watkins Ferry ... and whereas John Thomas and Else his wife for and in consideration of one Thousand pounds Silver and Gold paid by Richard Ridgway of County of Berkeley in Virginia doth release unto said Richard Ridgway part of the Land devised by the said Will ... We the said John Thomas and Else his wife appoint our Friends Able Walker and David Ross of the County of Frederick our True and Lawfull Attorneys for us and in our names ... to sign seal and acknowledge unto said Richard Ridgway a Good Lawfull and Sufficient Deeds of Lease & Release ...

Wit: Abraham Branson John (|) Thomas
    Cuthb.t Hayhurst Alce (X) Thomas
    Martha Walker
    Daniel Brown
    Timothy Brown
Recorded: 6 Aug. 1782

Bk 19, p. 317 - 17 Aug 1782

Between Lewis Stephens and Mary his wife of County of Frederick [to] Andrew Pitman of County aforesaid ... consideration of fifteen pounds ... all that Lott or half acre of Land in the Town of Stephensburg ... known by No. 32 ... which said half acre is part of a larger tract of 424 acres conveyed by deeds of L & R from Peter Stephens to Lewis Stephens the 2nd & 3rd May 1775 ... which said 424 acres is part of a greater tract of 674 acres granted by patent to said Peter Stephens the 3rd Oct. 1734 ...

Wit: John McGinnis Lewis Stephens
    John Taylor Mary (M) Stephens
Recorded: 6 Aug. 1782

Bk 19, p. 319 - 5 Aug. 1782

[Lease] Between Edward Rogers of the County of Frederick [to] John Brownley of the other part ... consideration of five shillings ... all that tract of Land lying and being in Frederick County containing by estimation one hundred and eighty one and a half Acres ... in the line of Thomas Bryan Martin Esq. ... all which said granted premises were invested in Edward Rogers Father to said Edward Rogers by virtue of a bequeath in the last Will and Testament of Benjamin Borden the same being part of a larger tract of Eight hundred acres ... Yielding and paying rent of one grain of Indian Corn on the last Day of the Year ...

Wit: Edmund Taylor Edward Rogers
    John Cordell
    Robert Catlett
Recorded: 6 Aug. 1782

Bk 19, p. 320 - 6 Aug. 1782

[Release] Between Edward Rogers of County of Frederick [to] John Brownley of aforesaid County ... consideration of Three hundred and Sixty three pounds ... 181 1/2 acres (same as above) ...
Wit: same as above   Edward Rogers
Recorded: 6 Aug. 1782

Bk 19, p. 321 - 16 Nov. 1780

Yohogania County - GREETINGS - Whereas David Vance and Sarah his wife by their Indenture of L & R the 26th and 27th Sept. 1780 have sold and conveyed unto David Brown the fee simple estate of and in certain tracts of Land situate in the County of Frederick, one of which contains four hundred and seven acres and the other one hundred and nineteen Acres and one fourth part of an Acre ... Sarah the wife of within named David Vance now releases Dower right to said Land ...
                                                      John Canon
Recorded: 6 Aug. 1782   Richard Yealy

Bk 19, p. 322 - 6 Aug. 1782

KNOW all men by these present that I William Helm am held and firmly bound unto his Excellency Benjamin Harrison Esq. Governor of Virginia in the Just and full sum of five hundred pounds ... The Condition of the above obligation is such that the above bound ___ is appointed a Commissioner for laying Taxes ...
Wit: none   William Helm
Recorded: 6 Aug. 1782

Bk 19, p. 323 - 6 Aug. 1782

KNOW all men by these present that I Lewis Stephens Jun. of Frederick County am held and firmly bound unto his Excellency Benjamin Harrison Esq. Governor of Virginia in the Just and full sum of five hundred pounds ... The Condition of the above obligation is such that the above bound Lewis Stephens is appointed a Commissioner for laying Taxes ...
Wit: none   Lewis Stephens
Recorded: 6 Aug. 1782

Bk 19, p. 323 - ? Sept. 1782

[Lease] Between William Smith Sen. of Berkeley County & State of Virginia [to] William Smith Jun. of the other Part ... consideration of five shillings ... Tract of Land on the waters of Sleepy Creek Granted by Patent unto William Smith Sen. 1760 ... Containing four hundred acres of Land more or less ... Yielding and paying yearly rent of one pepper corn at the Feast of St. Michaels the Archangle (sic) ...
Wit: Philip Bush   Wm Smith
Recorded: 8 Sept. 1782

Bk 19, p. 324 - ? Sept. 1782

[Release] Between William Smith Sen. of Berkeley County State of Virginia [to] William Smith Jun. of the same County and State ... consideration of Four Hundred Pounds ... 400 Acres (same as above) ...
Wit: Philip Bush　　　　　　　　　　　　　　Wm Smith
Recorded: 3 Sept. 1782

Bk 19, p. 325 - 12 June 1782

Between Martin Ashby of the County of Frederick [to] David Castleman of County aforesaid ... consideration of one hundred and twenty pounds specie ... tract of Land lying on Penningtons commonly called Bucks Marsh adjoining other Lands of the said Martin Ashby, Joseph Neil & others ... Containing fifty Acres; all which being a part of a Tract of Land Containing three hundred & forty six Acres ... conveyed by said Martin Ashby being son and Heir at Law to Nimrod Ashby dec'd.
Wit: Jno. Thomas　　　　　　　　　　　　　Martin Ashby
　　Stephen Johnson
　　David (A) Ashby
Recorded: 2 Sept. 1782

Bk 19, p. 326 - 18 June 1782

Washington County State of Pennsylvania - GREETINGS - know ye that I John Worth ... for diver good causes and conditions ... do nominate Ordain constitute and appoint (my brother) George Worth of Frederick County my true and Lawfull Attorney for me and in my name ...
Wit: J. Peyton Jun.　　　　　　　　　　　　Jno. Worth
Recorded: 3 Sept. 1782

Bk 19, p. 327 - 21 June 1782

KNOW all men by these presents that I John Ewing of County of Greenbrier and State of Virginia am held and firmly bound unto Wm Ewing Robert Ewing Samuel Ewing and Thomas Ewing in the Just and full sum of one Thousand pounds ... The Condition of the above obligation is such that the above John Ewing at the last Court held for this County proved himself the heir at Law of his Father Will Ewings estate ... Now the said John Ewing shall make a deed in fee simple for several lands hereafter mentioned (Viz): to William Ewing forever two hundred Acres of Land lying on Lord Fairfax Road the plantation whereon John Barr now lives ... to Robert Ewing forever two hundred Acres of Land known by the name of the Glebe on the Indian branch Both Tracts of Land is part of a Large Tract of Land Containing Six hundred and Twenty five Acres of Land ... also to Samuel Ewing forever one half of the plantation whereon John Cample now lives on a drain of Crooked Run to Thomas Ewing forever the other half of the said Land last mentioned ... Then the above obligation shall be void ...
Wit: Jno. McGinnis　　　　　　　　　　　　John Ewing
　　Elizabeth McGinnis

Jno. Taylor
Recorded: 3 Sept. 1782

Bk 19, p. 328 - 1 Sept. 1782
    [Lease] Between Alexander Drumgoole of Winchester in Frederick County [to] Roger Barton of County aforesaid ... consideration of five shillings ... equal moiety or half part of Lot No. 161 situate in Lord Fairfax's addition to the said Borough of Winchester containing in the whole half an Acre of Land ... in line of George Hardin ... containing one fourth part of an Acre of Land which was granted by Deed from Lord Fairfax to Jacob Fortney the 15th May 1753 by the said Fortney conveyed to the said Alexander Drumgoole by Deeds of L & R the 6th Feb. 1782 ... Yielding and paying rent of one pepper corn on Lady day next ...
Wit: none   Alexander Drumgoole
Recorded: 3 Sept. 1782

Bk 19, p. 328 - 2 Sept. 1782
    [Release] Between Alexander Drumgoole and Margt. Eliza. his wife of Winchester Virginia [to] Roger Barton of County of Frederick ... consideration of twenty Pounds ... half of Lot No. 161 in Winchester (same as above) ...
Wit: none   Alexander Drumgoole
Recorded: 3 Sept. 1782   Margret Elizabeth Drumgoole

Bk 19, p. 330 - 18 May 1782
    [Lease] Between Edmund Lindsey Sen. of County of Frederick [to] John Lindsey Sen. of the same place ... consideration of five shillings ... Tract of Land situate and lying on Long Marsh in the possession of John Lindsey Sen. ... Joining to Jacob Lindsey ... Joining to Robert Hodgen ... Joining to Francis McCormic ... Joining to Thomas Lindsey ... Joining to William Booths ... Joining to Robert Hollingsworth ... Containing in the whole 294 Acres ... Yielding and paying rent of one ear of Indian Corn on Lady day next ...
Wit: Jacob Lindsay   Edmund (X) Lindsay
    Elijah Landsay
    James Bulger
    William Shuter
Recorded: 3 Sept. 1782

Bk 19, p. 330 - 10 May 1782
    [Release] Between Edmund Lindsay Sen. of County of Frederick [to] John Lindsay Sen. of the same place ... consideration of Five Shillings ... 294 Acres (same as above) ...
Wit: same as above   Edmund (X) Lindsay
Recorded: 3 Sept. 1782

Bk 19, p. 332 - 10 May 1782

[Lease] Between Edmund Lindsey Sen. of County of Frederick [to] Thomas Lindsay of the same place ... consideration of Five Shillings ... Tract of Land situate and lying on Long Marsh in the possession of said Thomas Lindsay ... on Francis McCormic's line ... on Warner Washington's Land ... containing in the whole 294 Acres ... Yielding and paying rent of one year (sic) of Indian Corn on Lady day next.

Wit: Jacob Lindsey
    Elijah Lindsey
    James Bulger
    William Shuter
    William George Fraer
Recorded: 3 Sept. 1782

Edmund (X) Lindsey

Bk 19, p. 333 - 10 May 1782

[Release] Between Edmund Lindsey Senior of County of Frederick [to] Thomas Lindsey of the same place ... consideration of Five Shillings ... 294 acres (same as above) ...

Wit: same as above
Recorded: 3 Sept. 1782

Edmund (X) Lindsey

Bk 19, p. 334 - Jan. 1780

I Edward Snickers do by these presents Certify that in the Summer of 77 I sold for John Hatley Morton as his Agent and by his order to Charles Mynn Thruston a certain Tract of Land Called Kelley's in Shenandoah River containing four hundred acres at the rate of forty shillings per Acre the same being part of larger Tract which said Morton purchased of Nathaniel Burrell and I further Certify that I rcv'd. from Charles Mynn Thruston the sum of five hundred and four pounds ... and remitted the same to said John Hatley Morton ...

Wit: Danl. Morgan
    John Milton
    Tal. Stripling
Recorded: 4 Sept. 1782

Edwd. Snickers

Bk 19, p. 334 - 30 Sept. 1782

Between Patrick Quinn and Ann his wife & Ann Hawkins Widow and relict of Joseph Hawkins dec'd. all of the Parish and County of Frederick [to] Edward White of the Parish and County aforesaid ... consideration of Sixty pounds ... all that plantation situate lying and being in Parish & County aforesaid whereon said Patrick Quinn now lives which was granted to Joseph Hawkins by Deed from the late Proprietor the 24th March 1779 the said Jos. Hawkins departed this life Intestate leaving only his Widow the said Ann Hawkins and one Child the said Anne wife of said Patrick Quinn above mentioned his only Heirs ... in John Campbells line Thomas Churchmans corner ... Corner to the Manour of Greenway Court in William Hawkins line ... Containing one hundred and two Acres ...

Wit: Peter Catlett
  J. White
  Warnal White
Recorded: 1 Oct. 1782

    Patrick Quinn
    Ann ( ) Quinn
    Ann (+) Hawkins

Bk 19, p. 336 - 24 Sept. 1782

[Lease] Between John Barrow and Lydia his wife both of County of Frederick [to] Casper Mire of County aforesaid ... consideration of five shillings ... Tract of Land lying and being near the West Run ... therein contained Seven Acres and 28 Perches of land it being Part of a tract of 396 Acres granted to William and John Barrow by Patton (sic) the 15th Dec. 1778 which land being divided the said John Barrow became full possessed of the one half ... Yielding and paying rent of one Pepper Corn on lady Day next ...

Wit: Jno. McGinnis
  Wm Glascock
Recorded: 1 Oct. 1782

    John Barrow
    Lydia (+) Barrow

Bk 19, p. 337 - 25 Sept. 1782

[Release] Between John Barrow and Leaddy his wife of County of Frederick [to] Casper Mire of County aforesaid ... consideration of ten Pounds ... 7 Acres and 28 Perches (same as above) ...

Wit: same as above
Recorded: 1 Oct. 1782

    John Barrow
    Lydia (+) Barrow

Bk 19, p. 338 - 7 March 1782

[Lease] Between William Drew of Berkeley County in State of Virginia [to] John Kean Merchant of Winchester in County of Frederick ... consideration of five shillings ... a certain Lot of Land situate in the said Borough of Winchester known by Number 78 ... Also one other Lot of five Acres in the Commons of said Borough ... Lot above mentioned being the Number 38 the said Lots being the same which said William Drew purchased of Robert Aldridge ... Yielding and paying the rent of one pepper corn on lady day next ...

Wit: Joseph Holmes
  Edward Smith
  Alexander Drumgoole
Recorded: 2 Oct. 1782

    William Drew

Bk 19, p. 339 - 7 March 1782

[Release] Between William Drew and Hannah his wife of Berkeley County [to] John Kean of Winchester in Frederick County ... consideration of two hundred and twenty pounds in Gold and Silver ... Lot in Borough of Winchester and Lot in the Commons of said Borough (same as above) ...

Wit: same as above
Recorded: 2 Oct. 1782

    William Drew

Bk 19, p. 340 - 30 Sept. 1782

[Lease] Between William Drew of Berkely County and State of Virginia [to] Michael McKewn of County aforesaid ... consideration of five shillings ... Tract of Land lying and being in County of Frederick on the drains of Opeckon granted to a certain Richard Chapman by Deed from the Right Honorable Thomas Lord Fairfax the 26 Aug. 1766 and by sundry conveyances at last became vested in the said William Drew ... Corner to Thomas Helm ... Containing two hundred and ninety five Acres ... Yielding and paying rent of one pepper Corn on lady day next ...
Wit: none   Will Drew
Recorded: 2 Oct. 1782

Bk 19, p. 341 - 1 Oct. 1782

[Release] Between William Drew and Hannah his wife of County of Berkeley [to] Michael McKewn of County aforesaid ... consideration of Two hundred pounds ... 295 Acres (same as above) ...
Wit: none   Will Drew
Recorded: 2 Oct. 1782   Hannah Drew

Bk 19, p. 343 - 15 Dec. 1780

Between Mathias Sidler and Catharine his wife of the Town of Baltimore in Commonwealth of Maryland [to] Isaac Wilkes of the Town of Winchester of County of Frederick ... Consideration of Fifty pounds ... all that Lot No. 211 situate & being in the Town of Winchester in that part of Town commonly known by my Lords additional Survey ... containing in full one half acre all of which was granted to Christopher Lambert by Deed from the Proprietors Office the 15th May 1753 and by said Lambert conveyed to Benjamin Sidler by Deeds of Lease & Release the 7th & 8th May 1772 ...
Wit: Samuel May   Mathias Sidler
    Isaac Sitler   Catharine (X) Sidler
    Henry Baker
    Adam Anderson
Recorded: 5 Nov. 1782

Bk 19, p. 343 - 15 Nov. 1780

Between Matthias Sidler and Catharine his wife of the Town of Baltimore in the Commonwealth of Maryland [to] Jacob Grimm of Winchester in the County of Frederick ... consideration of eight hundred Pounds ... all that Lot No. 210 situate & being in the Town of Winchester in the part of said Town commonly known by My Lords addition Survey ... containing in full one half acre all of which was granted to Christopher Lambert by Deed from the Proprietors Office the 15th May 1753 ... and by said Lambert conveyed to Benjamin Sidler by Deeds of L & R the 7th & 8th May 1772 ...
Wit: Saml. May   Matthias Sidler
    Isaac Sitler   Catharine (X) Sidler

Henry Baker
Adam Anderson
Recorded: 5 Nov. 1782

Bk 19, p. 345 - 1 Oct. 1782
   Between Mordicai Beane and Judith his wife of Frederick County [to] Peter Hurbough of County aforesaid ... consideration of Thirty pounds ... Tract of Land situate on Paddy Run in the County aforesaid ... in Philip Blys line ... Containing two hundred and Sixty one Acres, which said Tract of Land was granted by the Proprietor of Northern Neck to said Mordicai Bean by a Deed the 3rd Oct. 1777 ...
Wit: Absalom Hammond   Mordicai (M) Bean
   John Frye   Judith Bane
   Moses Russell
Recorded: 5 Nov. 1782

Bk 19, p. 346 - 18 Aug. 1781
   KNOW All men by these present that I Fielding Lewis of Spotsylvania County Town of Fredericksbg. but now in Frederick do quit claim to a certain Tract of Land containing three hundred and Sixty nine Acres and eight shares Mortgaged to me by Edmond Taylor of said County of Frederick ... that I discharge said Edmond Taylor all dues and demands which I might have claimed ...
Wit: John Butler   Fielding Lewis
   George Lewis
   Fielding Lewis, Jun.
Recorded: 5 Nov. 1782

Bk 19, p. 346 - Nov. 1782
   Between Thomas Weekley of County of Frederick Gent. and Elizabeth his wife [to] John Dukes of the County aforesaid ... consideration of Five Shillings ... Tract of Land taken and situate on the Northwest side of the Blue Ridge being part of a Large tract of Land Taken up by Wm Rew ... Containing 44 Acres ...
Wit: none   Thomas Weekly
Recorded: 5 Nov. 1782   Libeth Weekly

Bk 19, p. 347 - 30 Aug. 1782
   Between Isaac Zane of County of Frederick [to] Lewis Stephens the elder of the same place ... consideration of Forty Pounds ... three Lots of Land hereafter mentioned situate lying and being in and adjoining to the town of Stephensburg in the County aforesaid ... One Lot or half acre of Land in the said Town distinguished by No. 10 ... also one other Lot of Land containing five acres adjoining the said Town called one of the out Lots known by No. 36 ... also one other out Lot of Land containing five Acres adjoining the said Town and known by No. 74 ... said three Lots were conveyed by Casper Larrick to said Isaac Zane the 3rd Dec. 1772 ...
Wit: none   Isaac Zane

Recorded: 1 Oct. 1782

Bk 19, p. 348 - 8 April 1779
    Between Nicholas Devault and Elizabeth his wife of County of Hampshire & State of Virginia [to] Michael Pierce of Frederick County ... consideration of One Hundred and fifty Pounds ... Tract of Land on the drains of Opeckon and part of a Tract of 460 Acres which was granted to William Cochran by Patent from under the hand and Seal of the Right Honorable Thomas Lord Fairfax Baron of Cameron Proprietor of Northern Neck the xxth day Sept. LXII ... the said 460 Acres of Land was by William Cochran conveyed unto David Houseman by Deeds of L & R the 3rd & 4th Aug. 1767 ... part of said 460 Acres being two hundred and Thirty acres was by said David Houseman and Mary his wife conveyed unto Nicholas Dewalt the 2nd March MDCCLXXI ... Corner to Abram Hollingsworth ... corner to Col. Benjamin Grason ... containing two hundred and thirty acres ...

Wit: Ben (B) Long	Nicholas (D) Devault
Daniel Sowers	Elizabeth (D) Devault
Will Kinkead	
John Sowers	
George Harden	
Rosman (X) Long	
Peter Luke	
1 wit. signed in German	

Recorded: 5 Nov. 1782

Bk 19, p. 350 - 13 April 1782
    Between James Tucker of that part of the County on the Western Waters called Ten Mile Creek a branch of the river Monongalia and supposed to be in the State of Pennsylvania and Elizabeth his wife [to] Mordicai Bean of County of Frederick ... consideration of Sixty five Pounds ... two undivided fourth parts of a certain Tract of Land containing one hundred Acres situate lying and being on the head Branch of Hog Creek ... being part of a greater Tract of Land of four hundred Acres which was granted to Ellis Thomas by Deed from the Proprietors Office the 22nd May 1751 and by said Ellis Thomas conveyed to John Thomas son of said Ellis Thomas which said one hundred Acres of Land was conveyed to said James Tucker and the said Mordicai Bean by John Thomas & Lydia his wife by Deeds of L & R the 3rd & 4th Dec. 1770 ... Also two undivided fourth parts of the other Tract of Land containing one hundred and eighty Acres adjoining the above mentioned Tract ... in the line of John Thomas ... line of Potts and Comp. now Isaac Zanes ... being the same Tract of Land which was granted to Isaac Zane by Deed from the Proprietors Office the 2nd Sept. 1769 and by said Isaac Zane conveyed to said James Tucker & the said Mordicai Bean by Deeds of L & R the 7th & 8th March 1771 ...

Wit: Jno. Craig	James Tucker
Patrick Allison	Elizabeth (X) Tucker
John Hughes	

Jno. Croudson
Bryan Fitzpatrick
Adam Albert
William Douglas
Recorded: 5 Nov. 1782

Bk 19, p. 352 - 5 Nov. 1782
 KNOW all men by these presents that we Robert White Marquis Calmes Thomas Berry James Ware William Frost and Richard Eastin are held and firmly bound unto James Gaml. Dowdall Elisha Williams George Noble and Jno. S. Woodcock Gentlemen Justices of the County of Frederick in the Just and full sum of five hundred Pounds ... The Condition of the above obligation is such that the above named Robert White is appointed Sheriff for the County of Frederick ...
Wit: none
                Robert White
                Marquis Calmes
                Thomas Berry
                James Ware
                William Frost
Recorded: 5 Nov. 1782   Richard Eastin

Bk 19, p. 353 - 4 March 1782
 [Lease] Between Bryan Bruin of Frederick County [to] James Gambl. Dowdall of the same place ... consideration of five shillings ... all three Lots of Land situate in the County of Frederick and known by No. 15, 19 & 20 ... Lot No. 15 containing twenty Acres ... Lot No. 19 containing twenty Acres and Lot No. 20 at Isaac Perkins line ... containing twenty four Acres ... which said three Lots of Land are part of a greater Tract of 369 Acres granted by Lord Fair Fax to Wm Cochran by Deed the 18th Nov. 1752 who divided the same into Lots & conveyed these three to said Bryan Bruin ... Yielding and paying rent of one pepper corn on Lady day next ...
Wit: J Peyton Jun.   Bryan Bruin
 William Campbell
 A. Magill
Recorded: 6 Nov. 1782

Bk 19, p. 354 - 4 March 1782
 [Release] Between Bryan Bruin of Frederick County [to] James Gamuel Dowdall of the same place ... consideration of Fifty pounds ... Three Lots of Land (same as above) ...
Wit: same as above   Bryan Bruin
Recorded: 6 Nov. 1782

Bk 19, p. 355 - 8 April 1782
 [Lease] Between Robert Rutherford of Berkeley County [to] John Glover of Frederick County ... consideration of five shillings ... Tract of Land situate on the

drains of back Creek in the said County ... containing three hundred and fifteen Acres ... Yielding and paying rent of one pepper Corn on Lady day next ...
Wit: David Deadwick   R. Rutherford
    George Hardin
    J Peyton Jun.
Recorded: 6 Nov. 1782

Bk 19, p. 356 - 9 April 1782
    [Release] Between Robert Rutherford of Berkeley County Esquire and Mary his wife [to] John Glover of County of Frederick ... consideration of Three hundred and Fifteen Pounds ... 315 Acres (same as above) ...
Wit: same as above   R. Rutherford
Recorded: 6 Nov. 1782

Bk 19, p. 358 - 8 April 1782
    [Lease] Between Robert Rutherford of Berkeley County Esquire [to] John Glover of Frederick County ... consideration of five shillings ... tract of Land situate on the drains of Back Creek in the said County of Frederick ... containing four hundred Acres ... Yielding and paying one pepper corn on Lady day next ...
Wit: David Deadwick   R. Rutherford
    George Hardin
    J Peyton Jr
Recorded: 6 Nov. 1782

Bk 19, p. 9 April 1782
    [Release] Between Robert Rutherford of Berkeley County [to] John Glover of Frederick County ... consideration of Four hundred Pounds ... 400 Acres (same as above) ...
Wit: same as above   R. Rutherford
Recorded: 6 Nov. 1782

Bk 19, p. 360 - 4 Sept. 1782
    WE the Subscribers, Col. John Hite, Jacob Moyers and John Taylor have laid off 96 2/3 Acres of Land being one third part of Elizabeth Reeds plantation where she lives - the part chosen by said Elizabeth as her Dower ...
                                                       Jno. Hite
                                                       Jacob Miers
Recorded: 3 Dec. 1782   Jno. Taylor

Bk 19, p. 361 - __ day of __ 1783
    Between William Glascock and Elizabeth his wife of County of Frederick [to] Henry Lewis of County aforesaid ... consideration of four pounds ... a Certain Lot of half acre of Land situate lying and being in the Town of Stevensburgh known by No. 62 ...

Wit: William McLeode   William   Glascock
    John Groves   Elizabeth Glascock
    Dennis Bush
Recorded: 4 March 1783

Bk 19, p. 362 - 3 March 1783
   [Lease] Between Elizabeth Myers of Frederick County [to] Philip Helphinstone of the same place ... consideration of five shillings ... Tract of Land situate in the said County ... Corner to Henry Fink ... Containing fifty one Acres ... the same being part of a larger Tract of Land which was conveyed to Philip Woolwine by Samuel Sample and by said Woolwine divided and conveyed the above mentioned part there of to Elizabeth Myers ... Yielding and paying rent of one pepper corn on Lady day next ...
Wit: none   Elizabeth (X) Miers
Recorded: 4 March 1783

Bk 19, p. 363 - __ March 1783
   [Release] Between Elizabeth Myers of Frederick County [to] Philip Helphinstine of the same place ... consideration of sixty pounds ... 51 Acres (same as above) ...
Wit: none   Elizabeth (X) Miers
Recorded: 4 March 1783

Bk 19, p. 364 - 3 March 1783
   [Lease] Between Edward Snickers of Frederick County [to] Richard Kidder Meade of County aforesaid ... consideration of five shillings ... all the Tract of Land or dividend of Land situate in the said County Containing Eight hundred Acres ... the same being part of a larger Tract of Land of Fifty thousand two hundred and twelve Acres which was Granted unto the Hon.ble George Carter and others by Deed poll for the Proprietor of the Northern Neck the 22nd Sept. 1730 ... by the last Will and Testament of said George Carter now dec'd. Trustees divided the same into Lots and Conveyed the above mentioned Eight Hundred Acres unto Ignatius Perry by deeds of L & R the 29th & 30th Nov. 1776 who conveyed same to Edward Snickers by Deeds of L & R the 3rd & 4th Jan. 1777 ... known by Lot No. 3 ... Yielding and paying rent of one pepper corn on Lady day next ...
Wit: none   Edward Snickers
Recorded: 4 March 1783

Bk 19, p. 365 - 4 March 1783
   [Release] Between Edward Snickers of Frederick County [to] Richard Kidder Meade of County aforesaid ... consideration of Five Hundred Pounds ... 800 Acres (same as above) ...
Wit: none   Edward Snickers
Recorded: 4 March 1783

Bk 19, p. 366 - 18 Dec. 1782

    Between Bryan Bruin of the Town of Winchester in the County of Frederick [to] John Neil of County aforesaid ... consideration of One hundred Pounds ... a full Moiety or half a lot of Ground in the Town of Winchester which Lot is known by No. 107 ... all of which Lot No. 107 was granted by the Rt. Hon.ble Thomas Lord Fair Fax to John Dougherty by Deed Poll ... one half of which Lot conveyed by Deeds of L & R to Peter Foreman by the said Dougherty who also conveyed the other half to Bryan Bruin by Deeds of L & R ...

Wit: Henry Beatty   Bryan Bruin
     John Reynolds
     Jno. Thomas
Recorded: 4 March 1783

Bk 19, p. 368 - __ March 1783

    [Lease] Between Philip Helphinstone of Frederick County [to] Elizabeth Myers of County aforesaid ... consideration of five Shillings ... two certain Lots of Land situate in the Lord Proprietors addition to the Town of Winchester known by Numbers 220 and 221 & contains half an Acre of Land each and situate Contiguous to each other ... said Lots were granted to Philip Helphinstine by separate deeds from the said Proprietor respectively 15th May 1753 ... Yielding and paying rent of one pepper corn on Lady day next ...

Wit: none   Philip Helphinstine
Recorded: 4 March 1783

Bk 19, p. 368 - 4 March 1783

    [Release] Between Philip Helphinstone and Rebecca his wife of Frederick County [to] Elizabeth Myers of the same place ... consideration of thirty pounds ... two Lots of Land No. 220 and 221 (same as above) ...

Wit: none   Philip Helphinstine
Recorded: 4 March 1793   Rebecca Helphinstine

Bk 19, p. 369 - 3 March 1783

    [Lease] Between William Baldwin of Berkeley County [to] Thomas Baldwin of Frederick County ... consideration of five shillings ... all that Tract of Land containing Five hundred acres situate lying and being in County of Frederick ... Being the same Tract of Land conveyed to said William Baldwin by Deeds of L & R from Francis Baldwin and Innocent his wife John Chenoweth and William Chenoweth Executors of the last Will and Testament of John Bosher dec'd. the 3rd & 4th April 1769 ... Originally granted to William and James Joliffe by Deed under the Hand and Seal of the Right Honorable Thomas Lord Fairfax the 7th April 1755 ... Yielding and Paying rent of one Ear of Indian Corn on Lady day next ...

Wit: none   Wm Baldwin
Recorded: 4 March 1783

Bk 19, p. 371 - 4 March 1783

[Release] Between William Baldwin and Jean his wife of Berkeley County [to] Thomas Baldwin of Frederick County ... consideration of Three Hundred Pounds ... 500 Acres (same as above) ...

Wit: none
Recorded: 4 March 1783

Wm Baldwin
Jean (J) Baldwin

Bk 19, p. 372 - 20 Aug. 1782

[Lease] Between John Littler of County of Frederick [to] David Johnston of County aforesaid ... consideration of five shillings ... Tract of Land on the drains of Opeckon Creek being part of the Tract of Land whereon said Littler now liveth ... Corner to Joseph Day ... in line of William Joliffe dec'd. ... in line of Lewis Neall ... Containing Twenty six and one Quarter of an Acre ... Yielding and paying rent of one pepper corn on Lady day next ...

Wit: Nath.l Pitney
    George Johnston
    Joseph Day
    1 wit. signed in German
Recorded: 4 March 1783

John Littler

Bk 19, p. 373 - 21 Aug. 1782

[Release] Between John Littler and Rosannah his wife of County of Frederick [to] David Johnston of County aforesaid ... consideration of One Hundred Pounds ... 26 1/4 Acres (same as above) ...

Wit: same as above
Recorded: 4 March 1783

John Littler

Bk 19, p. 374 - 20 Feb. 1783

Between John Wayman & Anne his wife of County of Frederick [to] Edward Snickers of the said County ... consideration of Twelve hundred pounds ... all that Tract of Land situate lying and being in County of Frederick ... by the side of the Road mentioned in Bartholomew Anderson's Will ... Containing three hundred and Seventy Acres more or less being the same which said John Wayman purchased of Edmund Taylor by Deed the 1st Sept. 1781 which said Jno. Wayman now lives ...

Wit: Benj. Berry
    John Kercheval
    J. Milton
Recorded: 5 March 1783

John Wayman
Anne Wayman

Bk 19, p. 376 - 5 Nov. 1782

Between Lewis Stephens and Mary his wife of Frederick County [to] James Henning of County aforesaid ... consideration of Sixty pounds ... all that Lot of Land Containing half an Acre situate in the Town of Stephensburg in the County aforesaid and known by No. 10 ... also two other Lots joining the said Town known by the No.

36 & 74 commonly called out Lots ... Lot No. 36 on the East side of Crooked Lane ... Containing eight Acres ... Lot No. 74 on the west side of Squirrel Lane ... containing five Acres ...
Wit: John Nisewanger
    William McLeod
    J. McGinnis
Recorded: 5 March 1783

Lewis Stephens
Mary (M) Stephens

Bk 19, p. 378 - 13 Dec. 1782
    Between Col. William Grayson and Elenora his wife of the Town of Dumfries in Prince William County [to] William Helm of County of Frederick ... consideration of Two hundred and fifty pounds ... all that Messuage or Tract of Land lying and being situate on the Waters of Opeccon (sic) in the County of Frederick ... corner to Frederick Conrads Land ... containing in the whole five hundred Acres ... all of which is a part of Eighteen hundred Acres granted by the Rt. Hon.ble Thomas Lord Fairfax by a Deed Poll to Col. Benjamin Grayson who granted and bequeathed the same by his last Will and Testament to his Son Col. William Grayson aforesaid ...
Wit: Alexander Drumgoole
    William Poyles
    John Thomas
Recorded: 5 March 1784 (?)

William Grayson

Bk 19, p. 380 - 10 Feb. 1783
    Between James Craik and Marianne his wife of County of Charles in State of Maryland [to] William Holliday of the Town of Winchester County of Frederick ... Consideration of one Hundred and Seventy Pounds ... all that Lott of Ground situate lying and being in that part of the Town of Winchester which was first laid out and described by No. 1 ... and also one lott of Ground containing five Acres situate lying and being in the Commons adjoining to and belonging to the said Town (No. 53) ...
Wit: Daniel Jenifer
    W H Jenifer
    Isaac Wilkes
Recorded: 5 March 1783

Jas. Craik
Marianne Craik

Bk 19, p. 382 - 26 Feb. 1783
    The within named Maryanne apart from her husband released Dower right to above land ...

Daniel Jenifer
W. H. Jenifer

Bk 19, p. 382 - 10 Feb. 1783
    Between James Craik and Maryanne his wife of Charles County in the State of Maryland [to] William Holladay of the Town of Winchester County of Frederick ... consideration of Seventy pounds ... all that Lot of Ground situate lying and being in the first addition made to the Town of Winchester described by No. 1 ...

Wit: Daniel Jenifer   James Craik
    W. H. Jenifer   Marianna Craik
    Isaac Wilkes
Recorded: 5 March 1783

Bk 19, p. 384 - 10 Feb. 1783
    Between James Craik and Marianne his wife of Charles County in the State of Maryland [to] Robert Gregg of Washington County in the State aforesaid ... consideration of Thirty Pounds ... All that Lot of Ground situate lying and being in the addition made to the Town of Winchester in the County of Frederick by James Wood dec'd. and known by No. 2 ...
Wit: Daniel Jenifer   James Craik
    W H Jenifer   Marianne Craik
    Isaac Wilks
Recorded: 5 March 1783

Bk 19, p. 386 - 26 Feb. 1783
    The within named Marianne apart from the said James her husband released Dower right to said Land ...   Daniel Jenifer
                                             W H Jenifer

Bk 19, p. 387 - 1 Feb. 1778
    Between Rachel Weaks of County of Frederick doth put and bind her daughter Ann Weaks, Apprentice unto James Sidwell and Hannah his wife of the same place to learn the Art and Mystery of Housewifery ... to serve from the date hereof untill she shall arrive to the age of Eighteen Years ... She shall do no damage to her Master or Mistress ... She shall not commit Fornication nor Contract Matrimony during the said Term, at Cards, Dice or any other unlawful Games she shall not absent herself Day or Night from her said Master or Mistress' Service unlawfully nor haunt Ale-Houses, Taverns or Play-Houses but in all things behave herself as a faithful Apprentice ought to do during the said Term ... etc ... etc ...
Wit: John Huff   Rachel Weaks
    Joseph (#) Parrel   James Sidwell
Recorded: 6 March 1783   Hannah Sidwell

Bk 19, p. 388 - 8 Feb. 1783
    Between Abraham Sovain of Winchester in the County of Frederick and Lydia his wife [to] Christian Stover of Strasburg in County of Shenandoah ... WHEREAS Abraham Sovain by his Bond of Obligation stands indebted to said Christian Stover in the Sum of one Hundred Sixty Pounds ... Now this Indenture for securing the payment of said Debt and also for and in consideration of five Shillings paid by said Christian Stover ... do grant bargain and sell unto said Christian Stover one certain Lot or half Acre of Land situate in an addition to the said Town of Winchester known by No. 203 & being the same said Abraham Sovain purchased from William Baylis.

Wit: J. Peyton Jr.   Abraham Sovain
   Bryce Hannah   Lydia (X) Sovain
   Adam Haymaker
Recorded: 7 March 1783

Bk 19, p. 390 - 3 March 1783
     [Lease] Between Alexander Dromgoole of Winchester in Virginia [to] Herden of the same place ... consideration of five shillings ... one Moiety or half part of a certain Lot of half an acre of Land situated in the said Town of Winchester and known by No. 161 ... by Roger Bartons other Moiety of the said Lot which said Lot was granted to Jacob Fortney by Deed for Lord Fairfax and by his conveyed to said Alexander Dromgoole ... Yielding and paying rent of one pepper corn on Ladyday next ...
Wit: none   Alexander Dromgoole
Recorded: 7 March 1783

Bk 19, p. 391 - 4 March 1783
     [Release] Between Alexander Dromgoole and Marg. Eliza. his wife of Winchester in the State of Virginia [to] George Hardin of the same place ... consideration of Fifteen Pounds ... Lot No. 161 in Winchester (same as above) ...
Wit: none   Alexander Dromgoole
Recorded: 7 March 1783

Bk 19, p. 392 - 5 Feb. 1783
     To all to whom these presents shall come Know ye that Sentence of Death having been passed by the Court of Frederick County against Joe a Negroe Man Slave the Property of William Hickman Jun. for felony execution whereof Still remaineth to be done and he having been recommended as a proper object of Mercy I have therefore thought fit by and with advice of Councill, hereby to Pardon the said Joe for the Felony aforesaid, hereby discharging him from all Paine and execution which might have been inflicted on him, but for these Letters of Pardon, given under my Hand and the Seal of the Commonwealth the 5th Day of February 1783 ...
Recorded: 7 March 1783   Benjamin Harrison

Bk 19, p. 393 - 24 March 1783
     [Lease] Between Thomas Bryan Martin Esq. of Parish of Frederick and County of Frederick [to] David Brown of Parish and County aforesaid ... consideration of Five Shillings ... All that Plantation Tract of Land situate on both sides of Opeckon Creek and which was granted to said Thomas B. Martin by a Deed from the late Proprietor of Northern Neck the 27th May 1763 ... in the line of Thomas Machen ... to William Curlett and Lewis Reno ... Containing two hundred and Seventy Acres ... Yielding and paying rent of one pepper corn on Lady day next ...
Wit: Wm Keys   B. Martin
   Wm (X) Taylor

Thos. Draper
Recorded: 1 April 1783

Bk 19, p. 394 - 25 March 1783
[Release] Between Thomas Bryan Martin Esq. of Parish of Frederick and County of Frederick [to] David Brown of Parish and County aforesaid ... for and in Consideration of Two hundred and Seventy pounds ... 270 Acres (same as above) ...
Wit: same as above   B. Martin
Recorded: 1 April 1783

Bk 19, p. 396 - 1 April 1783
Between David Marple of Frederick County [to] Robert White of the same place ... Consideration of Forty Pounds ... Parcel of Land containing Seventy Acres being part of Three Hundred and fifty Eight Acres granted to said David Marple by Deed from the Honorable Thomas Lord Fairfax the 3rd day of May 1774 ... in Major White's line ...
Wit: none   David Marple
Recorded: 1 April 1783

Bk 19, p. 397 - 1 April 1783
Between David Marple of Frederick County [to] Enoch Marple Jun. of the same place ... consideration of Twenty Pounds ... a certain parcel of Land Containing Forty Nine Acres & one Quarter of an Acre being part of Three hundred and Fifty Eight Acres that was granted to said David Marple by a Deed from the Right Honorable Thomas Lord Fairfax the 3rd May 1774 ... in Parson McKay's line ... to one of Major White's lines ...
Wit: none   David Marple
Recorded: 1 April 1783

Bk 19, p. 399 - 1 April 1783
Between Robert White and Elizabeth his wife of Frederick County [to] Enoch Marple Junior of County aforesaid ... consideration of Sixteen Pounds ... a certain parcel of Land Containing Thirty Six Acres and two Roods being part of a Tract of Land conveyed to said Robert White by John White and Ann his wife by Deeds of L & R the 2nd & 3rd days June 1761 ...
Wit: none   Robert White
Recorded: 1 April 1783

Bk 19, p. 400 - 29 March 1783
Between Warner Washington of Fairfield in County of Frederick and Hannah his wife [to] Warner Washington Jun. son of the said Warner Washington Sen. of the said County ... Consideration of that Natural Love and Affection which they bear unto said Warner Washington Jun. ... all that Tract of Land situate lying and being in County of Frederick being part of a Larger Tract belonging to said Warner

Washington Sen. and whereon said Warner Washington now liveth ... bound as by Survey made by William McPherson the 26th Feb. 1783 ... Corner to William Booth, Mrs. Calmes and Warner Washington Sen. ... Containing 250 Acres ...
Wit: Thos. Throckmorton   Warner Washington
   Rich. Willis Jun.
   John Lewis
Recorded: 1 April 1783

Bk 19, p. 402 - 29 March 1783
    KNOW all Men by these Presents that I Warner Washington the Elder of Frederick County out of Natural Love and Affection which I bear unto my son Warner Washington do give unto him the following Negroes, Anthony, Pompey, Mary, Nancy and Esther ...
Wit: Thos. Throckmorton   Warner Washington
   Rich. Willis Jun.
Recorded: 1 April 1783

Bk 19, p. 403 - 29 March 1783
    KNOW all Men by these Presents that I Warner Washington Sen. out of Natural Love and Affection which I bear unto my Grandson John Warner (?) of Bellmont have given unto the said John Washington a Negroe Boy named Davy ...
Wit: Thos. Throckmorton   Warner Washington
   Rich. Willis Jun.
Recorded: 1 April 1783

Bk 19, p. 403 - 29 March 1783
    KNOW all Men by these Presents that I Warner Washington Sen. out of Natural Love and Affection which I bear unto my Grandson Warner Washington of Bellmont have given unto said Warner Washington a Negroe Boy named Charles ...
Wit: Thos. Throckmorton   Warner Washington
   Rich. Willis Jun.
Recorded: 1 April 1783

Bk 19, p. 403 - 24 March 1783
    [Lease] Between John Shipler of County of Frederick [to] Jacob Hunsberry of County aforesaid ... consideration of Five Shillings ... all that Tract of Land lying and being on the Branches of Red Bud and Opeccon Creek which said Tract was granted to said John Shipler by Deed under the Hand and Seal of the Right Honorable Thomas Lord Fairfax the 29th April 1760 ... corner to Hugh Perrills Patent Land ... corner to William Albin ... Containing 211 Acres ...
Wit: Jos Day   John (S) Shipler
   Undril Barton
   Thomas Sperry /Perry
Recorded: 1 April 1783

Bk 19, p. 405 - 25 March 1783

    [Release] Between John Shipler and Magdalen his wife of County of Frederick [to] Jacob Hunsburry of County aforesaid ... consideration of Two hundred Pounds ... 211 Acres (same as above) ...

Wit: same as above   John (S) Shipler
Recorded: 1 April 1783   Magdalen ( ) Shipler

Bk 19, p. 406 - 23 March 1783

    [Lease] Between Earnest Enders of County of Frederick [to] George Burket of the County aforesaid ... consideration of five shillings ... Part of a Tract of Land laying and being on the drains of Opeccon Creek and is part of a Larger Tract containing 256 Acres which was granted to said Earnest Enders by Deed under the Hand & Seal of the Right Honorable Thomas Lord Fairfax the 6th May 1760 ... corner to Jacob Hunsberry ... Line of Matthias Mauk ... Containing twenty three and one quarter Acres ... Yielding and paying rent of one pepper corn on Lady day next.

Wit: Joseph Day   Earnest Enders
    Thomas Smith
    Henry Huntsberry
Recorded: 1 April 1783

Bk 19, p. 407 - 24 March 1783

    [Release] Between Earnest Enders and Christianna his wife of County of Frederick [to] George Burket of the County aforesaid ... consideration of Thirty four Pounds Seventeen Shillings and six pence ... 23 1/4 Acres (same as above) ...

Wit: same as above   Earnest Enders
Recorded: 1 April 1783

Bk 19, p. 409 - 23 March 1783

    [Lease] Between Thomas Sperry of County of Frederick [to] George Burket of County aforesaid ... consideration of five shillings ... part of a Tract of Land laying and being on the drains of Opeccon Creek and is part of the Tract granted to Thomas Sperry by Deed under the Hand and Seal of the Right Honorable Thomas Lord Fairfax the 3 March 1752 and by the last Will and Testament of said Thomas Sperry was bequeathed to his son Thomas Sperry ... Containing Nine and a half Acres ... Yielding and paying rent of one pepper corn on Lady day next ...

Wit: Undril Barton   Thomas Sperry
    John Donaldson
    Joseph Day
Recorded: 1 April 1783

Bk 19, p. 410 - 24 March 1783

    Between Thomas Sperry and Catharine his wife of County of Frederick [to] George Burket of County aforesaid ... consideration of Ten Pounds ... 9 1/2 Acres (same as above) ...

Wit: same as above
Recorded: 1 April 1783

Thomas Sperry
Catharine (X) Sperry

Bk 19, p. 411 - 27 Nov. 1782

[Lease] Between Daniel Dillon of County of Guilford in the State of North Carolina [to] Joseph Day of the County of Frederick ... consideration of five shillings ... part of a Tract of Land lying and being near the Dividing Ridge of Opeccon and Back Creek and was granted to said Daniel Dillon by Deed from the Proprietor of Northering (sic) Neck the 13th Aug. 1762 ... corner to Josiah Ridgway ... containing One hundred and Seventy one Acres ... Yielding and paying rent of one pepper corn on Lady day next ...

Wit: Pet. Ruble
   Isaac Thomas
   Henry Crumley
   Joseph Mooney
   Thomas Short
Recorded: 1 April 1783

Daniel Dillon

Bk 19, p. 412 - 28 Nov. 1782

[Release] Between Daniel Dillon and Lydia his wife of County of Guilford in State of North Carolina [to] Joseph Day of County of Frederick ... consideration of One Hundred Pounds ... 171 Acres (same as above) ...

Wit: same as above
Recorded: 1 April 1783

Daniel Dillon

Bk 19, p. 414 - 28 Nov. 1782

Guilford County - Lydia Dillon apart from Daniel Dillon her Husband released Dower right to above land ...

Robert McKemie
Charles Bruce

Bk 19, p. 415 - 31 March 1783

[Lease] Between John Glover of County of Frederick [to] William Duncan of the same Place ... consideration of five shillings ... Tract of Three Hundred and fifty Seven and a half Acres of Land lying on Isaac's Creek ... being on one equal Moiety or half part of two tracts of Land which were conveyed to said John Glover by deed from Robert Rutherford containing in the whole Seven Hundred and fifteen Acres ... corner to Land surveyed for Matthew Harrison ... Yielding and paying rent of one pepper corn on Lady day next ...

Wit: none
Recorded: 2 April 1783

John Glover

Bk 19, p. 416 - 1 April 1783

[Release] Between John Glover and Sophia his wife of County of Frederick [to] William Duncan of the same Place ... consideration of Fifty Pounds ... 357 Acres

(same as above) ...
Wit: none
Recorded: 2 April 1783
John Glover

Bk 19, p. 418 - 2 April 1783
    Between John Emet and Mary his wife of County of Frederick [to] Henry Lewis of County aforesaid ... Consideration of Six Pounds ... a certain Lott or half an Acre of Land lying and being in the Town of Stevensburgh, known by No. 61 ...
Wit: Wm Glascock
John Emett
Recorded: 2 April 1783

Bk 19, p. 419 - April Court 1783
    Pursuant to an Order of the April Court 1783 for Laying off the Dower of Mary Chambers, widow of William Chambers dec'd. ... We have laid out in the manner following: (to wit) her Dower includes all the Land (herein described - acreage not given) ...

Robt. White
Ger.d Briscoe
Joseph Jones
Recorded: 6 May 1783
Joseph Longacre

Bk 19, p. 420 - 27 March 1783
    [Lease] Between Henry Hunter of County of Frederick [to] George Steip of County aforesaid ... consideration of Five Shillings ... Part of a Tract of Land Laying on the drains of Opeccon Creek and is Part of a Larger Tract granted to Andrew Milbourn by Deed under the Hand and Seal of the Right Honorable Thomas Lord Fairfax ... And by the said Andrew Milbourn conveyed to Thomas McClun and by said McClun conveyed to Henry Hunter ... corner to John Littler ... near the Waggon Rhoad ... Containing 27 3/4 Acres ... Yielding and paying rent of one Pepper Corn on Lady Day next ...
Wit: none
Henry Hunter
Recorded: 6 May 1783

Bk 19, p. 421 - 28 March 1783
    [Release] Between Henry Hunter of County of Frederick [to] George Steip of County aforesaid ... consideration of Fifty five Pounds ... 27 3/4 Acres (same as above) ...
Wit: none
Henry Hunter
Recorded: 6 May 1783

Bk 19, p. 422 - 31 April 1783
    Between Elizabeth Lehew of County of Frederick [to] William Lehew of County aforesaid ... consideration of Fifteen Pounds ... Tract of Land containing Thirty five Acres situate lying and being in County aforesaid ... corner to Jeremiah Lehew ... It being part of a Tract of Three Thousand Acres granted to William

Russell Esq. by Patent the 17th Dec. 1735 ... The said Russell granted and sold four hundred Acres thereof to Christopher Marr ... the said Marr granted and conveyed Two hundred Acres thereof to Peter Lehew by Deed the 2nd Feb. 1754 and the said Peter Lehew by his last Will and Testament Willed and bequeathed to his daughter Elizabeth Lehew Thirty five Acres ...
Wit: Charles Payton   Elizabeth (X) Lehew
   Jeremiah Lehew
   Frances Lehew
Recorded: 6 May 1783

Bk 19, p. 424 - 21 Oct. 1782
    Between Joseph Self and Abigail his wife in County of Frederick [to] Henry Adams of County aforesaid ... consideration of Ten Pounds ... Tract of Land lying and being near Hunting Ridge on the Drains of Hoge Creek ... Containing in the Whole fifty six Acres all of which is part of a Tract of Land containing Four Hundred Acres granted by deed Poll by the Rt. Honorable Thomas Lord Fairfax to the said Joseph Self ...
Wit: Robert Denny   Joseph Self
   Aaron Mercer   Abigail Self
   Philip Babb
Recorded: 6 May 1783

Bk 19, p. 425 - 27 March 1783
    Between Gabriel Jones of Rockingham County [to] Alexander White of Frederick County ... WHEREAS Henry Heth late of said County of Frederick and Agnes his wife by their Indenture the 4th Nov. 1767 for securing the Payment of Three Hundred Pounds to John Carlyle and John Dalton of Fairfax County and for Securing the Payment of Two Hundred Pounds to Jacob Hite late of Frederick County ... did sell and confirm unto said John Dalton and John Carlisle (sic) and Jacob Hite Lots and Tracts of Land ... And Whereas said Alexander White on the 21st June last paid said Gabriel Jones the sum of One Hundred and Eighty one Pounds five Shillings the Principal & Interest then due on the last mentioned and hath paid the further sum of Three Hundred and forty one Pounds three Shillings and ten pence ... Now this Indenture for (the above sums) hath granted unto said Alexander White the Lots and Tracts of Land above mentioned ...
Wit: And. Wodrow   Gabriel Jones
   F. Keyes
Recorded: 6 May 1783

Bk 19, p. 427 - 15 April 1783
    [Lease] Between Jacob Huntsburry of County of Frederick [to] Palser Foulks of County aforesaid ... consideration of Five Shillings ... Part of a Tract of Land Laying and being in said County and is part of the Tract whereon said Jacob Huntsberry now liveth ... Containing 50 Acres ... Yielding and paying rent of one

Pepper Corn on Lady Day next ...
Wit: Earnest Enders
   Henry Huntsberry
   Conrad Huntsberry
Recorded: 6 May 1783

Jacob (J) Huntsberry

Bk 19, p. 428 - 16 April 1783
   [Release] Between Jacob Huntsberry and Elizabeth his wife of County of Frederick [to] Palser Foulks of County aforesaid ... consideration of Fifty Pounds ... 50 Acres (same as above) ...
Wit: same as above
Recorded: 6 May 1783

Jacob (J) Huntsberry
Elizabeth ( ) Huntsberry

Bk 19, p. 430 - 8 May 1783
   Between Isaac Hite Sen. of County of Frederick [to] Isaac Hite Jun. of the same place ... consideration of Five Shillings ... all those Two Tracts of Land contiguous to and adjoining each other Containing four Hundred and Eighty Three Acres ... Three Hundred Acres of which was conveyed to said Isaac Hite Senior by Deeds of L & R the 28th & 29th March 1748 from James Hogg and Agnes his wife ... North side of the lone Meadow ... The remainder one Hundred and Eighty three Acres was conveyed to said Isaac Hite Senior by Deeds of L & R the 5th & 6th March 1770 from William Vance ... in the line of the said Isaac Hite and corner to William Vance's Survey ... in Michael Lee's line ... to James Hogg's line ...
Wit: none
Recorded: 8 May 1783

Isaac Hite

Bk 19, p. 432 - 8 May 1783
   Between Isaac Hite of County of Frederick [to] William Booth of County of Shanandoah ... Consideration of Natural Love and Affection which he doth bear the said William Booth and also further consideration of five Shillings ... all that Tract of Land containing Ninety five Acres situate lying and being in County of Frederick ... on the East side of Cedar Creek corner to Bowman's land ... in the Line of Lewis Smaltzhover's Land ...
Wit: none
Recorded: 8 May 1783

Isaac Hite

Bk 19, p. 434 - 16 April 1783
   KNOW all Men by these presents that I John McGinnis of Stephensburg for and in consideration of fifty Pounds have Sold in plain and open Market one Sorrel Horse and also one Waggon and Gears and one Cow unto Edmd. McGinnis ...
Wit: John Windsor (#) Driver
   Robert McBean
   Stephen Miers
Recorded: 8 May 1783

J. McGinnis

Bk 19, p. 434 - 31 May 1783

    Between John Snapp of County of Shanandoah [to] John Wincor Driver of County of Frederick ... consideration of Forty Pounds ... the several Lots of Land situate Lying and being in the Town of Stephensburg ... that is to said one Lot in the Town on the East side of Mulberry Street known by Number 72 ... Containing half an Acres ... also out Lot No. 23 on the East side of Crooked Land ... Containing five Acres of Land ... Lot No. 86 on the W. side of Squirrel Lane ... Containing five Acres of Land ... Which said three Lots of Land was conveyed in Fee Simple from Lewis Stephens and Mary his wife to Lawrence Snapp ... And then by the Death of said Lawrence Snapp was put in possession of John Snapp, he being Heir at Law to his Father the said Lawrence Snapp ...

Wit: Joel Reese   John Snap
   Henry Bengle
Recorded: 3 June 1783

Bk 19, p. 436 - 2 June 1783

    [Lease] Between Daniel Zuber of York County and State of Pennsylvania [to] Jacob Sherman of County aforesaid ... consideration of Five Shillings ... all that Tract of Land Lying and being on the Drains of back Creek ... which was granted to a certain Joseph Bridges by Deed under the Hand and Seal of the Right Honorable Thomas Lord Fairfax and granted by said Joseph Bridges unto said Daniel Zuber ... corner to Absolum Hayworths ... Containing three ___ and Ninety Acres ... Yielding and paying rent of one pepper Corn on Lady Day next ...

Wit: none   Daniel Zuber
Recorded: 3 June 1783

Bk 19, p. 437 - 3 June 1783

    [Release] Between Daniel Zuber of York County in State of Pennsylvania [to] Jacob Sherman of County aforesaid ... Consideration of One Hundred Pounds ... in a Hollow of William White's ... 390 Acres (same as above) ...

Wit: none   Daniel Zuber
Recorded: 3 June 1783

Bk 19, p. 439 - 5 May 1783

    Between Jacob White and Agnes his wife of Frederick County [to] Michael White of County aforesaid ... Consideration of Fifty Pounds ... Tract of Land situate lying and being in aforesaid County ... containing One Hundred and Thirty Three Acres and one third ... (in his actual possession now being by virtue of a Deed Granted by the Proprietor of the Northern Neck to John Stitler, Jacob White and Michael White the 10th Jan. 1767) ...

Wit: Richard Longacre   Jacob White
   Aaron Mercer   Agnes (X) White
   John Longacre
Recorded: 3 June 1783

Bk 19, p. 441 - 5 May 1783

Between Michael White of Frederick County [to] Jacob White of County aforesaid ... consideration of Fifty Pounds ... Tract of Land situate lying and being in the aforesaid County ... containing Two Hundred and Sixty Six Acres and Two thirds ... (in his actual possession now being by virtue of a Deed granted by the Proprietor of Northern Neck to John Stitler, Jacob White and Michael White the 10th Jan. 1767) ...
Wit: Richard Longacre   Michael White
    Aaron Mercer
    John Longacre
Recorded: 3 June 1783

Bk 19, p. 442 - 26 May 1783

[Lease] Between Thomas Edmondson of County of Frederick [to] Joseph Holmes Gent. of aforesaid ... consideration of Five Shillings ... a certain Lot in the Borough of Winchester ... containing one fourth of an Acre of Land in Loudon Street known by No. 75 ... Also one out Lot belonging to the same known by No. 29 containing two Acres and one half ... Yielding and paying rent of one Pepper Corn on Lady day next ...
Wit: Frederick Conrad   Thos. Edmondson
    William Edmondson
    Isaac Littler
Recorded: 3 June 1783

Bk 19, p. 443 - 27 May 1783

[Release] Between Thomas Edmondson of Frederick County [to] Joseph Holmes of the aforesaid ... consideration of one Hundred and Thirty Pounds ... Lot No. 75 and Lot No. 29 in the Borough of Winchester (same as above) ...
Wit: same as above   Thos. Edmondson
Recorded: 3 June 1783

Bk 19, p. 445 - 2 June 1783

[Lease] Between Thomas Edmondson of Winchester in County of Frederick [to] Nicholas Mesmore of the same place ... consideration of Five Shillings ... a certain Lot or half Acre of Land situate in the said Town of Winchester known by the No. 59 the same being the Lot which Bryan Bruin with other Lands Mortgaged to Courtney & Howard Merchants of Baltimore to secure the Payment of a Sum of Money ... And by a decree of the Court, the said Lot together with the out Lot of five Acres (which has since been separated & divided into sundry Lots) were conveyed to said Thomas Edmondson by Angus McDonald high Sheriff ... Yielding and paying rent of one Pepper Corn on Lady day next ...
Wit: J. Peyton Jr.   Thos. Edmondson
    Lewis Hoff
    Thomas Peyton

Recorded: 3 June 1783

Bk 19, p. 446 - 3 June 1783
    [Release] Between Thomas Edmondson of Winchester in County of Frederick [to] Nicholas Mesmore of the same place ... consideration of fifty five pounds ... Lot No. 50 in the Borough of Winchester (same as above) ...
Wit: same as above   Thos. Edmondson
Recorded: 3 June 1783

Bk 19, p. 448 - 2 June 1783
    [Lease] Between Peter Hurbough late of the County of Frederick but now of County of Shenandoa [to] Lawrence Schnepp of County of Shenandoa ... consideration of five pounds ... tract of Land which he the said Peter Humbough purchased of John Bachelor by Deeds of L & R the 3rd & 4th April 1775 containing Twenty five Acres and a Half ... situate lying and being on a Branch of Cedar Creek joining Joseph Wesant's and Michael Poker's Land ... Yielding and paying therefore one Ear of Indian Corn in and upon the feast of Christmas ...
Wit: Joseph Longacre   Peter Hurbough
   Jacob Havely
Recorded: 3 June 1783

Bk 19, p. 449 - 3 June 1783
    [Release] Between Peter Hurbough and Katharine his wife late of County of Frederick but now of Shanandoa [to] Laurence Schnepp of the said County of Shanandoa ... consideration of One Hundred and Twenty Pounds ... 25 1/2 Acres (same as above) ...
Wit: same as above   Peter Hurbough
Recorded: 3 June 1783   Katharine Hurbough

Bk 19, p. 451 - 3 June 1793
    Between John Wincor Driver and Eleanor his wife of County of Frederick [to] Samuel Weeks of place aforesaid ... consideration of Twelve Pounds ... the whole half Acre Lot situate Lying and being in the Town of Stephensburgh that is to said Lot No. 72 ... East side of Mulberry Street ... which said Lott of Land was conveyed in Fee Simple from John Snapp of Shanandoah County to John Wincor Driver ...
Wit: none   John Wincor (#) Driver
Recorded: 3 June 1783   Ellenor Driver

Bk 19, p. 453 - 21 April 1783
    [Lease] Between Lewis Stephens and Mary his wife of County of Frederick [to] John Hite, Jr. of the same Place ... consideration of Five Shillings ... all that Tract of Land lying in Frederick County containing one half Acre, being part of a greater Tract of Land containing 42 (424) Acres and conveyed by Deed of L & R the 2nd & 3rd May 1755 from Peter Stephens to Lewis Stephens ... which said 424 Acres of Land

is part of a greater Tract of 674 Acres granted by Patent to sd Peter Stephens the 3rd Oct. 1734 ... Line between Lewis Stephens and John Hite, Jr. ... corner to Richard Stafford's two acres ... Yielding and paying therefore one Ear of Indian Corn in and upon the feast of Christmas ...
Wit: none
Recorded: 5 Aug. 1783

Lewis Stephens
Mary (M) Stephens

Bk 19, p. 454 - 21 April 1783
    [Release] Between Lewis Stephens and Mary his wife of County of Frederick [to] John Hite Jr. of the same place ... Consideration of Ten Pounds ... 1/2 Acre (same as above) ...
Wit: none
Recorded: 4 Aug. 1783

Lewis Stephens
Mary (M) Stephens

Bk 19, p. 456 - 24 July 1783
    WITNESSETH that John Cottrall son of Elizabeth Cottrall late of Hampshire hath put Himself ... doth voluntarily and of his own free will and accord put himself apprentice to Nathan Nicholas shoemaker to learn the Shoemaking trade or Mystery ... to Serve him from the day of the Date hereof for and during the Term of three Years ...
Wit: John Hodgson
   Elizabeth Hodgson
   Hannah Hodgson
Recorded: 3 April 1783

John Cottrill

THE END

DEED BOOK 19

FREDERICK COUNTY, VIRGINIA

FREDERICK COUNTY, VIRGINIA

DEED BOOK 20 [1783 - 1785]

(Abstracted)

Bk 20, p. 1 - 5 March 1783
    Between Lewis Stephens and Mary his wife of Parish and County of Frederick [to] Dennis Bush of the same Parish and County ... WHEREAS Lewis Stephens sometime in the month of May 1760 sold and conveyed to George McCall a certain Lot or half Acre of Land in the Town of Stephensburg commonly called or known by No. 58 under certain Conditions ... one of which said George McCall should erect and build on said Lott No. 58 a certain Dwelling House ... that sd George McCall should pay yearly to sd Lewis Stephens ten Shillings ... Whereas neither of the aforesaid Conditions were fulfilled or complyed with ... Now this Indenture for and in consideration of One Hundred & Eighty pounds paid by Dennis Bush ... the aforesaid Lott or half Acre of Land in the sd Town of Stephensburg No. 58 ...
Wit; Vane Bush   Lewis Stephens
   Geo. W. Stephens   Mary (M) Stephens
   Abraham Nisewanger
   Christian Snipe
Recorded: 5 Aug. 1783

Bk 20, p. 3 - 21 April 1783
    Between Lewis Stephens & Mary his wife of County of Frederick [to] Richard Stafford of the same Place ... consideration of ten pounds ... all Lott of two Acres of Land lying near the Town of Stephensburg ... by the side of the Road leading (from) Winchester to Stephensburg ... Corner to a half Acre Lott purchased by John Hite ... between John Groves & James Hennings Lotts ... line between Maj. Lewis Stephens & John Hite ... which two Acre of Land are part of a larger Tract of Land containing 424 Acres & conveyed by Deed of L & R the 2nd & 3rd May 1755 from Peter Stephens to Lewis Stephens ... which sd 424 Acres of Land is part of a greater Tract of 674 Acres Granted by Patent to sd Peter Stephens the 3rd Oct. 1734 ...
Wit: none   Lewis Stephens
Recorded: 5 Aug. 1783   Mary (M) Stephens

Bk 20, p. 5 - 21 April 1783
    [Lease] Between John Hite Jr. and Susanna his wife of County of Frederick [to] Lewis Stephens of the same Place ... consideration of Five Shillings ... All that parcel of Land containing one Acre of Land part of a larger Tract of Land containing Twelve Hundred & three Acres & Conveyed by Deed of L & R from John Hite to John Hite, Jr. which sd 1203 (Acres) of Land is part of a Greater Tract of 5018 Acres granted by Pattent to Jost Hite the 3rd Oct. 1734 ... petition line between Maj. Lewis

Stephens & John Hite Jr. ... Yielding and paying therefore one Ear of Indian Corn in & upon the first day of Christmas ...
Wit: none
Recorded: 5 Aug. 1783
Jno. Hite jr
Susanna Hite

Bk 20, p. 6 - 21 April 1783
[Release] Between John Hite Jr & Susanna his wife of County of Frederick [to] Lewis Stephens of the same Place ... consideration of Ten Pounds ... one acre (same as above) ...
Wit: none
Recorded: 5 Aug. 1783
Jno. Hite jr
Susanna Hite

Bk 20, p. 8 - 1 Aug. 1783
[Lease] Between John Haggin son & heir at Law of James Haggin dec'd. of County of Lincoln in State of Virginia [to] Michael Fraker of the County of Frederick ... consideration of five Shillings ... part of a Tract of Land laying and being on the drains of Opeccon being part of a Tract Granted to James Haggin by Deed under the Hand and Seal of the Right Honorable Thomas Lord Fairfax ... corner to Robert Rutherford ... containing 49 3/4 Acres and twenty four poles ... Yielding and paying rent of one pepper Corn on Lady day next ...
Wit: none
Recorded: 5 Aug. 1783
John Haggin

Bk 20, p. 9 - 2 Aug. 1783
[Release] Between John Haggin Son & Heir at Law of James Haggin dec'd. of County of Lincoln in State of Virginia [to] Michael Fraker of the County of Frederick ... consideration of Forty five Pounds ... 49 3/4 Acres & 24 poles (same as above) ...
Wit: none
Recorded: 5 Aug. 1783
John Haggin

Bk 20, p. 11 - 2 Aug. 1783
[Lease] Between John Haggin son and Heir at Law of James Haggin dec'd. of County of Lincoln in State of Virginia [to] Jacob Rogers Jr of County of Frederick ... consideration of Five Shillings ... Tract of Land lying and being on the drains of Opeccon & being part of a Tract Granted to James Haggin by Deed under the Hand and Seal of the Right Honorable Thomas Lord Fairfax ... in the line of Edward Dodd ... containing twenty four and three quarters of an Acre ... Yielding and paying rent of one pepper Corn on Lady day next ...
Wit: Jonathan Ross
  David Ross
  Joseph Day
Recorded: 5 Aug. 1783
John Haggin

Bk 20, p. 3 Aug. 1783

[Release] Between John Haggin Son and Heir at Law of James Haggin dec'd. of County of Lincoln in State of Virginia [to] Jacob Rogers Jr of County of Frederick ... consideration of fourteen Pounds seventeen Shillings ... 24 3/4 Acre (same as above) ...
Wit: same as above   John Haggin
Recorded: 5 Aug. 1783

Bk 20, p. 13 - 5 Aug. 1783

Between David Nisewanger of Frederick County [to] Robert Gamble of the same place ... WITNESSETH that whereas said Robert Gamble was indebted to said David Nisewanger in the sum of three thousand and eighty pounds ... for the better securing the payment said Robert Gamble did by Indenture the 7th March 1780 Grant bargain & sell unto said David Nisewanger ... a certain plantation situate in said County of Frederick Containing Two hundred and twenty two Acres ... WHEREAS said Robert Gamble having paid the said David Nisewanger the sum (above mentioned) with all Interest due ... whereof said David Nisewanger hath granted and released said Indenture of Mortgage ... in and to the tract of Land ...
Wit: Willm. Vance   David Nisewanger
  John Gilkeson
  Cassamar May
Recorded: 5 Aug. 1783

Bk 20, p. 14 - 3 May 1783

KNOW all men by these presents that I George Pierce of County of Frederick for and in consideration of Twenty five pounds paid by Spencer Lehue of County aforesaid ... One Red Cow with a white face, Two yearlings with crop on Left Ear, three yearlings with crop on Right ear and One Sorrel Mare ...
Wit: James Browning   George Pierce
  Jacob Utterback
  Wm (X) Little
Recorded: 5 Aug. 1783

Bk 20, p. 15 - 5 March 1783

[Lease] Between Benjamin Blackburn of County of Hampshire [to] Francis McCormick of County of Frederick ... consideration of five shillings ... a Certain Tract of Land left by Will to the said Benjamin Blackburn by his Uncle Samuel Blackburn dec'd. situate lying and being on South West Marsh in the County of Frederick ... in the whole One Hundred and Seventy four Acres and Twenty eight poles ... Yielding and paying rent of one Ear of Indian Corn on the last day of said Term ...
Wit: John Rice   Benjamin Blackburn
  Saml. Baker
Recorded: 5 Aug. 1783

Bk 20, p. 17 - 5 March 1783

[Release] Between Benjamin Blackburn of County of Hampshire [to] Francis McCormick of County of Frederick ... consideration of Four Hundred and fifty Pounds ... 174 Acres 28 poles (same as above) ...
Wit: same as above   Benjamin Blackburn
Recorded: 5 Aug. 1783

Bk 20, p. 18 - 4 Aug. 1783

[Lease] Between Meridith Helm Senior of County of Frederick [to] William Helm of County aforesaid ... consideration of Five Shillings ... two Tracts of Land called the rich Ridge situate and lying on the drains of Opeckon ... the first Tract Containing four hundred Acres ... Also another Tract of Land joining the former and being contiguous thereto ... Containing two hundred Acres ... Yielding and paying therefore one Pepper corn Yearly ...
Wit: none   Meridith Helm Sen.
Recorded: 5 Aug. 1783

Bk 20, p. 20 - 5 Aug. 1783

[Release] Between Meridith Helm Sen. and Sarah his wife of County of Frederick [to] William Helm of County aforesaid ... consideration of One thousand Pounds ... Two Tracts of Land - one containing 400 Acres ... the other 200 Acres (same as above) ...
Wit: none   Meridith Helm
Recorded: 5 Aug. 1783   Sarah (X) Helm

Bk 20, p. 22 - 6 Aug. 1783

Between James Walker of Winchester in County of Frederick [to] Rev. Alexander Balmain of the same place ... consideration of two hundred pounds ... a Certain Lot or half Acre of Land situate in Winchester and known by No. 74 ... Also one other Lot of five Acres situate in the Common of said Borough Contiguous to above Lot 74 and is known by No. 34 which said lots were Granted to John Carlyle by Deed the 15th May 1753 from the Proprietor of Northern Neck and by said Carlyle conveyed to said James Walker by Deed the 4th Aug. 1779 ...
Wit: David Kennedy   James Walker
   James Limrall
   John Reynolds
Recorded: 6 Aug. 1783

Bk 20, p. 24 - 14 June 1783

Between Thomas Edmondson of Winchester in County of Frederick [to] Martin Reilley of the same place ... consideration of Sixty five pounds ... one equal half part of a certain Lot of half Acre of Land situate in the Borough of Winchester the same being part of a Greater Tract of Land of Five acres which was formerly laid out in the Common of the said Borough and which said Thomas Edmondson obtained

by the annexing of the said Borough being allowed ... known by No. 1 and is situate on the No. side of Fairfax Road ...
Wit: John Thomas   Thomas Edmondson
　Henry Prince
　Jacob Kiger
　J Peyton Jr
Recorded: 6 Aug. 1783

Bk 20, p. 25 - 14 June 1783
　　　Between Thomas Edmondson of Winchester in State of Virginia [to] Jacob Keyger of the same place ... consideration of thirty pounds ... one equal moiety of lot No. 1 situate in the Borough of Winchester aforesaid the same being part of a Lot of five Acres which said Thomas Edmondson obtained and was formerly an out Lot ... the moiety hereby conveyed contains one fourth part of an Acre of Land ...
Wit: John Thomas   Thomas Edmondson
　Henry Prince
　Martin Riyle /Riley
　J Peyton Jr.
Recorded: 6 Aug. 1783

Bk 20, p. 26 - 5 Aug. 1783
　　　[Lease] Between Robert Rutherford of Berkeley County in State of Virginia Esquire [to] Edward Smith of Winchester Frederick County ... consideration of five Shillings ... Tract of Land situate in the County of Frederick ... Corner to Land surveyed for Isaac Hollingsworth also for Land surveyed for Enoch Pearson ... North side of the Great Road leading from Winchester to Snickers Ferry ... Containing Forty six Acres which sd Tract of land is part of a Greater Tract of One hundred Acres which the said Rutherford received when he made sundry Sales to Col. John Smith out of a certain Tract of Four hundred Acres Granted by Deed from Lord Fairfax to said Rutherford the 11th April 1760 ... Yielding and paying rent of one pepper corn on Lady day next ...
Wit: David Deadwick   Robert Rutherford
　J. Peyton
　Thomas Peyton
Recorded: 6 Aug. 1783

Bk 20, p. 28 - 6 Aug. 1783
　　　[Release] Between Robert Rutherford and Mary his wife of Berkeley County [to] Edward Smith of Winchester in County of Frederick ... consideration of One hundred pounds ... 46 Acres (same as above) ...
Wit: same as above   R. Rutherford
Recorded: 6 Aug. 1783

Bk 20, p. 30 - 15 July 1784 (?)

GREETINGS - Whereas Joseph Steer and Grace his wife by their Indenture the 14th Dec. 1780 have sold and conveyed unto Isaac Sitler the Fee Simple estate in a certain part of lott No. 22 in the Borough of Winchester together with part of the Out lott No. 76 in the Common to the said Borough ... Grace now releases Dower right to said Lotts ...   Joseph Holmes
Recorded: 7 Aug. 1783   Edward McGuire

Bk 20, p. 31 - 7 June 1783

Between Hannah Onion widow and Relict of Zachius Onion late of Hartford County in State of Maryland dec'd. and Stephen Onion Eldest son and Heir at Law of said Zachius Onion [to] Alexander Robison of Baltimore County in Maryland ... consideration of Twelve hundred pounds ... Tract of Land called and known by the name Back Creek in the County of Frederick ... in a Valley on the East side of Hog Creek ... 1200 Acres of Land more or less as by patent thereof Granted to a certain Stephen Onion on the 6th March 1753 ...
Wit: Philip Bush   Hannah Onion
  Isaac Wilke   Stephen Onion
  James Holliday
Recorded: 8 Aug. 1783

Bk 20, p. 33 - 25 May 1780

TO ALL CHRISTIAN PEOPLE Greetings ... Know ye that I the said James Grinning for divers good Causes and Considerations but Especially for the Good will and Love I bear to my Neighbour Robert Haines also the consideration of five Shillings paid by said Robert Haines ... Grant bargain and Sell unto said Robert Haines a Parcell of Land Containing one hundred and twenty five Acres situate lying and being in (Parish and County of Frederick) and being the Plantation whereon I now live and which I formerly purchased of John Painter ...
Wit: Anthony Moor   James (+) Grinning
  Robert Rea
  Thomas Fawcett

This Indenture was proved by the affirmation of the Witnesses thereto (being people Called Quakers) and ordered to be Recorded ...
Recorded: 2 Sept. 1783

Bk 20, p. 34 - 18 Aug. 1783

[Lease] Between George Kellar of County of Frederick [to] George Sheaver late of County of Shenandoah ... consideration of five shillings ... Tract of Land situate lying and being on a branch of Ceader (sic) Creek containing one hundred and twenty nine Acres and a half and part of a Greater Tract Granted to Jacob Gibson by a Deed from Proprietors Office the 10th March MDCCLII and said Jacob Gibson conveyed the same by L & R the 20th & 21st Jan. MDCCLIII to Lewis Smaltzhavin and said Lewis Smaltzhavin by his Deed conveyed same to said George

Kellar in March MDCCLXXX ... Yielding and paying rent of one Pepper corn on Lady day next ...
Wit: David Nisewanger George Kellar
    Jacob Trout
Recorded: 2 Sept. 1783

Bk 20, p. 36 - 19 Aug. 1783
    [Release] Between George Keller and Margarad his wife of County of Frederick [to] George Sheaver late of the County of Shenandoah ... consideration of One Hundred Pounds ... 129 1/2 Acres (same as above) ...
Wit: same as above George Keller
Recorded: 2 Sept. 1783 Margared (X) Keller

Bk 20, p. 38 - 2 Sept. 1783
    Between Robert Gamble and Elizabeth his wife of Frederick County [to] John Gilkeson and William Vance of County aforesaid ... consideration of four hundred pounds ... Tract of Land situate in County of Frederick adjoining the Lands of Jacob Chrisman Edward Whitehead and Isaac Zane ... corner to the Land patented by Yost Hite and corner to Charles McDowell ... Containing two hundred and seventy two Acres which said Tract of Land was conveyed to William Gowdy by Jacob Chrisman and by said Gowdy to said Gamble ...
Wit: none Robert Gamble
Recorded: 2 Sept. 1783 Elizabeth Gamble

Bk 20, p. 40 - 2 Sept. 1783
    Between Thomas Cochran and Phebe his wife of Winchester in County of Frederick [to] Philip Woolwine of the same place ... Whereas said Thomas Cochran by his two Bonds stands indebted to said Philip Woolwine in the Sum of One hundred pounds ... Now this Indenture for better Securing the payment of said sums of money also for and in consideration of five Shillings ... doth bargain and sell unto said Philip Woolwine a certain part of Lot No. 15 situate on the East side of Loudoun Street in said Borough of Winchester and being the same said Philip Woolwine purchased from Benjamin Shreve and by said Woolwine conveyed to said Thomas Cochran ... to John Haymakers line ... to the line of Martin Riley ... Also two Acres and a half of Land in the said borough on the north side of Martin Rileys out Lot and adjoining Henry Bakers Lot ... being one moiety of Lot No. 22 ... Lot No. 15 & 22 is part of the purchase which the aforesaid Shreve made of Meshack Sexton ...
Wit: none Thomas Cochran
Recorded: 2 Sept. 1783 Phebe Cochran

Bk 20, p. 42 - 21 June 1783
    Between John Barnett of County of Frederick [to] William Helm, Stephen Johnston, Thomas Berry, Joseph Berry & Jacob LaRue of County aforesaid ... consideration of the full sum of one Shilling ... Being Babtist (sic) and members of

the Baptist Church at Trap Hill ... piece of Land situate lying and being near bucks marsh on Trap Hill ... in William Booths line ... Containing in a whole three rods and thirty perches all of which is part of a Tract of Land containing One Hundred and Eighty Acres which said Tract of Land containing 180 Acres was part of a larger Tract Containing three Hundred and Seventy eight acres which said 378 Acres was Granted by what is commonly known as King's Patent to a certain Samuel Maurice who in his last Will and Testament gave and devised same to Benjamin Maurice his son and the said Benjamin Maurice sold and conveyed by deeds of L & R the Tract of One Hundred and Eighty Acres aforementioned to James Barnett dec'd. who in his last Will and Testament gave and devised same to said John Barnett ...
Wit: John Kerchival
    William Davis
    Nathaniel Ashby
    John LaReu
John Barnell
Recorded: 7 Oct. 1783

Bk 20, p. 45 - 20 Oct. 1779
    Between Henry Heth and Agnes his wife of Winchester in County of Frederick [to] William Heth of the same place ... Consideration of fifty pounds ... one half part of a certain Lott of Land containing one half an Acre situate in the said Town of Winchester and known by No. 42 ... the other half said Lott now being the property of Thomas McDugal with one half of a certain lott of five Acres on the common of the said Town ... the same being the half lotts which said Henry Heth purchased of Hugh West ... Also another lott of Land situate in an addition to the said Town of Winchester known by the No. 154 being the lott which said Henry Heth purchased of Thomas Rutherford ...
Wit: J. Peyton Jr.
    Robt. Macky
    Saml. Gilkeson
Henry Heth
Agnes Heth
Recorded: 7 Oct. 1783

Bk 20, p. 47 - 9 Sept. 1783
    [Lease] Between John Carter of County of Craven and Commonwealth of South Carolina [to] Charles Johnson /Johnston and Susannah Chambers of County of Frederick ... consideration of five shillings ... One undivided eighth part of a parcell of Land ... Containing 592 Acres granted to Wm. Chambers by two Deeds the 4th & 8th Nov. 1754 ...
Wit: George Kiger
    George Overacre
    William Swords
John Carter
Recorded: 7 Oct. 1783

Bk 20, p. 48 - 8 Sept. 1783 (?)
    [Release] Between John Carter and Rachel his wife of Craven County and

Commonwealth of South Carolina [to] Charles Johnston and Susannah Chambers of County of Frederick ... consideration of Sixty pounds ... 592 Acres (same as above).
Wit: same as above
Recorded: 7 Oct. 1783

John Carter
Rachel (X) Carter

Bk 20, p. 50 - 21 Aug. 1783

KNOW all men by these presents that we William Darlington & John Darlington of County of Frederick are held firmly bound unto Gabriel Darlington, David Darlington, Margaret Darlington, Joseph Darlington and Meridith Darlington in the sum of Four thousand pounds ... WHEREAS Meridith Darlington the Elder lately deceased father to the above bound William Darlington and John Darlington being willing and desirous to do Justice by dividing the Estate of his Father Equally among all his Children and said John Darlington second son of said Meridith Darlington having also consented to same Division in case of Death of said William Darlington the heir in Line ... when the sd division shall be made will make over and Convey to each of the Children of the said Meridith Darlington such proportions of Land or such said sums of money as shall be determined and with out further delay.

Wit: John Capper
    Josiah Jackson
    John Lupton
    Jos. Steer Jr.
    David Davis
    Jno. Davis
Recorded: 7 Oct. 1783

William Darlington
John Darlington

Bk 20, p. 51 - 7 Aug. 1783

Between John Ashby of Fauquier County and Parish of Hambleton [to] Nathaniel Ashby of County of Frederick ... consideration of the natural love and affection that he hath to his son Nathaniel Ashby ... Tract of Land containing four hundred and Seven Acres the said Land being Granted to George Carter Esq. late of the Middle Temple of London Esq. and by his Trustees Charles Carter & Peter Hedgman conveyed by L & R to said John Ashby the 22nd & 23rd April 1762 ... The said four hundred and seven Acres joining to Thomas Bryley, John Bell, dec'd., Richard Mede, Alex. Henderson ... (Reserving the natural life of said John Ashby).

Wit: John Coe
    Lewis Ashby
    John (J) Jones
    Franklin (X) McKensey
Recorded: 7 Oct. 1783

John Ashby

Bk 20, p. 52 - 15 Sept. 1783

Between Frederick Slusher and Ann Galihar his wife of County of Frederick [to] Geo. Fulkes of County aforesaid ... consideration of Two hundred pounds ... Tract of Land situate lying and being in County aforesaid ... on the west side of a

branch of Crooked Creek in the line of Lorone (Lawrence ?) Snapp ... Containing 430 Acres ...
Wit: Wm Glascock Jun.
   Jacob Leonard
   Henry Poose (?)
Recorded: 7 Oct. 1783

Frederick Slusher
Anna Galihar (A) Slusher

Bk 20, p. 54 - 4 Oct. 1783
    Between Lewis Stephens and Mary his wife of County of Frederick [to] Jacob Leonard of County aforesaid ... consideration of Twenty four Shillings ... all that Messuage of Lot of Ground situate near Stephensburgh ... Containing in the whole Two Acres and thirty perches which said Messuage or Lot is part of a Large Tract of Land Containing four hundred and twenty four Acres conveyed by Deeds of L & R the 2nd & 3rd May 1755 from Peter Stephens to Lewis Stephens ... which said 424 Acres of Land is part of Six Hundred & Twenty four Acres granted by Patent to said Peter Stephens the 3rd Oct. 1734 ...
Wit: John Grove
   Daniel Mylinger
Recorded: 7 Oct. 1783

Lewis Stephens
Mary (M) Stephens

Bk 20, p. 57 - 1 May 1783
    [Lease] Between Francis Lehew and Leanah his wife John Lehew and Frances Lehew widow of Peter Lehew dec'd. of County of Frederick [to] Solomon Vanmeter of County of Shanandoe ... Consideration of five Shillings ... Tract or Lott of Land lying and being in County aforesaid and on Great Happy Creek ... Corner of George Cheeks Lot ... in which Bounds there is contained One Acre and three quarters & seven Perches of Land it being part of a Tract of 3000 Acres Granted to William Russel Esq. by Patton (sic) the 17th Dec. 1733 ... the sd Russel being so possessed conveyed 400 acres thereof to Christopher Mar by Deed ... said Mar conveyed 200 Acres thereof to Peter Lehew by his deed the 2nd Feb. 1754 the said Peter Lehew being so possessed with said Land did by his Last Will and Testament give and bequeath 35 Acres thereof to his son Francis Lehew and the rest of his children ... Yielding and paying rent of one pepper corn on Lady day next ...
Wit: Mason Jones
   John Lehew
Recorded: 7 Oct. 1783

Francis Lehew
Frances (+) Lehew

Bk 20, p. 58 - 2 May 1783
    [Release] Between Francis Lehew and Leanah his wife John Lehew and Franes Lehew Widow of Peter Lehew dec'd. of County of Frederick [to] Solomon Vanmeter of County of Shanandoe ... consideration of five Pounds ... 1 3/4 Acres and 7 perches (same as above) ...
Wit: same as above

Francis Lehew
Leanna Lehew

Recorded: 7 Oct. 1783   Frances (+) Lehew

Bk 20, p. 61 - 7 Oct. 1783
    Between George Noble of County of Frederick [to] Thomas Noble of the same County ... consideration of Two Hundred pounds ... Tract of Land situate lying and being in County of Frederick ... Containing two hundred acres according to a Survey made by Mr. Benjamin Berry on 24 April 1783 and which such Survey is part of two Lotts of Land purchased out of Mercer's Land and Distinguished by No. 11 & 14 ...
Wit: none   Geo. Noble
Recorded: 7 Oct. 1783

Bk 20, p. 62 - 2 April 1783
    Between Mary Wood widow and Devisee of Colonel James Wood late of County of Frederick dec'd. [to] Alexander White of said County Attorney at Law ... Whereas the Remains of Elizabeth the much beloved and affectionate Wife of said Alexander White and Daughter of James and Mary Wood by interred in a Space of Ground of said James Wood supposed to Contain One Hundred & forty square feet and whereas the said Alexander White hath earnestly requested that said Space of Land be conveyed to him for purpose of a Burying Ground ... Now this Indenture ... in consideration of five Shillings ... doth grant bargain and sell the Space of Ground above Described ...
Wit: James Wood   Mary Wood
   Robt. White Jun.
   Robert Wood
Recorded: 7 Oct. 1783

Bk 20, p. 64 - __ Oct. 1774
    Between Daniel Benezet of the City of Philadelphia in the Province of Pennsylvania Merchant and Elizabeth his wife [to] Peter Op of Stevensburg in Frederick County ... Consideration of Seventy five pounds ... a Certain Lot or half Acre of Land situate in the Town of Stevensburg known by No. 48 ... on the East side of Market Street ... Also one other Lot Containing five Acres adjoining to part of the said Town ... on the East side of High Lane ... in Lawrence Stephenson line ... Also the other Lot of half an acre in the said Town of Stevensburg known by No. 47 together with an out Lot of Five Acres joining the said Town ... being the same Lots of Land which George Cabbage and Catharine his wife by Indenture the 7th May 1767 did grant to said Daniel Benezet ...
Wit: Martin Noll   Danl. Benezet
   C. Messemer   Eliza. Benezet
   Vance Bush
   Reuben Allen Sen.
Recorded: 8 Oct. 1783

Bk 20, p. 66 - 6 June 1770

    Between Thomas Ewing and Samuel Brown of the Town of Baltimore in province of Maryland Merchants and partners [to] Daniel McPherson of County of Frederick ... Whereas Joseph Beeler and Margaret his wife in and by a certain Indenture the 13th July 1768 ... Did grant bargain and sell unto said Thomas Ewing and Samuel Brown a Tract of Land situate lying and being in County of Frederick ... Viz: to Jacob Penningtons corner ... Containing five hundred Acres ... And also one other Tract of Land Adjoining the before mentioned ... near the House of the said Joseph Bealor ... Corner to Mr. John Harden ... Containing Sixty seven Acres ... Whereas said Thomas Ewing and Samuel Brown did Grant to said Joseph Beeler that if he the said Joseph Beeler should well and truly pay the full sum of Eight Hundred pounds together with Interest the said Indenture should be none Effect and said Thomas Ewing and Samuel Brown should reconvey the Interest vested in them by said Indenture ... which said Tract of Land sd Joseph Beeler hath sold and conveyed unto said Daniel McPherson ... Now this Indenture for and in consideration of three hundred and ninety pounds paid by said Daniel McPherson ... all the Right Title and Interest of the said Thomas Ewing and Samuel Brown of the before part recited Indenture ...

Wit: Jas. Keith   Thos. Ewing
    Andrew Bradley   Samuel Brown
    1 wit. signed in German
Recorded: 8 Oct. 1783

Bk 20, p. 68 - 5 Sept. 1783

    Between George Hite Adm. of the Estate of Jacob Hite late of Berkeley County [to] Daniel McPherson of County aforesaid ... Whereas said Joseph Beeler late of Frederick County was Indebted unto aforesaid Jacob Hite in the sum of money for securing the payment whereof said Joseph Beeler and Margaret his wife did by an Indenture by Indenture the 11th Oct. 1769 Grant unto said Jacob Hite a Tract of Land situate in County of Berkeley (then Frederick) ... corner to Jacob Pennington ... Containing five hundred Acres ... Also one other tract adjoining the before mentioned ... near the said Beeler House ... Containing seven acres ... which said Tracts of Lands the said Joseph Beeler afterwards by Indenture of L & R the 13th & 14th March 1770 conveyed unto said Daniel McPherson ... Now this Indenture for and in consideration of Two hundred and twenty three pounds seven Shillings and ten pence ... surrender unto said Daniel McPherson ...

Wit: J. Peyton Jr.   G. Hite
    Jas. Keith
    David Deadwick
    Thomas Peyton
Recorded: 8 Oct. 1783

Bk 20, p. 71 - 18 Oct. 1770

    Joseph Beeler's Account with Jacob Hite - 148 Pounds 8 Shillings 10

Pence ... I do certify that the above is a True Copy of Mr. Joseph Beelers Acct. as it Stands on Mr. Jacob Hites Books (Vide Leagr. G. 172) ... and that it was this day settled ...   Thos. Hite
Recorded: 8 Oct. 1783

Bk 20, p. 72 - __ day of __ 1783
    [Lease] Between Robert Craigan the Elder of Winchester in County of Frederick [to] Robert Craigan the younger of the same place ... consideration of Five Shillings ... Tract of Land situate on one of the branches of Sleepy Creek on the Easterly side of warm Spring Ridge ... corner to Henry Lewis former Survey ... Containing three hundred and thirteen Acres which said Tract of Land was Granted to said Robert Craigan Sen. by Deed from the Proprietor of the Northern Neck the 16th July 1765 ... Yielding and paying one pepper corn on Lady day next ...
Wit: none   Robert Craigan
Recorded: 4 Nov. 1783

Bk 20, p. 73 - 4 Nov. 1783
    [Release] Between Robert Craigan Sen. of Winchester in County of Frederick and Susanna his wife [to] Robert Craigan Jun. of the same place ... Consideration of One Hundred pounds ... 313 Acres (same as above) ...
Wit: George Sommerville   Robert Craigan
    John Duffield   Susanna Craigen
    John Collin Crockwell
Recorded: 4 Nov. 1783

Bk 20, p. 76 - 3 Nov. 1783
    [Lease] Between Robert Craigan of Winchester in County of Frederick [to] Robert Craigan Jun. of the same place ... consideration of Five Shillings ... a Certain Lot or half Acre of Land situate in the said Borough of Winchester known by Number 68 together with one other lot of Eight Acres two rods & thirty four perches Situate in the Common of said Borough ... known by Number 58 ... Yielding and paying one pepper corn on Lady day next ...
Wit: none   Robert Craigan
Recorded: 4 Nov. 1783

Bk 20, p. 77 - 4 Nov. 1783
    [Release] Between Robert Craigan Sen. and Susanna his wife of Winchester in County of Frederick [to] Robert Craigan Jun. of the same place ... consideration of One Hundred pounds ... Lots No. 68 & 58 in Winchester (same as above) ...
Wit: George Sommerville   Robert Craigan
    John Duffield   Susanna Craigan
    John Collin Crockwell
Recorded: 4 Nov. 1783

Bk 20, p. 79 - 25 Sept. 1783

[Lease] Between Benjamin Haines of the Township of Evesham in County of Burlington and in the Western Division of New Jersey Cordwinder [to] Robert Haines of Frederick County ... consideration of Five Shillings ... Tract of Land situate lying and being in Frederick County aforesaid containing Two Hundred Acres ... which said Tract of Land was conveyed to said Benjamin Haines from Charles Buck and Lettice his wife by Deeds of L & R the 3rd & 4th June 1765 ... and was conveyed to said Charles Buck from Thomas Postgate and Mary his wife by Deeds of L & R the 12th & 13th Nov. 1750 ... Yielding and paying rent of one pepper corn on Lady Day next ...

Wit: Abel Walker   Benjamin Haines
　　 Evan Rogers
　　 Elizabeth Jolliffe
　　 Levi Haines
　　 Isaac Parkins
Recorded: 4 Nov. 1783

Bk 20, p. 80 - 26 Sept. 1783

[Release] Between Benjamin Haines of Township of Evesham in County of Burlington in the Western Division of New Jersey Cordwinder [to] Robert Haines of Frederick County ... consideration of Two Hundred pounds ... 200 Acres (same as above) ...

Wit: same as above   Benjamin Haines
Recorded: 4 Nov. 1783

Bk 20, p. 82 - 30 Oct. 1783

[Lease] Between Thomas Neill of County of Frederick [to] John Buchanan of Berkeley County ... Consideration of yearly rent of Seven pounds ten Shillings granted to farm let ... all that Tract of Land situate on the drains of Opequan (sic) Creek ... Containing one hundred and Ninety six Acres Granted to Lewis Neill by Deed from the proprietors office ... for and During the natural life of said John Buchanan and during the natural life of Elizabeth his wife and John Blackford son of Benjamin Blackford and during the life of the longest liver of them ...

Wit: Thomas Horbert   Thomas Neill
　　 Jos. Neill   John Buchanan
　　 Lewis Neill
Recorded: 4 Nov. 1783

Bk 20, p. 84 - 4 Nov. 1783

[Lease] Between Charles Buck and Mary his wife of County of Shenandoah [to] Thomas Buck of County of Frederick ... consideration of Five Shillings ... all that Tract of Land lying at the mouth of Passage Creek running down the North River ... Containing one hundred Acres ... Yielding and paying rent of one pepper corn on Lady Day next ...

Wit: William Davis
  Saml. Price
  Charles Catlett
Recorded: 4 Nov. 1783

Charles Buck
Mary Buck

Bk 20, p. 85 - 4 Nov. 1783
    [Release] Between Charles Buck and Mary his wife of county of Shannandoah [to] Thomas Buck of County of Frederick ... consideration of Two Hundred and twenty five pounds ... 100 Acres (same as above) ...
Wit: same as above
Recorded: 4 Nov. 1783

Charles Buck
Mary Buck

Bk 20, p. 87 - 29 May 1769
    [Lease] Between John Gillaspy of North Carolina [to] John Lyle of Frederick County ... consideration of Ten Shillings ... Tract of Land lying and being under the North Mountain on the Drains of Opeckon ... Bounded as by a Survey made thereof by William Baylis ... Corner to John Boyd ... to Hugh Lyles line ... Containing one hundred & ninety two and a half Acres ... Yielding and paying yearly rent of one pepper corn at the feast of St. Michael the Archangle (sic) ...
Wit: Hugh Lyle
  John Hayes
  Jas. Morrison
Recorded: 4 Nov. 1783

John Gillaspy

Bk 20, p. 89 - 30 May 1769
    [Release] Between John Gillaspy of North Carolina [to] John Lyle of Frederick County ... consideration of Thirty Pounds ... 192 1/2 Acres (same as above). ...
Wit: same as above
Recorded: 4 Nov. 1783

John Gillaspy

Bk 20, p. 91 - 29 May 1769
    [Lease] Between John Gillaspy of North Carolina [to] John Hays Jun. of County of Frederick ... consideration of Ten Shillings ... Tract of Land lying and being under the North Mountain on the drains of Opeckon and bounded by a Survey made by William Baylis ... in Hugh Lyles line and Corner to John Lyles ... Containing one hundred and ninety and a half Acres ... Yielding and paying yearly rent of one pepper corn at the feast of St. Michael the Archangle ...
Wit: Hugh Lyle
  John Lyle
  Robert Lyle
Recorded: 4 Nov. 1783

John Gillaspy

Bk 20, p. 92 - 30 May 1769

[Release] Between John Gillaspy of North Carolina [to] John Hays Jun. of County of Frederick ... consideration of Fifty Pounds ... 190 1/2 Acres (same as above) ...
Wit: same as above John Gillaspie
Recorded: 4 Nov. 1783

Bk 20, p. 94 - 1 June 1779

Between Meredith Helm & Joseph Helm Executors of the last Will and Testament of Thomas Helm dec'd. of County of Frederick [to] William Drew of said County ... consideration Seventeen Hundred & fifty pounds ... Tract of Land on the drains of Opeckon being the same which was granted by Patent from the Proprietor of Northern Neck to Rich. Chapman the 26th Aug. 1766 and by said Chapman conveyed by Deeds of L & R the 3rd & 4th Aug. 1768 to sd Thomas Helm dec'd. ... Containing two hundred and Ninety five Acres ...
Wit: Joseph Holmes Meredith Helm
 John Kain Joseph Helm
 J. Peyton Jr.
Recorded: 4 Nov. 1783

Bk 20, p. 95 - 28 Oct. 1783

Between David Kennedy of the Borough of Winchester in County of Frederick [to] Daniel Morgan Esq. of said County ... consideration of One Thousand and fifty pounds ... Two parcels of Land situate lying and being in the Borough of Winchester aforesaid containing each of them the eight part of an Acre and being each of them the fourth part of a Lot of the sd Borough and also two other pieces of Land situate lying and being in the Common and each of them also containing and being one fourth part of a Lot of the said Commons ... they being the same parcels of Land or Lots which were conveyed to Henry Keppele Sen. by Philip Bush and Catharine his wife by Deed the 22nd July 1778 ...
Wit: Edward McGuire David Kennedy
 J. Milton
 John Kerchival
Recorded: 4 Nov. 1783

Bk 20, p. 97 - 9 April 1783

[Lease] Between George Brinker of County of Frederick [to] Edward Smith of County aforesaid ... consideration of Five Shillings ... part of a Tract of Land lying and being in the said County and is part of the Tract which was bequeathed to said Brinker by the last Will and Testament of Henry Brinker dec'd. ... Containing ten and a half Acres ... Yielding and paying one pepper corn on Lady day next ...
Wit: none George Brinker
Recorded: 4 Nov. 1783

Bk 20, p. 98 - 10 April 1783

[Release] Between George Brinker and Rebeccah his wife of County of Frederick [to] Edward Smith of County aforesaid ... consideration of thirty pounds ... 10 1/2 Acres (same as above) ...
Wit: none
Recorded: 4 Nov. 1783
George Brinker
Rebeccah Brinker

Bk 20, p. 100 - 30 Nov. 1783

[Lease] Between John Keyzer of County of Hampshire and State of Virginia [to] Joseph Wood of Frederick County ... consideration of Five Shillings ... a certain Tract of Land containing One Hundred and Eighty Acres of Land on both sides of Hogs Creek in Frederick County ... the same being granted to Robert Rutherford by Deed from the Proprietor the 8th Aug. 1765 ... and conveyed by said Robert Rutherford and Mary his wife by L & R the 6th & 7th Feb. 1769 (to said John Keyzer) ... on the Indian Grave hill ... Yielding and paying rent of one pepper corn on Lady day next ...
Wit: Joseph Holmes
   David Kennedy
   John Davis
   David Hunter
Recorded: 5 Jan. 1784
John (K) Keyzer

Bk 20, p. 102 - 1 Dec. 1783

[Release] Between John Keyzer and Sally his wife of County of Hampshire [to] Joseph Wood of Frederick County ... consideration of One hundred pounds ... 180 Acres (same as above) ...
Wit: same as above
Recorded: 5 Jan. 1784
John (K) Keyzer
Sally (X) Keyzer

Bk 20, p. 104 - 6 Dec. 1783

Sally Keyzer released Dower right to above land ...
Joseph Holmes
David Kennedy

Bk 20, p. 105 - 6 Feb. 1784

GREETINGS - Know ye that I Joseph Berry Esq. of the Parish and County of Frederick for and in consideration of the love Goodwill and affection I have and bear towards Francis Berry of the same Parish and County ... Grant unto said Francis Berry three hundred and eight Acres of Land formerly belonging to Thomas Ashby.
Wit: Miles W. Conway
   Moley Berry
   William (X) Hanes
Recorded: 2 March 1784
Jos. Berry

Bk 20, p. 105 - 6 Feb. 1784

    GREETINGS - Know ye that I Joseph Berry Esq. of Parish & County of Frederick for and in consideration of the Love Goodwill and affection which I have and do bear Towards my Daughter Moley Berry of the same Parish and County have given and granted unto said Moley Berry Two Negroes Named Peg & Hanner they & their increase of which I present have Delivered the said Moley Berry ...

Wit: Miles W. Conway   Jos. Berry
    Francis Berry
    James (X) Dent
Recorded: 2 March 1784

Bk 20, p. 106 - 6 Feb. 1784

    GREETINGS - Know ye that I Joseph Berry Esq. of Parish & County of Frederick for and in consideration of the Love Goodwill and affection which I have and do bear towards Miles Withers Conway of the same Parish and County have given and granted unto said Miles Withers Conway two Negroes Judy and Jane ...

Wit: Francis Berry   Joseph Berry
    James (X) Dent
    Hulda Hullet
    Moley Berry
Recorded: 2 March 1784

Bk 20, p. 107 - 25 Feb. 1784

    [Lease] Between Martin Ashby of County of Frederick [to] Edward Snickers of County aforesaid ... consideration of five Shillings ... Tract of Land lying and being on Penningtons or Buck Marsh in County aforesaid ... line of Carters Tract ... Containing three hundred and six Acres ... Yielding and paying therefore one pepper Corn upon the 24th Feb. next ...

Wit: Taliaferro Stribling   Martin Ashby
    Jno. Thomas
    Danl. Morgan
Recorded: 3 March 1784

Bk 20, p. 108 - 26 Feb. 1784

    [Release] Between Martin Ashby and Miriam his wife of County of Frederick [to] Edward Snickers of County aforesaid ... consideration of five hundred pounds ... 306 Acres (same as above) ... all of which Tract of Land is a part of a greater Tract containing Three hundred and fifty six Acres all of which was granted to Nimrod Ashby by the Rt. Honorable Thomas Lord Fairfax by Deed Poll and was legally possessed by Martin Ashby son & heir at law of said Nimrod Ashby ...

Wit: same as above   Martin Ashby
Recorded: 3 March 1784

Bk 20, p. 110 - 9 Feb. 1784

    KNOW all Men by these presents that I Martin Ashby of County of Frederick for and in consideration of One Hundred pounds to me paid by John Milton of County aforesaid ... Do bargain and sell unto said John Milton One Negro Woman Named Cate ...

Wit: Fra. Obanion   Martin Ashby
    Mary Higgers
    Jno. Thomas
    Taliaferro Stribling
    Danl. Morgan
Recorded: 3 March 1784

Bk 20, p. 111 - 28 Oct. 1783

    THIS is to Certify that whereas their is an Intention of Marriage between John Leith of Frederick County and Martha Alder of Shenandoah County ... which marriage to be celebrated between said John Leith and Martha Alder on this proviso that said John Leith doth give up all Claim to any and every thing Viz: Goods and chattles or anything else by her possessed before the Celebration of marriage between them ... Vesting her with authority to dispose of same amongst her Children either before or after her death ...

Wit: George (X) Harding   John Leith
    John H. Gray
Recorded: 3 March 1783

Bk 20, p. 112 - 20 Feb. 1784

    Between Gabriel Jones of County of Rockingham [to] John McDonald of parish and County of Frederick ... WHEREAS by Indenture of L & R between sd John McDonald and Mary his wife of Town of Winchester to Gabriel Jones of County of Augusta on 1st and 2nd Sept. 1766 for consideration of Two Hundred Pounds therein mentioned to by paid by said Gabriel Jones to said John McDonald ... did sell unto said Gabriel Jones Tract of Land Containing three Hundred & thirty Six Acres being the same Tract of Land which sd John McDonald purchased of the said Gabriel Jones ... and whereas sum of two hundred pounds paid by sd John McDonald ... sd Gabriel Jones hath surrendered unto sd John McDonald the above mentioned Indenture ...

Wit: none   Gabriel Jones
Recorded: 3 March 1784

Bk 20, p. 113 - 3 March 1784

    Between Adam Kerns and Esther his wife of Frederick County [to] Henry Eley of the same place ... consideration of ten pounds ... a certain Lot of Ground situate in the said County ... in the line of Henry Hoover ... Containing 10,400 square feet and being part of the Tract whereon the said Adam Kerns now lives ...

Wit: none   Adam Kerns

Recorded: 3 March 1784   Esther (X) Kerns

Bk 20, p. 114 - 3 Oct. 1783
    Between Robert Kite and Sarah his wife of Stephensburg in County of Frederick [to] William McLeed of the same place ... consideration of Sixty pounds ... a certain Lot or half acre of land situate in the said Town of Stephensburg and known by No. 19 ... the same being the Lot which said Robert Kite purchased of John Taylor who purchased the same of one Peter Upp ...

Wit: Joseph Stevens   Robert Kite
    John W. (#) Driver   Sarah (X) Kite
    John Grove
Recorded: 3 March 1784

Bk 20, p. 115 -
    KNOW all men by these presents that I Samuel Gilkeson of County of Frederick ... Have ordained Constituted and Appointed John Gilkeson of County aforesaid my True and lawful Attorney for me and in my name ... but to use of him the said John Gilkeson untill the sum of Six hundred and forty eight pounds Seven Shillings Principal due and Owing by two Bonds as Security to Samuel Glass & Joseph Glass Exors. of David Glass dec'd. ... also sum of One Hundred & twenty four pounds Eleven Shillings & four pence due and owing by a Settled Account to said John Gilkeson by sd Samuel Gilkeson be fully satisfied from John Wayman Robert Cochran, James Cochran, Isabella Cochran and Andrew Jack & in default of payment thereof ...

Wit: Jno. Magill   Saml. Gilkeson
    Saml. Boyd
    Phil Pendleton
Recorded: 4 March 1784

Bk 20, p. 117 - 1 Dec. 1775
    Between Peter Richards and Mary Richards of Budleigh in County of Devon Children of Peter Richards of the same place dec'd. by their Attorney John Lee ... John Lee now of the City of Burlington and Western Division of province of New Jersey and Alice his wife is one other of his Daughters of said Peter Richards dec'd. [to] Thomas P. Hawlings of the City of Burlington Esq. ... Whereas John Richards late of County of Frederick dec'd. was in his life time seized of several Tracts of Land situate in Frederick County and made his last Will and Testament the 28th Nov. 1749 and therein died give and devise unto his Brother Peters Children all his Estate real and personal to be equally divided between them and soon after died ... And whereas Henry Richards one of the sons of said Peter Richards came over to this Country which by Will aforesaid entitled to one moiety of said Estate ... and whereas Jonathan Richards one other of the sons of said Peter Richards did constitute and appoint said Henry Richards his lawful Attorney to sell and dispose or other wise divide ... NOW THIS INDENTURE that the said Parties of the first for and in

consideration of two hundred and ninety two pounds ten Shillings paid by Party of the second ... all those two Tracts of Land lying and being in County of Frederick ... on Both sides of Cedar Creek ... Containing three hundred and fifty three Acres ...
Wit: Daniel Ellis
   Abrm. Hewlings
   William Smith
   Thos. Rodman
John Lee
Alice Lee
Peter Richards
Mary Richards
Recorded: 6 April 1784

Bk 20, p. 120 - 1 Dec. 1775
   Burlington County, New Jersey - Alice Lee wife of the said John released Dower right to the above land ...
Thomas Redman
Daniel Ellis

Bk 20, p. 121 - 30 Oct. 1776
   Between Thomas P. Hawlings of City of Burlington and Western Division of New Jersey Esq. [to] Henry Richards of Cedar Creek in County of Frederick ... consideration of Two hundred and Sixty four Pounds ... all those two Tracts of Land situate lying and being in County of Frederick ... the first on both sides of Cedar Creek ... by the line of Robert Marney ... Containing three hundred and fifty three Acres ... The other Tract adjoining situate on the north side of Cedar Creek containing One Hundred and Fifty Acres ...
Wit: Moses Kempton
   Edward Black
   Abrm. Hewlings
Thomas P. Hewlings
Recorded: 6 April 1784

Bk 20, p. 124 - 18 Nov. 1783
   Between Nicolus Sperry Jun. of Frederick County [to] Joseph Stover of Shenandoah County ... for and in consideration of Fifty pounds ... all that plantation or Tract of Land Containing four Hundred & thirty Acres situate lying and being on the Drains of the North River of Shenandoah the same which hath been granted by Deed from the proprietors office to Nicholaus Sperry Sen. the 29th June 1778 and the said Nicholas Sperry Sen. conveyed the same by Deed the 2nd & 3rd Aug. 1781 to his son Nicholas Sperry Jun. ... at the line of George Boroman ... Lawrence Stephens corner ... at the sd Gasper Mires Line ... Containing four Hundred & thirty Acres of Land ...
Wit: Alexander Hite
   David Deadwick
Nicholas Sperry
Recorded: 6 April 1784

Bk 20, p. 126 - 6 April 1784
   Between Thomas Sperry and Catharine his wife of County of Frederick [to] Isaac Sidler of the Town of Winchester in County aforesaid ... Consideration of full

sum of Four Hundred (Pounds) ... Tract of Land situate and being on the water of Red Bud in County aforesaid ... containing in the whole Two Hundred Acres all of which is a part of a Larger Tract Containing four Hundred Acres granted by the Right Honorable Thomas Lord Fairfax to Thomas Spiry (sic) who upon his decease by his last Will and Testament devised and bequeathed the same to his son the sd Thomas Spiry ...

Wit: Nathaniel Ashby
  Thomas Williamson
  1 wit. signed in German
Recorded: 6 April 1784

Thomas Sperry
Catharine (X) Sperry

Bk 20, p. 129 - 5 April 1784

[Lease] Between Evan Thomas Elder Brother and Heir at Law of John Thomas dec'd. of Frederick County [to] Richard Ridgway of Berkeley County ... consideration of Five Shillings ... all that Tract of Land containing three Hundred and twenty nine Acres being part of a Tract of Four Hundred Acres more or less Devised to said John Thomas by the last Will and Testament of his Father Evan Thomas dec'd. the 18th June 1753 ... It being part of a Tract of One thousand and fourteen Acres granted to said Evan Thomas dec'd. by Pattent the 12th Nov. 1735 ... lying and being on the Drains of Opeccon Creek in the said County ... Corner to the Land belonging to the Heirs of Enos Thomas dec'd. ... Corner to the Land belonging to the Heirs of Henry Rees dec'd. ... corner to Abel Walkers Land ... in the line of Land belonging to John Joliffe dec'd. ... Yielding and paying rent of one pepper corn on Lady day next ...

Wit: Nathan Littler
  David Ross
  John Tremble
Recorded: 6 April 1794

Evan (E) Thomas

Bk 20, p. 130 - 6 April 1784

[Release] Between Evan Thomas elder Brother and heir at Law of John Thomas dec'd. of County of Frederick and Margaret his wife [to] Richard Ridgway of Berkeley County ... consideration of Six Hundred Pounds ... 329 Acres (same as above) ...

Wit: same as above
Recorded: 6 April 1784

Evan (E) Thomas
Margaret (Marg.) Thomas

Bk 20, p. 133 - 5 April 1784

[Lease] Between Richard Ridgway of Berkeley County [to] Abel Walker of County of Frederick ... consideration of five Shillings ... Tract of Land containing forty seven Acres 2 rods 14 perches being part of a Tract containing three hundred & twenty nine Acres conveyed to said Richard Ridgway by Deeds of L & R under the hand and seal of Evan Thomas Heir at Law of John Thomas dec'd. and Margaret his wife the 5th & 6th April being part of a Tract of Four Hundred Acres more or less devised to said John Thomas by the last Will and Testament of Evan Thomas dec'd.

his father the 18th June 1753 ... It being part of a Tract Containing One thousand and fourteen Acres granted to said Evan Thomas by Patton the 12th Nov. 1735 ... Lying and being on the drains of Opeckon Creek ... Yielding and paying rent of one pepper corn on Lady day next ...
Wit: John Tremble   Richard Ridgway
  Nathan Littler
  Mord. Walker
Recorded: 6 April 1784

Bk 20, p. 134 - 6 April 1784
   [Release] Between Richard Ridgway of Berkeley County [to] Abel Walker of Frederick County ... consideration of ninety four pounds ... 47 Acres 2 Rods 14 Perches (same as above) ...
Wit: same as above   Richard Ridgway
Recorded: 6 April 1784   Marget Ridgway

Bk 20, p. 136 - 5 April 1784
   [Lease] Between Richard Ridgway of County of Berkeley [to] David Ross of Frederick County ... consideration of five Shillings ... all that Tract of Land containing fifty four Acres 3 Rods being part of a Tract Containing three Hundred and twenty nine Acres conveyed to said Richard Ridgway by Deeds of L & R under the hand and seal of Evan Thomas Heir at Law of John Thomas dec'd. and Margaret his wife the 5th & 6th April being part of a Tract of Four Hundred Acres more or less devised to said John Thomas by the last Will and Testament of his Father Evan Thomas dec'd. the 18th June 1753 ... It being part of a Tract of One thousand and fourteen Acres Granted by Pattent the 12th Nov. 1735 Lying and being on the Drains of Opeckon Creek in the said County of Frederick ... Yielding and paying rent of one pepper corn on Lady day next ...
Wit: John Tremble   Richard Ridgway
  Nathan Littler
  Mord. Walker
Recorded: 6 April 1784

Bk 20, p. 138 - 6 April 1784
   [Release] Between Richard Ridgway of County of Berkeley [to] David Ross of Frederick County ... consideration of One Hundred and eight pounds ... 54 Acres 3 Rods (same as above) ...
Wit: same as above   Richard Ridgway
Recorded: 6 April 1784   Margaret Ridgway

Bk 20, p. 140 - 21 Nov. 1783
   [Lease] Between George Harden of Winchester in Frederick County [to] Philip Bower of the same place ... consideration of five Shillings ... one equal moiety or half part of Lot No. 161 situate in Lord Fairfaxs addition to Winchester aforesaid

containing one fourth part of an Acre of Land and being the same that George Hardin purchased from Alexander Dromgoole by his Deeds of L & R the 3rd & 4th May 1783 who purchased the whole Lot from Jacob Fortney who obtained a Deed for same from Lord Fairfax ... Yielding and paying rent of one pepper corn on Lady day next ...
Wit: David Deadwick George Hardin
    George Summerville
    Jno. Peyton Jr.
Recorded: 7 April 1784

Bk 20, p. 141 - 22 Nov. 1783
    [Release] Between George Hardin and Ann his wife of Winchester in Frederick County [to] Philip Bower of the same place ... consideration of Ten pounds ... one half of Lot No. 161 in addition to the Town of Winchester (same as above) ...
Wit: same as above George Hardin
Recorded: 7 April 1784 Ann Hardin

        [there are no page numbers 142 and 143]
Bk 20, p. 145 - Part of Deed missing
    [last page of a Mortgage Deed between Robert Cochran & James Cochran [to] John Cochran] ...
Wit: none Robert Cochran
Recorded: 7 April 1784 James Cochran

Bk 20, p. 146 - 6 April 1784
    Between Jacob Kenderick of County of Frederick [to] Thomas Allen of County of Shenandoah ... consideration of one hundred and fifty pounds ... parcel of Land Containing Two hundred and forty eight acres situate lying and being in the fork of Shanendo in County of Frederick ... Corner to Benjamin Kenderick ... John Cuns & Joseph Kings Corner ... Bequeathed to sd Jacob Kenderick by the Last Will and Testament of his Father Abraham Kenderick dec'd. ...
Wit: none Jacob Kenderick
Recorded: 7 April 1784

Bk 20, p. 148 - 8 April 1784
    Between Abraham Sovain and Lydia his wife of Winchester in County of Frederick [to] Christian Stover of Strawsburg in County of Shenandoah ... Witnesseth that for better Securing the payment of One hundred pounds which said Abraham Sovain stands indebted to him Christian Stover exclusive of one other Mortgage heretofore entered and further sum of five Shillings ... do grant bargain and sell unto said Christian Stover ... a certain Lot or half acre of Land situate in an Addition made to said Town of Winchester by Lord Fairfax ... known by No. 203 ...
Wit: Marmaduk Magson Abraham Sovain
    Michael Copenhaver Lidia Sovain

Jacob Kenderick
Recorded: 8 April 1784

Bk 20, p. 149 - 10 Sept. 1783
    KNOW all Men by these presents that I Tavener Beale of Shanandoah County for and in consideration of Eighty pounds paid by Leonard Erkstine of Winchester ... Hath bargained and sold two Negroe slaves one of which is a lad of about fourteen years of age named Tom and the other a girl of about Eleven years of age named Grace ...
Wit: J. Milton   Tavener Beale
    J. Peyton
    J. C. Stroebel
Recorded: 4 May 1784

Bk 20, p. 150 - 1 May 1784
    Between Jacob Stearley and Mary magdilen his wife of County of Frederick [to] John Neill Lewis Neill Abraham Neill and Joseph Neill of County aforesaid ... consideration of One hundred and Seventy five pounds ... all that tract of Land situate upon the waters of Opekon Containing two Hundred and three Acres ... Commonly known by the name of Stewarts Tract being part of a Tract of Land Containing three hundred and fifty three Acres formerly granted to Robert Stewart by Deed the 13th June 1760 ... The said 203 acres conveyed by said Robert Stewart and Catharine his wife to Bryan Bruin by Deeds of L & R the 17th Sept. 1764 ... by virtue of a ___ of the County Court of Hampshire sold and conveyed by Thomas Rutherford Sheriff of County of Frederick to said Lewis Neill by Deed the 5th Aug. 1772 ... conveyed by said Lewis Neill to the above mentioned Jacob Stearly by Deeds of L & R the 2nd Nov. 1772 ...
Wit: John Lee   Jacob Stearly
    John Lupton   Mary Magdalin (+) Stearly
    Cuthbert Hayhurst
Recorded: 4 May 1784

Bk 20, p. 153 - 3 May 1784
    [Lease] Between Nicholas Sperry Jun. of Frederick County [to] George Gudehunst of County aforesaid ... consideration of five Shillings ... Tract of Land situate lying and being in said County ... the same being (part) of a Greater Tract or Tracts conveyed and a plot laid out by Joseph Bowman dec'd. the 11th Dec. 1773 containing one thousand and twenty one Acres from several Tracts ... Granted by Deeds from the Proprietors office to Thomas Sperry Senior dec'd. and to Nicholas Sperry Senior form which the said Nicholas Sperry Senior conveyed the intended tract of Two Hundred and ninety eight acres to his son Nicholas Sperry Jun. the 1st March 1774 ... corner to James Hoge, Thomas Sperry dec'd. and Isaac Hite ... containing two hundred and ninety eight acres ... Yielding and paying rent of one pepper Corn on Lady day next ...

Wit: Arch. Magill   Nicholas Sperry
   David Keeler
Recorded: 4 May 1784

Bk 20, p. 154 - 4 May 1784
   [Release] Between Nicholas Sperry Jun. of County of Frederick [to] George Gudehunst of County aforesaid ... consideration of One Hundred pounds ... 298 Acres (same as above) ...
Wit: same as above   Nicholas Sperry
Recorded: 4 May 1784

Bk 20, p. 156 - 14 Dec. 1780
   Between Joseph Steer Sen. of Frederick County and Grace his wife [to] Isaac Sidler of Winchester in County aforesaid ... consideration of Sixty nine pounds ... a part of a Lot being situated on the East side of Loudon Street in the Town of Winchester known by No. 22 ... also part of a Lot of Ground situate and being on the common of the said Town containing five Acres and twenty perches known by No. 76 ... all of which Lots was formerly the property of Andrew Caldwell dec'd. and conveyed to said Joseph Steer Sen. by Andrew Caldwell's son of and heir of Andrew Caldwell dec'd. by Deeds of L & R the 1st & 2nd May 1775 ...
Wit: Jos. Steer Jun.   Joseph Steer
   Thomas Price   Grace Steer
   Mashack Sexton
Recorded: 4 May 1784

Bk 20, p. 158 - 26 May 1783
   Between Henry Ellison Esquire of Whiteheaven in the Kingdom of Great Britain [to] Alexander White of County of Frederick Attorney at Law ... WHEREAS Henry Heth late of County of Frederick was indebted to said Henry Ellison in the sum of three Hundred and Six pounds Sixteen Shillings and Seven pence for Securing the payment thereof did by Indenture the 3rd Oct. 1769 Between Henry Heth and Agnes his wife of one part to Henry Ellison on the other part ... a Tract of Land in said County joining the plantation whereon said Heth then lived Containing Two hundred and Sixty acres being part of a Tract of three hundred and thirty Acres Granted to William McMahen by Deed from the proprietor of Northern Neck the said William McMahen conveyed to said Henry Heth by Deeds of L & R the 19th & 20th Oct. 1765 ... NOW THIS INDENTURE that said Henry Ellison for and in consideration of three hundred and Seventy three pounds Six Shillings and three pence to said Charles Yates his Attorney in fact ... hath transferred to said Alexander White the said Indenture of Mortgage ...
Wit: William Lovell   Henry Ellison
   Godlove Heiskill
   Fielding Lucas
   Peter Michlenburg

James Sommerville
William Helm
C. M. Thruston
Edmund Taylor
Recorded: 5 May 1784

Bk 20, p. 160 - 4 May 1784
    [Lease] Between Joseph Thompson of Berkley County and State of South Carolina [to] James Dillon of Frederick County ... consideration of Five Shillings ... all that Tract of Land containing three Hundred and ninety eighty Acres being the same Tract conveyed to said Joseph Thompson by Deed of L & R under the seal of William Dillon which he held by Deed under the Hand and Seal of the Right Honorable Thomas Lord Fairfax the 16th Nov. 1752 ... being on both sides of the dividing Ridge of Opeccon and Back Creek as by a Survey made thereof by Mr. John Mazey ... Yielding and paying rent of one pepper corn on Lady day next ...
Wit: none
Recorded: 5 May 1784
James Steer
Attorney in fact for Joseph Thompson

Bk 20, p. 162 - 5 May 1784
    [Release] Between Joseph Thompson of Berkley County and State of South Carolina [to] James Dillon of Frederick County ... consideration of two hundred and fifty pounds ... 398 Acres (same as above) ...
Wit: none
Recorded: 5 May 1784
James Steere
Attorney in fact for Joseph Thompson

Bk 20, p. 164 - 2 May 1784
    GREETINGS - Know ye that I John Smith reposing especial trust and confidence in my friend John Peyton of Winchester for diver good causes and considerations ... have nominated constituted and appointed him the said John Peyton my true and lawfull attorney for me and in my name ... to sell and dispose of the Estate real and personal which I now hold in sd County of Frederick and Hampshire particular a Tract of Land in the former of one hundred and ninety two acres known by the name of Battletown and One undivided fourth part of two Certain Tracts of Land in the last mentioned County ...
Wit: J. Drew
  G. Hite
Recorded: 5 May 1784
John Smith

Bk 20, p. 165 - 9 Nov. 1783
    [Lease] Between John Gilkeson & Samuel Gilkeson of Frederick County [to] William Gilkeson Sen. of the same place ... Consideration of Five Shillings ... Tract of Land situate on the Head of Opeckon Creek ... Corner to Nathl. Cartmill and John Bicket ... Containing Two hundred and eighty five acres the same more or less Granted or Conveyed to said John & Samuel Gilkeson by Robert Bicket who

purchased the same from Samuel Bicket ... Also one other Tract of Land adjoining the Tract above mentioned ... Containing one hundred and fifty Acres which said Tract is part of a Larger Tract Granted to Jost Hite by Patent and by him conveyed to Samuel Glass by Deeds of L & R recorded in Orange County Court and by him conveyed to John Bicket who by his last Will and Testament bequeathed the same to Robert Bicket and by said Robert Bicket conveyed to the said John Gilkeson and Samuel Gilkeson ... Yielding and paying rent of one pepper corn on Lady day next.
Wit: David Deadwick   John Gilkeson
    George Sommerville   Saml. Gilkeson
    Jno. Peyton
Recorded: 5 May 1784

Bk 20, p. 166 - 10 Nov. 1783
    [Release] Between John Gilkeson and ___ his wife and Samuel Gilkeson and Susannah his wife of Frederick County [to] William Gilkeson Sen. of the same place ... consideration of four hundred pounds ... 285 Acres and 150 Acres (same as above).
Wit: same as above   John Gilkeson
                                        Saml. Gilkeson
Recorded: 5 May 1784   Susanna Gilkeson

Bk 20, p. 169 - 10 Nov. 1783
    Susannah Gilkeson apart from Samuel Gilkeson released Dower right to said Land ...
                                        Joseph Holmes
                                        Edward McGuire

Bk 20, p. 169 - 24 Jan. 1784
    Between Abraham Kenderick of County of Frederick [to] Thomas Allen of County of Shannando ... Consideration of One Hundred and fifty pounds hard money ... all that parcel of Land Containing Two hundred and One Acres and one Quarter Situate lying and being in fork of Shannando in County of Frederick ... (Land) bequeathed to him the said Abraham Kenderick by the last Will and Testament of his Father Abraham Kenderick dec'd. ...
Wit: George Ryan   Abraham Kenderick
    Rebekah Miller
    Mary Gennings
Recorded: 6 May 1784

Bk 20, p. 172 - 9 Nov. 1783
    Between Wm. Glascock Jun. & Elizabeth his wife of County of Frederick [to] Henry Armistead of County of Spotsylvania and Town of Fredericksburg ... Consideration of the love and affection which they have and do bear unto said Henry Armistead (he having intermarried with their Niece Winifred Peachey) and also for consideration of Ten pounds ... all my Lotts in the Town of Stevensburg in County of Frederick ...

Wit: La Mackintosh Wm Glascock Jun.
   Robt. Thomas
   Armistead Long
Recorded: 7 May 1784

Bk 20, p. 173 - 29 Jan. 1784
    [Lease] Between Joshua Pyles of the Borough of Winchester in Frederick County [to] Elias Holding of the same place ... consideration of Five Shillings ... proportion of Lot No. 155 situate in the said Borough of Winchester ... Containing one fourth part of an acre of Land and four square feet which was Granted by Patent from Lord Fairfax to Jacob Castleman by him conveyed to Francis Tygart and by him conveyed to said Joshua Pyles ... Yielding and paying rent of one pepper corn on Lady day next ...
Wit: Jno. Peyton Joshua (P) Pyles
   Andrew Kyger
   William Swords
Recorded: 7 May 1784

Bk 20, p. 174 - 30 Jan. 1784
    [Release] Between Joshua Pyles and Sarah his wife of the Borough of Winchester in County of Frederick [to] Elias Holding of the same place ... for and in consideration of thirty pounds ... proportion of Lot No. 155 (same as above) ...
Wit: same as above Joshua (P) Pyles
Recorded: 7 May 1784 Sary (+) Pyles

Bk 20, p. 177 - 4 May 1784
    Between Thomas Wood and Mary his wife of Winchester in County of Frederick [to] John Hite Sen. of the said County ... consideration of twenty pounds ... One certain Lott or half acre of Land situate in Lord Fairfaxs addition to the said Town of Winchester and known by No. 129 the same which was granted to said Thomas Wood by Deed for Lord Fairfax the 15th May 1753 ...
Wit: none Thos. Wood
Recorded: 7 May 1784 Mary (X) Wood

Bk 20, p. 178 - 1 June 1784
    Between Adam Kerns and Hester his wife of Frederick County [to] Henry Huver of the same place ... Consideration of eleven pounds ... parcel of Land situate in said County ... East side of the great Road leading form Winchester to Stephensburg ... Containing one acre and twenty four poles together with one half part of the run ... the said Tract of Land is part of and taken from the Original Tract of Adam Kerns ...
Wit: J. Peyton Adam Kerns
Recorded: 1 June 1784 Hester (X) Kerns

Bk 20, p. 180 - 15 May 1784
    Between John Nisewanger and Margaret his wife of County of Frederick [to] Vance Bush of County aforesaid ... consideration of forty five pounds ... Parcel of Land situate lying and being on the south side of Stephens Run ... Containing four and a half acres 7 rods which said Parcel of Land is part of a Large tract of Land Containing four hundred & thirty five acres Granted by Yoest Hite to Jacob Nisewanger by Deeds of L & R the 21st & 22nd Feb. 1738 ...
Wit: Jno. McGinnis   John Nisewanger
    Peter Upp   Margaret (X) Nisewanger
    Kassamer Plum
    John Marburger
Recorded: 1 June 1784

Bk 20, p. 182 - 29 May 1784
    Margaret Nisewanger apart from her husband released Dower right to said Land ...   Joseph Longacre
                                                                  Elisha Williams

Bk 20, p. 182 - 1 June 1784
    Between John Edmondson of County of Frederick [to] John Adams of aforesaid County ... consideration of Sixty pounds ... all that Tract of Land situate on the north side of Back Creek Containing three Hundred and Twenty Six Acres and the same which was Granted to Isaac Foster by Deed from the Proprietor of Northern Neck the 8th Sept. 1776 (?) and by said Isaac Foster conveyed to Achillis Foster by Deeds of L & R the 1st & 2nd June 1767 (?) ... Corner to Jesse Pugh and Mary Mullin ... in Barrack Fisher's line ... in William Pickerings line ...
Wit: A. Waggoner   John Edmondson
    Jno. Rogers
Recorded: 1 June 1784

Bk 20, p. 184 - 4 July 1774
    [Lease] Between Thomas Rees of County of Frederick [to] William House of the same place ... consideration of five Shillings ... all that Tract of Land containing Four Hundred Acres of Land lying and being on the Timber Ridge ... the said Tract of Land being granted to said Thomas Rees by pattent from the proprietor of Northern Neck the 4th Sept. 1766 ... Yielding and paying rent of one Ear of Indian Corn in and upon the feast of Christmas ...
Wit: Robert Rees   Thomas (TR) Rees
    Joseph Mooney
    Solomon Rees
Recorded: 3 Aug. 1784

Bk 20, p. 186 - 5 July 1774
    [Release] Between Thomas Rees of County of Frederick [to] William House

of the same place ... consideration of One Hundred and Seventy one pounds ... 400 Acres (same as above) ...
Wit: same as above
Recorded: 3 Aug. 1784

Thomas (TR) Rees
Margaret (X) Rees

Bk 20, p. 188 - 22 April 1784
    Between George Volk late of the County of Frederick [to] George Mock and Michael Gardiner of the same place ... Whereas said George Volk by his Bond or Obligation stands Bound to Christopher Kriser in the full sum of Seventy pounds ... Now this Indenture the said George Mock and Michael Gardner in consideration of the said debt & Interest owing to said Christopher Kraiser aforesaid Securing the payment according to the condition of the Bond and also consideration of five Shillings ... doth grant bargain and sell unto said George Mock and Michael Gardner all that plantation containing four Hundred and thirty Acres the same which I have purchased of Frederick Shlosser and in my possession ...
Wit: Alexander Hite
    George Brinker
    Benjamin Langley
Recorded: 3 Aug. 1784

George Volk

Bk 20, p. 190 - 3 Sept. 1783
    [Lease] Between Henry Hunter of County of Frederick [to] Meredith Helm of County aforesaid ... consideration of five Shillings ... part of a Tract of Land situate on the Drains of Opecon Creek ... which said Tract was granted to Andrew Millbourn by Deed under the Hand and Seal of the Right Honorable Thos. Lord Fairfax the 22nd May 1766 and by the same Andrew Millbourn conveyed to Thomas McClum and by said Thos. McClum conveyed to said Henry Hunter ... corner to John Littler and the Heirs of Robert Millbourn ... Containing one hundred and Seventy two and a Quarter Acres ... Yielding and paying rent of one pepper corn on Lady next ...
Wit: Wm Slaughter
    John Donaldson
    Jos. Day
Recorded: 3 Aug. 1784

Henry Hunter

Bk 20, p. 192 - 4 Sept. 1783
    [Release] Between Henry Hunter and Ann his wife of County of Frederick [to] Meredith Helm of County aforesaid ... consideration of three Hundred and forty four pounds ten Shillings ... 172 1/4 Acres (same as above) ...
Wit: same as above
Recorded: 3 Aug. 1784

Henry Hunter
Ann (X) Hunter

Bk 20, p. 194 - 4 Sept. 1783
    Ann Hunter apart from Henry Hunter released Dower right to said Land ...

Edward McGuire

Bk 20, p. 195 - 2 Aug. 1784
 [Lease] Between John Rees of County of Frederick [to] Jonas Likins of County aforesaid ... consideration of Five Shillings ... Tract of Land lying and being on Opecon Creek containing Two Hundred and eighty Six Acres ... which said Tract was Granted to Simeon Taylor by Deed under the Hand and Seal of the Right Honorable Thomas Lord Fairfax the 3rd April 1760 and by said Simeon Taylor was conveyed to said John Rees by Deeds of L & R the 30th April & 1st May 1764 ... Yielding and paying rent of one pepper corn on lady day next ...
Wit: Wm Slaughter   John Rees
   Thos. Edmondson
   Joseph Day
Recorded: 3 Aug. 1784

Bk 20, p. 196 - 3 Aug. 1784
 [Release] Between John Rees and Lydia his wife of County of Frederick [to] Jonas Likins of County aforesaid ... consideration of Five hundred and Seventy pounds ... 286 Acres (same as above) ...
Wit: same as above   John Rees
Recorded: 3 Aug. 1784   Lydia Rees

Bk 20, p. 199 - 31 July 1784
 Between James Mann Foley and Elizabeth his wife of County of Frederick [to] Edwin Young of County of Shanandoah ... consideration of One Hundred and Sixty pounds ... Tract of Land lying and being in County of Frederick Containing by Estimation thirty one Acres and three quarters ... in the division line laid off for Richard Foley Jun. ... being part of a Larger Tract Bought by Richard Foley of James McKay and Charles Buck Exors. of Thomas Chester and sold by them to said Richard Foley ... also part of one other Tract of Eighty Acres ... corner to Richard Foley ... corner to Selby Foley ...
Wit: Nathan McPherson   James Man (X) Foley
   Charles Catlett   Elizabeth (X) Foley
   Selby Foley
   James Miller
Recorded: 3 Aug. 1784

Bk 20, p. 201 - 8 June 1784
 KNOW all men by these presents that I George Ashby of County of Frederick for and in consideration of Twenty five pounds paid by David Smith of County aforesaid ... do bargain and sell One Negro Boy named Solomon about fourteen years Old ...
Wit: Arg. Taylor   George Ashby
   Francis Lehew

John (+) Hughs
Recorded: 3 Aug. 1784

Bk 20, p. 202 - 2 Aug. 1784
    [Lease] Between Adam Reagley of Frederick County [to] David Nicewanger of County aforesaid ... consideration of Five Shillings ... Tract of Land containing nearly Twenty Acres 2 Rood 26 poles ... situate lying and being in aforesaid County on a drain of Cedar Creek being part of a Tract whereon he now liveth and adjoining to land of the said David Nicewanger ... which said Tract is part of a Larger Tract of 133 Acres conveyed by Deeds of L & R from William Evans and Dorothy his wife to said Adam Reagley by their Deeds the 17th & 18th May ... which said 133 Acres is part of a larger Tract of 400 acres Granted to said William Evans by Patent the 14th March 1753 ... Yielding and paying rent of one pepper corn on Lady day next. ...
Wit: none   Adam Reagley
Recorded: not given

Bk 20, p. 203 - 3 Aug. 1784
    [Release] Between Adam Reagley of Frederick County [to] David Nisewanger of County aforesaid ... consideration of Ten pounds ... nearly 20 Acres 2 Roods and 26 poles (same as above) ...
Wit: none   Adam Reagley
Recorded: 3 Aug. 1784

Bk 20, p. 205 - 9 July 1784
    [Lease] Between Philip Babb heir at law of Sampson Babb late of Frederick County dec'd. and Joseph Babb [to] Joseph Lupton of County aforesaid ... for and in consideration of five Shillings ... Tract of Land situate in the said County ... Containing One Hundred & Eighty Acres which was by the last Will and Testament of Thomas Babb dec'd. devised to the aforesaid Sampson Babb dec'd. who dying Intestate and without Issue the same descended to said Philip Babb his Eldest Brother and heir at Law ... Yielding and paying rent of one pepper Corn on Lady day next ...
Wit: J. Peyton   Philip Babb
    D. Norton   Joseph (X) Babb
    Jonah Hollingsworth
Recorded: 3 Aug. 1784

Bk 20, p. 206 - 10 July 1784
    [Release] Between Philip Babb Heir at Law of Sampson Babb late of Frederick County and Mary his wife and Joseph Babb & Hannah his wife [to] Joseph Lupton of County aforesaid ... consideration of Six hundred and fifty pounds ... 180 Acres (same as above) ...
Wit: J. Peyton   Philip Babb
    D. Norton   Mary (M) Babb

Jonah Hollingsworth   Joseph (X) Babb
George Sommerville   Hannah (+) Babb
Recorded: 3 Aug. 1784

Bk 20, p. 209 - 3 Aug. 1784
    [Lease] Between Brian Bruin of Winchester in County of Frederick [to] David Kennedy of the same place ... consideration of Five Shillings ... a certain Tract or lot of Land situate in County of Frederick ... in the line of Isaac Parkins ... Containing seventeen Acres being part of a larger Tract of 369 acres which the Rt. Hon.ble Thomas Lord Fairfax Granted by Patent to William Cochran who laid out Sundry lots and conveyed the lot above described to said Brian Bruin and which is known by No. 21 ... Yielding and paying rent of one pepper corn on Lady day next ...
Wit: none   Bryan Bruin
Recorded: 3 Aug. 1784

Bk 20, p. 210 - 2 Aug. 1784 (?)
    [Release] Between Bryan Bruin of Winchester in County of Frederick [to] David Kennedy of the same place ... consideration of Fifty pounds ... 17 Acres (same as above) ...
Wit: none   Bryan Bruin
Recorded: 3 Aug. 1784

Bk 20, p. 212 - 2 Aug. 1784
    [Lease] Between David Kennedy of Winchester in Frederick County [to] John Donaldson of the same place ... consideration of Five Shillings ... Tract or Lot of Land situate in said County ... in the line of Isaac Perkins ... Containing Seventeen Acres being part of a larger Tract of 369 Acres which the Rt. Hon.ble Thomas Lord Fairfax Granted by Patent to William Cochran who laid out Sundry Lots there upon and conveyed the above described to Bryan Bruin and Bryan Bruin conveyed to said David Kennedy by Deeds of L & R the 2nd Aug. 1784 ... Yielding and paying rent of one pepper Corn on Lady day next ...
Wit: none   David Kennedy
Recorded: 3 Aug. 1784

Bk 20, p. 213 - 3 Aug. 1784
    [Release] Between David Kennedy of Winchester in Frederick County [to] John Donaldson of the same place ... Consideration of Fifty Pounds ... 17 Acres (same as above) ...
Wit: none   David Kennedy
Recorded: 3 Aug. 1784

Bk 20, p. 215 - 10 Dec. 1783
    [Lease] Between Robt. Wilson Jun. of Frederick County [to] Samuel May of the Borough of Winchester in County aforesaid ... consideration of five Shillings ...

Tract of Land situate lying and being in County of Frederick containing three hundred and fifty three acres ... in line of Mr. Colverts land ... which said Tract of Land Robert Wilson Sen. by his Deeds of L & R the 2nd & 3rd March 1761 conveyed to said Robert Wilson Jun. ... Yielding and paying rent of one pepper Corn on Lady day next ...
Wit: J. Peyton   Robt. Wilson
  Michael Deadwick
  David Deadwick
Recorded: 3 Aug. 1784

Bk 20, p. 216 - 11 Dec. 1783
    [Release] Between Robert Wilson Jun. and Mary his wife of County of Frederick [to] Samuel May of Borough of Winchester and County aforesaid ... consideration of nine hundred and forty pounds ... 353 Acres (same as above) ...
Wit: same as above   Robt. Wilson
Recorded: 3 Aug. 1784   Mary Wilson

Bk 20, p. 219 - 5 April 1784
    Between Isaac Wilkes and Jean his wife of Winchester in County of Frederick [to] Cornelius Baldwin late of New Jersey ... Consideration of ninety pounds ... a certain Lot or half acre of Land situated in Lord Fairfax's addition to the said Town of Winchester and known by No. 211 being the same whereon said Isaac Wilkes now lives which said Lot of Land was granted to Christopher Lambert by Deed from the said Lord Fairfax the 15th May 1753 and by said Lambert conveyed to Benjamin Sidler by Deeds of L & R the 7th & 8th May 1772 and by said Benjamin conveyed to Mathias Sitler by Deeds of L & R the 7th & 8th May 1772 who conveyed the same to Isaac Wilkes by Deed the 15th Dec. 1780 ...
Wit: Wm McGuire   Isaac Wilks
  Joseph Holmes   Jean (X) Wilks
  Edward McGuire
Recorded: 3 Aug. 1784

Bk 20, p. 220 - 5 April 1784
    Jean Wilks respecting her right of Dower to above land ...
                                                  Joseph Holmes
                                                  Edward McGuire

Bk 20, p. 221 - 23 June 1784
    Between Alexander Dromgoole and Margaret Elizabeth his wife of Winchester in County of Frederick [to] Lewis Wolf of the same place ... consideration of two hundred pounds ... part of Lot No. 16 situate in the Borough of Winchester ... which said Lot No. 16 was Granted to Marquis Calmes dec'd. by Deed the 15th May 1753 by Lord Fairfax and said Marquis Calmes dying Intestate the same descended to William Calmes his Eldest son and Heir at Law who by his last Will & Testament

bequeathed the same to Miriam Calmes and by said Miriam Calmes conveyed to said Alexander Dromgoole by Deed the 2nd July 1782 ...
Wit: Goldsmith Chandler Alexander Drumgoole
  Nicholas Sperry M. Elizabeth Drumgoole
  Mahlon Smith
Recorded: 4 Aug. 1784

Bk 20, p. 223 - 4 Aug. 1784
  KNOW all men by these presents that I Jacob Hackney of Berkley County in consideration of the natural love and affection which I have and doth bear unto my son William Hackney have granted and delivered unto him one negro boy named Dick about nine year old and one negro Girl named Jane about eight years old ...
Wit: none Jacob Hackney
Recorded: 4 Aug. 1784

Bk 20, p. 223 - 24 June 1784
  Between William Glascock Jun. & Elizabeth his wife of County of Frederick [to] Henry Armistead of County of Spotsylvania ... for and in consideration of three hundred and fifty pounds ... all that Lot or half Acre of Land in the Town of Stephensburg known by No. 60 ...
Wit: Micajah Hughes Wm Glascock Jun.
  Peter Crider Elizabeth Glascock
  John Croff
Recorded: 4 Aug. 1784

Bk 20, p. 225 - 3 Aug. 1784
  [Lease] Between William Barratt of Frederick County [to] George Scott and Philip Pendleton as Tenants in Common of Berkley County ... consideration of five Shillings ... all that Tract of Land Situate lying and being at the Gap of the north mountain on both sides of the big Spring branch a branch of Back Creek ... in James Hayworths line ... Containing three hundred & five acres ... It being the same Tract of Land granted to said William Barrett by Deed under the Hand and Seal of the Right Honorable Thomas Lord Fairfax the 21st Nov. 1760 ... (Reserving thereout on behalf of Thomas Thompson and Sinah his wife the use and Occupation of about Twenty Acres thereof and so much longer as the said Sinah shall live and to be Divided by a line agreed upon by said George Scott and Mordicai Walker) ... Yielding and paying rent of one pepper Corn on Lady day next ...
Wit: Goldsmith Chandler William Barrett
  Jona Lupton
  Lewis Walker
Recorded: 4 Aug. 1784

Bk 20, p. 227 - 4 Aug. 1784
  [Release] Between William Barrett of Frederick County [to] George Scott and

Philip Pendleton (as Tenants in common and not Joint Tenants) of County of Berkley ... consideration of four Hundred pounds ... 305 Acres (same as above) ...
Wit: same as above   William Barrett
Recorded: 4 Aug. 1784

Bk 20, p. 230 - 3 Aug. 1784
     [Lease] Between Jacob Kiger and Mary his wife of Winchester in County of Frederick [to] John Donaldson of the same place ... consideration of five Shillings ... all his full equal moiety or half part of Lot No. 1 being part of a Lot of five acres which Thomas Edmondson obtained an Act of Assembly for annexing the said Borough of Winchester ... said Lot was granted to said Jacob Kiger by Deed the 14th June 1783 from the said Thomas Edmondson ...
Wit: none   Jacob Kiger
Recorded: 4 Aug. 1784

Bk 20, p. 231 - 4 Aug. 1784
     [Release] Between Jacob Kiger & Mary his wife of Winchester in County of Frederick [to] John Donaldson of the same place ... consideration of Twenty five pounds ... a half part of Lot No. 1 (same as above) ...
Wit: none   Jacob Kiger
Recorded: 4 Aug. 1784   Mary (M) Kiger

Bk 20, p. 233 - 23 June 1783
     Between Thomas Rutherford of Berkley County Esquire and Drusilla his wife [to] John Shultz of Winchester of County of Frederick ... consideration of Sixty Pounds ... one equal moiety or half part of a certain portion of two acres and forty square pole of land situate in Col. Woods addition to the Town of Winchester which was conveyed to said Thomas Rutherford by Deed from Mrs. Mary Wood Executrix and Devisee of said Col. Wood ... Containing one acre and twenty square poles ...
Wit: G. Hite   Thomas Rutherford
     Edw. Smith   Drusilla Rutherford
     J. Peyton Jr.
Recorded: 4 Aug. 1784

Bk 20, p. 235 - 3 Oct. 1783
     Berkley County - Rutherford apart from within mentioned Thomas Rutherford released Dower right to above land ...   John Cooke
                                                                      Cato. Moore

Bk 20, p. 235 - 5 April 1777
     [Lease] Between Robert Blackburn of County of Augusta [to] John Cowgill of County of Berkeley ... consideration of five Shillings ... part of a Tract of Land lying on the drains of Opecon ... and is part of a larger Tract Granted to said Robert Blackburn by Deed under the Hand and Seal of the Right Honorable Thomas Lord

Fairfax the 6th Aug. 1768 Containing five Hundred acres ... in the line of Widow Siere ... corner to Reason Reagon ... Corner to his Lordship ... Corner of John Mouser ... containing three Hundred acres ... Yielding and paying rent of one pepper Corn on Lady day next ...
Wit: John Littler   Robert Blackburn
 John Tremble
 Abram Taylor
 Jos. Day
Recorded: 4 May 1784

Bk 20, p. 237 - 6 April 1777
 [Release] Between Robert Blackburn and Margaret his wife of County of Augusta [to] John Cowgill of County of Frederick [in Lease - Berkeley Co.] ... consideration of three Hundred Pounds ... 300 Acres (same as above) ...
Wit: same as above   Robert Blackburn
Recorded: 5 Aug. 1784

Bk 20, p. 240 - 25 Aug. 1777
 Margaret Blackburn wife of within mentioned Robert released Dower right to above land ...   John Smith
                Jos. Holmes

Bk 20, p. 240 - 21 Nov. 1783
 Between Benjamin Fry of County of Frederick [to] David Whitemore of County of Lancaster in Commonwealth of Pennsylvania ... consideration of three hundred & thirty six pounds ... all those Tracts of Land lying and being situate on the waters of Cedar Creek ... containing three hundred acres being part of John Bransons Patent for one thousand acres ... another Tract joining the former containing two hundred & fourteen acres ... Corner to Paul Frowmans Patent Land ... in the line of Joseph Fawcett ... And also another Tract of Land adjoining the former tracts being part of a Larger Tract of three hundred and fifty three Acres lying on Frowmans Run one of the Drains of Cedar Creek ... all three Tracts of Land containing on the whole Five hundred & Seventy four acres as was conveyed by Abraham Fires (?) to said Benjamin Fry by Deeds of L & R ...
Wit: David Kennedy   Benj. (B) Fry
 Robt. Jamison
 Jno. Thomas
Recorded: 5 Aug. 1784

Bk 20, p. 244 - 14 Dec. 1779
 Between Mason Jones and Mary his wife of County of Shannando [to] George Cheek of County of Frederick ... consideration of two hundred pounds ... one Tract of Land containing one acre & half of an acres situate lying and being near happy Creek ... in the line of Baylis Ashbys ...

Wit: Charles Peyton   Mason Jones
      Francis Lehew   Mary (+) Jones
      James (+) Cheek
Recorded: 3 Aug. 1784

Bk 20, p. 247 - 4 Aug. 1784
    [Lease] Between Thomas Jones of County of Frederick [to] Barnet Williams of the same County ... consideration of five Shillings ... Tract of Land near the dry Marsh in sd County ... on Fairfax Road ... corner to John Maddins Survey ... Containing two hundred acres ... Yielding and paying rent of one pepper corn on Lady day next ...
Wit: none   Thomas Jones
Recorded: 5 Aug. 1784

Bk 20, p. 248 - 5 Aug. 1784
    [Release] Between Thomas Jones and Ann his wife of County of Frederick [to] Barnet Williams of the same County ... consideration of Two hundred pounds ... 200 Acres (same as above) ...
Wit: none   Thomas Jones
Recorded: 5 Aug. 1784   Ann Jones

Bk 20, p. 250 - 23 March 1784
    [Lease] Between Samuel May of Winchester in Frederick County [to] William Grayham of the Town of Baltimore in the State of Maryland ... consideration of five Shillings ... Tract of land situate on the drains of Back Creek and known by the name of Brush Creek ... Containing one Hundred and twenty Seven Acres which said Tract of Land was Granted to Joseph Howbridge /Trowbridge by the proprietor of Northern Neck and said Howbridge conveyed to John Lawison who conveyed the same to David Heaton and by said Heaton to Dennis Oran and by him Transferred to Peter Helphenstone now Dec'd. and by the Exors. of said Peter Helphenstine dec'd. was conveyed to said Samuel May ... Also one other Tract of Land situate at the forks of Brush Creek and adjoining to the Tract above mentioned ... in Joseph Watsons line ... Corner to Dennis Orian ... Containing four hundred and ninety eight Acres which last mentioned Tract was Granted to said Peter Helphinstine dec'd. by Deed from Lord Fairfax and by the Exors. of him conveyed to said Samuel May ... Yielding and paying rent of one pepper corn on Lady day next ...
Wit: none   Saml. May
Recorded: 6 Aug. 1784

Bk 20, p. 252 - 24 March 1784
    [Release] Between Samuel May and Rosanna his wife of Winchester in Frederick County [to] William Grayham of Baltimore Town in the State of Maryland ... consideration of One hundred and Sixty pounds ... 120 Acres [Lease states 127 Acres] and 498 Acres (same as above) ...

Wit: none
Recorded: 6 Aug. 1784

Saml. May
Rosanna May

Bk 20, p. 255 - 20 Feb. 1784
    Between Joshua Piles and Sarah his wife of Winchester in Frederick County [to] Daniel Miller of the same place ... consideration of Fifty pounds ... proportion of Lot No. 155 situate in Lord Fairfax's addition to Winchester ... Containing one fourth part of an Acre of Land wanting four Square feet which said lot was granted by Patent from Lord Fairfax to Jacob Castleman by him conveyed to Francis Tygart and by him to said Joshua Pyles ...
Wit: J. Peyton
  William Swords
  John White
Recorded: 6 Aug. 1784

Joshua (P) Pyles
Sarah (|) Pyles

Bk 20, p. 256 - 22 April 1784
    KNOW all Men by these presents that I George Volk late of Frederick County have constituted and appointed George Mock of the above said County my true and Lawful Attorney for me and in my name ... to Enter into and upon my Land Now in the occupation of Peter Miller as a Tenant thereof containing Four Hundred & Thirty Acres by agreement Entered into with Frederick Slusher the 20th or 21st May 1779 for which Tract said Frederick Slusher is to make a good Deed ...
Wit: Alexander Hite
  Michael (X) Gardner
Recorded: 7 Sept. 1784

George Volk

Bk 20, p. 257 - 7 Sept. 1784
    Between David Ashby and Jane his wife of Frederick County [to] John Milton of the same place ... consideration of three hundred & forty five pounds ... Tract of land whereon said David Ashby now lives ... in line of Carters Patent ... corner to Francis Stripling by the road leading from Battletown to Berry's ferry ... line of Edward Snickers ... Containing one hundred and fifteen acres the same being part of a larger Tract of land which was by the last Will and Testament of Samuel Isaacs dec'd bequeathed to Godfrey Isaacs and by the said Godfrey conveyed to said David Ashby by Deeds of L & R the 2nd & 3rd Sept. 1767 ...
Wit: none
Recorded: 7 Sept. 1784

David (A) Ashby
Jane (|) Ashby

Bk 20, p. 260 - 7 Sept. 1784
    [Lease] Between Joshua Baker late of Frederick County [to] Alexander McDougal of Bath, Berkeley County ... consideration of Five Shillings ... One lott of Ground in the Town of Winchester on the west side of Cameron Street adjoining to lott formerly belonging to John Greenfield dec'd. on the north side and on the south side the lott of James Wood, Jun. ... known by lott No. 25 ... also one lott in the

Common annexed to the aforesaid Town ... Lott known by No. 21 which said lotts were granted by Deed poll form the proprietor of Northern Neck to John Howard the 15th May 1753 and conveyed by said John Howard unto Joshua Baker dec'd. Father to said Joshua Baker here in named by L & R the 6th & 7th Dec. 1757 and conveyed to said Joshua Baker by virtue to the last Will and Testament of Joshua Baker dec'd. the 12th Aug. 1764 when he bequeathed said Lotts unto his son Joshua Baker ... Yielding and paying rent of one Ear of Indian Corn on the last day of said Term ...
Wit: Fra.s Stribbling   Joshua Baker
   Jos. Stewart
Recorded: 7 Sept. 1784

Bk 20, p. 261 - 8 Sept. 1784
   [Release] Between Joshua Baker late of Frederick County Black Smith [to] Alexander McDougal of Berkley in the Town of Bath Taylor ... consideration of One hundred and fifty pounds ... Lots No. 25 and 21 (same as above) ...
Wit: same as above   Joshua Baker
Recorded: 7 Sept. 1784 (?)

Bk 20, p. 263 - 31 Aug. 1784
   [Lease] Between Peter Palser of County of Shannando [to] Archibald Rutherford of County of Frederick ... consideration of Five Shillings ... part of a tract lying and being on the Drains of Opeckon Creek and is part of a larger Tract which was granted to Jonathan Taylor by Deed from under the Hand & Seal of the Right Honorable Thomas Lord Fairfax and by Taylor was conveyed to said Peter Palser ... Corner to John Littler and John Millburns Survey by a Waggon Road ... Containing Two Hundred acres ... Yielding and paying rent of one pepper corn on Lady day next.
Wit: Joseph Holmes   Peter Palser
   John Donaldson
   David Hunter
   Nicholas Mesmer
Recorded: 7 Sept. 1784

Bk 20, p. 265 - 1 Sept. 1784
   [Release] Between Peter Palser of County of Shannandoa [to] Archibald Rutherford of County of Frederick ... consideration of Five hundred pounds ... 200 Acres (same as above) ...
Wit: same as above   Peter Palser
Recorded: 7 Sept. 1784

Bk 20, p. 267 - 8 Sept. 1784
   Between Jacob Grimm and Mary his wife of Borough of Winchester [to] Henry Moore of Frederick County ... consideration of Forty Pounds ... one full equal Moiety or half part of a certain Lot or half acre of Land situate in Lord Fairfax's addition to the Town of Winchester known by No. 210 ... which said Lot was Granted by Patent

from Lord Fairfax to Christopher Lambert who conveyed same to Benjamin Sitler and by said Benjamin conveyed to Matthias Sitler who conveyed same to said Jacob Grimm ...

Wit: none
Recorded: 8 Sept. 1784

Jacob Grimm
Mary (+) Grimm

Bk 20, p. 269 - 7 June 1784

 Between Henry Deaney & Barbara his wife of the Town of Winchester in County of Frederick [to] John Magill of Gilhall in said County Esquire Attorney at Law ... consideration of two Hundred and forty pounds ... One Lot of Land lying and being in the Town of Winchester Numbered (10) on the East side of Braddock Street Containing One hundred and five feet fronting the said Street & one hundred eighty eight feet fronting Wolf Street ... the said Lot being part of a Tract of Land Granted to said James Wood by Deed from the proprietor of Northern Neck and by him devised in his last Will and Testament to Mary Wood ... and conveyed by said Mary Wood to said Henry Deaney by Deeds of L & R the 3rd & 4th Aug. 1762 ...

Wit: David Deadwick
 John Brady
 Christopher Witsel
Recorded: 8 Sept. 1784

Henry Deaney
Margaret (+) Deaney ?
(listed as Barbara in Deed)

Bk 20, p. 271 - __ day of __ 1784

 Between John Neill and Lydia his wife of County of Frederick [to] Lewis Neill of the County aforesaid ... consideration of One hundred and fifty pounds ... all that tract of Land containing Two hundred Acres lying in the County aforesaid being part of a greater tract of Land Containing three hundred Acres which John Neill son of John Neill obtained by Deed from the proprietors office the 8th May 1760 ... south side of Wilkerson's Marsh near the Fairfax Road ...

Wit: John Donaldson
 Joseph Day
 Thomas Jones
Recorded: 8 Sept. 1784

John Neill
Lydia (X) Neill

Bk 20, p. 274 - 8 Sept. 1784

 Between John Rees of Frederick County [to] Joseph Holmes of the aforesaid ... consideration of Two hundred and fifty pounds ... all that Messuage or Tenement of land containing One hundred Eighty nine Acres situate and lying in County aforesaid Adjoining the Lands of Doct. John McDonald & Ignatious Perry & Others.

Wit: John S. Woodcock
 David Hunter
 James Young
Recorded: 8 Sept. 1784

John Rees

Bk 20, p. 276 - 3 Sept. 1784

[Lease] Between Joseph Horner of County of Frederick [to] John Tremble of County aforesaid ... consideration of Five Shillings ... all that Land which was formerly granted unto William Gilliam by Deed under the Hand and Seal of the Right Honorable Thomas Lord Fairfax the 15th June 1754 and by said Gilliam conveyed to said Joseph Horner by Deeds of L & R the 2nd & 3rd Sept. 1755 ... on a Branch of Opeccon Called Littlers Branch and joining Littlers Patent Land ... Corner to Joseph Carter in the line of Robert Stewart ... in the line of John Littler dec'd. ... corner to said Littler and John Briscoe ... Containing 276 Acres ... Yielding and paying rent of one Ear of Indian Corn on Lady day next ...
Wit: none   Joseph Horner
Recorded: 5 Oct. 1784

Bk 20, p. 278 - 4 Sept. 1784

[Release] Between Joseph Horner and Margary his wife of County of Frederick [to] John Tremble of County aforesaid ... consideration of Three hundred pounds ... 276 Acres (same as above) ...
Wit: none   Joseph Horner
Recorded: 5 Oct. 1784   Margary (M) Horner

Bk 20, p. 281 - 5 Oct. 1784

WITNESSETH that I Roger Williams Orphan of George Williams late of Frederick County dec'd. ... with the consent and approbation of the Court of said County bind my self an Apprentice to George Clopton of County aforesaid untill I the said Roger Williams arrive to the Age of Twenty One years ...
Wit: none   Roger Williams
Recorded: 5 Oct. 1784   Geo. Clopton

Bk 20, p. 281 - 28 July 1783

[Lease] Between Azariah Pugh of County of Berkeley in State of South Carolina [to] John Dillon of Frederick County ... Consideration of five Shillings ... all that Tract of Land lying on the Drains of Back Creek ... which said Tract was Granted to Luke Dillon by Deed under the Hand and Seal of the Right Honorable Thomas Lord Fairfax the 1st Oct. 1761 and conveyed by said Luke Dillon to said Azariah Pugh by Deeds of L & R the 1st March 1763 ... Corner to William Dillon ... Corner to John Cromly and Woolrey Ruble ... in James Hayworths line ... Containing Eighty six Acres ... Yielding and paying rent of one pepper corn on Lady day next ...
Wit: Saml. Edwards   Azariah Pugh
    William Aspinal
    John Edwards
Recorded: 5 Oct. 1784

Bk 20, p. 283 - 29 July 1783

[Release] Between Azariah Pugh of Berkeley County in State of South

Carolina [to] John Dillon of Frederick County ... consideration of Forty Pounds ... 86 Acres (same as above) ...
Wit: same as above Azariah Pugh
Recorded: 5 Oct. 1784

Bk 20, p. 285 - 10 Sept. 1784
 [Lease] Between Isaac Sutherland of Frederick County [to] Martin Triece of the same place ... consideration of Five Shillings ... part of a Tract of Land which was granted to said Isaac Southerland by Deed under the Hand and Seal of the Right Honourable Thomas Lord Fairfax the 2nd July 1777 ... corner to the meeting House Lot ... Containing two hundred and three and a half Acres ... Yielding and paying rent of one pepper corn on the feast of St. Michael the Archangle (sic) ...
Wit: Samuel Wickersham Isaac (I) Southerland
   Thomas Barrett
   John Dillon
   Richd. Barrett
Recorded: 5 Oct. 1784

Bk 20, p. 286 - 10 Sept. 1784
 [Release] Between Isaac Southerland and Sarah his wife of Frederick County [to] Martin Triece of the same place ... consideration of Fifty eight pounds ... 203 1/2 Acres (same as above) ...
Wit: same as above Isaac (I) Southerland
Recorded: 5 Oct. 1784 Sarah (X) Southerland

Bk 20, p. 289 - 2 Oct. 1784
 Between John Hite Jun. and Susanna his wife of County of Frederick [to] William Sydnor of County of Lancaster in State of Virginia ... Consideration of One Thousand pounds ... a certain Plantation or Tract of Land lying and being in Frederick County ... Containing five hundred and Eighty eight Acres ...
Wit: Wm Glascock Jun. Jno. Hite
   Thads. McCarty Susanna Hite
   John Poker
Recorded: 5 Oct. 1784

Bk 20, p. 290 - 20 Sept. 1784
 [Lease] Between Robert Hodgen and Jacob Lindsey of County of Frederick [to] Edmond Clare of County aforesaid ... consideration of Ten Shillings ... Several small Tracts of Land lying and being on a Branch of Shannado River Called the Long Marsh ... Corner to Lindsey and Bartholomew Smith ... Corner to Hezekiah Lindsey ... corner to John Lindsey ... corner of Jacob Lindsey ... line of John Rice ... Containing three hundred and fifty two Acres ... Yielding and paying rent of one pepper corn on Lady day next ...
Wit: John Kerchival Robert Hodgen

Saml. Kerchival   Jacob Lindsey
Fran.s Stribling
Edw. Snickers
Recorded: 6 Oct. 1784

Bk 20, p. 292 - 21 Sept. 1784
    [Release] Between Robert Hodgen and Sarah his wife and Jacob Lindsey and Elizabeth his wife of County of Frederick [to] Edmond Clare of County aforesaid ... consideration of One thousand and thirty Pounds ... 352 Acres (same as above) ...
Wit: same as above   Robert Hodgen
                                         Sarah (S) Hodgen
                                         Jacob Lindsey
Recorded: 6 Oct. 1784   Elizabeth (X) Lindsey

Bk 20, p. 295 - 25 Sept. 1784
    Sarah & Elizabeth apart from Robert and Jacob their husbands released Dower right to above land ...   Joseph Berry
                                         Wm Helm

Bk 20, p. 295 - 10 April 1784
    KNOW all Men by these presents that I John Cooke of County of Frederick for and in consideration of Fifty pounds to me in hand paid by William Aldridge of the same place ... Doth grant bargain and sell One Feather bed and bedding & bedstead, One Chaff bed, One black Cow, One black yearling, One pide (sic) Cow, Six Chairs etc ... etc ... etc ...
Wit: Nicholas Porter   John Cooke
     James Lindsey
Recorded: 6 Oct. 1784

Bk 20, p. 296 - 7 April 1784
    Between Robert Cockrane and James Cockrane and Sarah his wife of Frederick County [to] John Cockrane of the same place ... consideration of two hundred pounds ... Tract of Land situate on the east side of Opeckon Creek ... line of Robert Glass ... Containing one hundred and seven Acres including two Acres on the lower end of the meadow ... which said tract of Land is part of a larger Tract of 429 Acres which was conveyed to said Robert Cockrane & James Cockran by deed from Samuel Gilkeson the 7th May 1782 ...
Wit: none   Robt. Cochran
Recorded: not dated   James Cockran

Bk 20, p. 298 - 8 June 1784
    [Lease] Between John Millburn of County of Frederick [to] George Ship of County aforesaid ... consideration of five Shillings ... all that Lott or parcel of Ground Laying and being on the Drains of Opecon & is part of the Tract whereon

said John Millburn now liveth ... line of Nathan Littler and corner of John Millburn ... Containing Six acres ... Yielding & paying one pepper corn on Lady day next ...
Wit: Richard Carter
    William Milburn
    Meshack Sexton
Recorded: 2 Nov. 1784

John Millburn

Bk 20, p. 299 - 9 June 1784
    [Release] Between John Millburn and Mary his wife of County of Frederick [to] George Sheip of County aforesaid ... consideration of Eighteen pounds ... Six Acres (same as above) ...
Wit: same as above
Recorded: 2 Nov. 1784

John Millburn
Mary Millburn

Bk 20, p. 301 - 2 Nov. 1784
    Between Lewis Stephens Sen. of Frederick County and Mary his wife [to] Lewis Stephens Jun. of the same place ... consideration of One hundred Pounds ... Tract of Land situate near the Town of Stephensburg ... corner to Col. John Nicewanger and the Heirs of Henry Stephens dec'd. ... corner to said Lewis Stephens Sen. ... along said Lewis Stephens Jun. line ... in the line of John Taylors lot ... Corner to James Hennings lott ... Containing Eighty seven Acres and one fourth part of an Acre ...
Wit: none
Recorded: 2 Nov. 1784

Lewis Stephens
Mary (M) Stephens

Bk 20, p. 303 - 2 Nov. 1784
    Between Isaac Sitler and Barbara his wife of Winchester in County of Frederick [to] Jacob Kiger of the same place ... consideration of One hundred and twenty five pounds ... one full equal moiety or half part of the proportion of Lot No. 22 situate on the East side of Loudoun Street in Winchester aforesaid which Joseph Steer by his Deed of Bargain the 14th Dec. 1780 conveyed to said Isaac Sitler ... at the north corner of Meshask Sextons Stone House ... in the line of John Sperry ... which said Lots were conveyed to said Joseph Steer by Deeds of L & R the 1st & 2nd May 1775 from Andrew Caldwell Eldest son & Heir at Law of Andrew Caldwell dec'd. ...
Wit: none
Recorded: 2 Nov. 1784

Isaac Sittler

Bk 20, p. 305 - 2 Nov. 1784
    Between Isaac Sitler and Barbara his wife of Frederick County [to] John Sperry of the same place ... consideration of One hundred and twenty five Pounds ... one full equal moiety or half part of that proportion of Lott No. 20 situate in the Borough of Winchester on the Easterly side of Loudoun Street which Joseph Steer by his Deed the 14th Dec. 1780 conveyed to said Isaac Sitler ... corner to Jacob Kiger ... Corner of James Walkers Lot ... which said Lots were conveyed to said Joseph

Steer by Deeds of L & R the 1st & 2nd May 1775 from Andrew Caldwell eldest son and heir at Law of Andrew Caldwell dec'd. ...
Wit: none   Isaac Sitler
Recorded: 2 Nov. 1784

Bk 20, p. 307 - 6 March 1784
    Between Joseph Day of County of Frederick and Catharine his wife [to] Gavan Lawson of County of Culpepper ... Whereas said Joseph Day is Indebted to said Gavan Lawson in the sum of six hundred and ninety three pounds nineteen Shillings ... NOW this Indenture for better Securing the payment & in consideration of five Shillings ... the several Lots of Land hereafter mentioned ... Six acres and one half acre where said Joseph Day now lives being the same which he purchased of Stephen Ross ... Twenty three acres and one quarter of an acre joining the former being the same which he purchased of John Littler ... Twenty seven acres near the former on the opposite side of the Great Road the same which he purchased of George Ross ...
Wit: Mary Jolliffe   Joseph Day
   Lewis Walker
   Alex. White
   Solomon Hoge
   Thomas Campbell
   Robt. White Jun.
Recorded: 2 Nov. 1784

Bk 20, p. 309 - 27 Oct. 1784
    Between Jeremiah Lehew and Milly his wife of County of Frederick [to] Allen Wily of the County aforesaid ... consideration of Twenty five pounds ... one certain Lot of Land lying and being on the East side of Happy Creek ... corner to Wilys other Land purchased of John Lehew ... in William Lehews line ... Containing Ten Acres One Quarter and twenty perches of Land it being part of a larger Tract Granted to William Russell Esq. by patent the 17th Dec. 1755 the said Russell convaid (sic) four hundred Acres thereof to Christopher Marr and said Marr convaid two hundred Acres thereof to Peter Lehew being possessed with the said Land did by his last Will and Testament bequeath to said Jeremiah Lehew 33 Acres thereof ...
Wit: Chareles Peyton   Jeremiah (X) Lehew
   John Kerchival   Milly (X) Lehew
Recorded: 2 Nov. 1784

Bk 20, p. 311 - 20 Oct. 1784
    [Lease] Between Jeremiah Lehew and Milly his wife of County of Frederick [to] Charles Paton of County aforesaid ... consideration of five Shillings ... Tract or Lot of Land in County aforesaid ... in which Bounds there is contained two Acres of Land it being part of a larger Tract Granted to William Russell Esquire by Paton (sic) the 17th Dec. 1735 [1755 in above Deed] ... The said Russell convaid (sic) 400 Acres thereof to Christopher Marr who conveyed 200 acres thereof to Peter Lehew

... the said Lehew by his last Will and Testament did bequeath 33 Acres thereof to said Jeremiah Lehew ... Yielding and paying one pepper corn on Lady day next ...
Wit: Allen Wiley
  John Kerchival
Recorded: 2 Nov. 1784

Jeremiah (X) Lehew
Milley (X) Lehew

Bk 20, p. 312 - 21 Oct. 1784
   [Released] Between Jeremiah Lehew and Milly his wife of County of Frederick [to] Charles Paton of County aforesaid ... consideration of ten pounds ... 2 Acres (same as above) ...
Wit: same as above
Recorded: 2 Nov. 1784

Jeremiah (X) Lehew
Milley (X) Lehew

Bk 20, p. 314 - 28 Oct. 1784
   [Lease] Between John Donaldson of the Borough of Winchester in County of Frederick [to] Isaac Littler of the Borough & County aforesaid ... consideration of Five Shillings ... all his full equal moiety or half part of Lott No. 1 being part of a Certain Lott of Five Acres which Thomas Edmondson obtained an Act of Assembly for annexing the said Borough of Winchester and is the uppermost half of the said Lott & was conveyed by said Thomas Edmondson by Deed the 14th June 1783 to Jacob Kiger and by said Kiger conveyed to said John Donaldson by Deeds of L & R the 3rd & 4th Aug. 1784 ... Yielding and paying one pepper corn on Lady day next ...
Wit: Gabriel Throckmorton Jun.   John Donaldson
  Saml. Baker
  Joseph Day
Recorded: 2 Nov. 1784

Bk 20, p. 315 - 29 Oct. 1784
   [Release] Between John Donaldson of the Borough of Winchester in County of Frederick [to] Isaac Littler of Borough & County aforesaid ... consideration of Fifty Pounds ... One half of Lot No. 1 (same as above) ...
Wit: same as above   John Donaldson
Recorded: 2 Nov. 1784

Bk 20, p. 317 - 2 Nov. 1784
   KNOW all Men by these presents that we Joseph Holmes Edward Smith Battaile Muse Thos. Throckmorton and Thomas Berry are held and firmly Bound unto Jno. S. Woodcock Elisha Williams David Kennedy Robert Mackey Gentlemen Justices of County of Frederick in the just and full sum of Five hundred pounds ...
   The Condition of the above obligation is such that the above Bound Joseph Holmes is appointed Sheriff for the County of Frederick ...
Wit: J. Peyton   Joseph Holmes
     Edw. Smith
     Battaile Muse

Recorded: 2 Nov. 1784

Thos. Throckmorton
Thos. Berry

Bk 20, p. 319 - 4 Nov. 1784
    Between John McGinnis and Elizabeth his wife of Town of Stephensburg and County of Frederick [to] Henry Carver of place aforesaid ... consideration of Thirty five Pounds paid to Edm. McGinnis (a debt due to said Edm. McGinnis by said John McGinnis) ... a Certain Lot of Land in the Town of Stephensburgh known by No. 14 ... containing half an Acre of Land which said lot was conveyed by the last Will and Testament of Christian Foglesong to John Marburger in the year 1780 and was conveyed to John McGinnis the said year ...

Wit: Dennis Bush
    Philip Trout
    Anthony Kline
Recorded: 3 Nov. 1784 (?)

John McGinnis
Elizabeth McGinnis

Bk 20, p. 320 - 8 Sept. 1784
    [Lease] Between Micajah Hughes and Mary his wife of Frederick County [to] Jacob Marker of the same place ... consideration of five Shillings ... a Certain Lot of half an Acre of Land situate in the Town of Stephensburg and known by No. 27 which said Lot were conveyed to sd Micajah Hughes and Mary his wife by Deed from Col. John Hite ... Yielding and paying one pepper corn on Lady day next ...

Wit: J. McGinnis
    James Hening
    Henry W. Carver
Recorded: 3 Nov. 1784

Micajah Hughes

Bk 20, p. 321 - 9 Sept. 1784
    [Release] Between Micajah Hughes and Mary his wife of Frederick County [to] Jacob Marker of the same place ... consideration of Ten Pounds ... Lot No. 27 (same as above) ...

Wit: same as above
Recorded: 3 Nov. 1784

Micajah Hughes
Mary (+) Hughes

Bk 20, p. 323 - 9 Sept. 1784
    Between Micajah Hughes and Mary his wife of Stephensburgh in County of Frederick [to] Henry Carver of place aforesaid ... consideration of Six pounds ten Shillings ... a Certain Lot of Land in the Suburbs of Stephensburg commonly called Out Lots ... known by No. 125 which said five acres of Land was conveyed from Lewis Stephens and Mary his wife to John Hite and afterwards conveyed from John Hite to Micajah Hughes ...

Wit: J. McGinnis
    James Hening
    Jacob O. Marker

Micajah Hughes
Mary (+) Hughes

Recorded: 3 Nov. 1784

Bk 20, p. 325 - 18 Sept. 1765
    Between James Hall and his wife Sarah Ann Hall [to] Richard Hall of the other part ... consideration of thirty pounds ... all that Lands that is intitled (sic) by Will to said James Hall and his wife Sarah Ann Hall by said James Hall Father dec'd.
Wit: John Suell   James (JH) Hall
   William Hall   Sarah Ann Hall
   David Suell
   Thomas Hall
Recorded: 3 Nov. 1784

Bk 20, p. 326 - 13 Nov. 1784
    Between Samuel Griffith and Mary his wife of Frederick County [to] Thomas Campbell of the same place ... consideration of Twenty eight pounds ... two certain Tracts of Land situate on Evan Thomas's Run one of the drains of Opeckon ... in the line of Robert Stewart ... at the line of Mary Littler ... Containing twenty three acres and three roods ... The other sd Tract ... line of Mary Littler ... line of Evan Thomas ... Containing one hundred Acres ...
Wit: David Deadwick   Samuel Griffith
   Thos. Cochran
   J. Peyton
Recorded: 7 Dec. 1784

Bk 20, p. 328 - 28 Feb. 1785
    Between Mary Wood Relict and Devisee of James Wood late of Frederick County [to] John Hatley Norton of Winchester in County aforesaid ... Consideration of one hundred and Seventy pounds ... Eight Lots of Land Situate in the addition made to the Town of Winchester and known by the Numbers 4, 4, 5, 5, (?) ... two said Lots 6 & 6 lying contiguous & adjoining to each other ... three other of the said Lots adjoining to each other and are known by the No. 4, 5 & 6 ... each which Lots contains half an Acre of Land ...
Wit: Wm McGuire   Mary Wood
   John Heth
   Robert Wood
   D. Norton
Recorded: 1 March 1785

Bk 20, p. 330 - 1 March 1785
    Between James Williams and Mary his wife of County of Frederick [to] Barnett Williams of County aforesaid ... WHEREAS the Hon.ble George Washington and Fielding Lewis Esq. should make sale of Certain lands which George Carter died seized to such persons as shall be willing to purchase ... in 1774 conveyed unto Mordicai Redd by Deeds of L & R all that Tract of Land Containing eight hundred

& Twenty seven Acres lying and being in Frederick County known by No. 4 ... it being part of a larger Tract of Fifty thousand two Hundred and twelve Acres Granted to said George Carter & Others by Deed Poll by the Proprietor of Northern Neck the 22nd Sept. 1730 ... the said Mordicai Redd & Aggatha his wife sold and conveyed by Deeds of L & R three Hundred Acres (of aforementioned Eight Hundred and Twenty seven Acres) ... Consideration of three Hundred and fifty pounds ... Corner to late John Bell, John Ashby & Richard K. Meade ... corner to late John Bell and Edward Reed dec'd. ... Containing three hundred Acres ...
Wit: none   James Williams
Recorded: 1 March 1785   Mary Williams

Bk 20, p. 332 - __ March 1785
Between Jacob Marker of County of Frederick [to] Daniel Smith of County of Shanandoah ... consideration of Twenty pounds ... a certain Lot or half Acre of Land situate in the Town of Stephensburg and known by No. 27 ...
Wit: John Swearingen Williams   Jacob Marker
    Adam Albert
Recorded: 1 March 1785

Bk 20, p. 333 - 1 March 1785
Between Nicolaus Sperry Junior and Elizabeth his wife of County of Frederick [to] John Sperry son of said Nicolaus of County aforesaid ... consideration of One hundred pounds ... [Tract of Land] in his actual possession by virtue of his said Fathers Deeds for two Tracts from the proprietors Office and of Thomas Sperry Dec'd. for a Greater Tract and resurveyed by Joseph Bowman dec'd. the 11th Dec. 1773 for One thousand & Seventy One Acres from which said Nicholas Sperry now conveys part thereof by this Deed Two hundred and Sixty nine Acres ... Line to Jacob Sperrys and William Evans ... Corner to William Legett now Peter Sensenigs ... Line of Nicholas Sperrys own Land ... Containing two hundred and Sixty nine Acres ...
Wit: Nicholas Sperry   Nicholas (NSP) Sperry Jr.
    John Lentz   Elizabeth (D) Sperry
Recorded: 1 March 1785

Bk 20, p. 336 - 1 March 1785
Between Nicholas Sperry Junior and Elizabeth his wife of County of Frederick [to] Jacob Sperry son of said Nicholas Sperry and County aforesaid ... consideration of One hundred pounds ... [tract of Land] in his actual possession Now being by virtue of his said Father Nicholas Sperry who by Deeds granted by the proprietor and Thomas Sperry dec'd. in two Tracts and by a resurvey One Tract by Joseph Bowman dec'd. the 11th Dec. 1773 of One thousand and Seventy One Acres conveys now apart of said Tract Two hundred and thirteen acres thereof to said Jacob Sperry forever ... corner to George Goodykunt dec'd. and corner to John Sperry son of said Nicholas Sperry ... corner to Nicholas Sperry's own Land ... Corner to Daniel McCans ... at line of Mr. Isaac Hite ... Containing two hundred and thirteen Acres ...

Wit: Nicholas Sperry   Nicholas (NSP) Sperry Jr.
Recorded: 1 March 1785   Elizabeth (D) Sperry

Bk 20, p. 339 - 10 Jan. 1785
    Between William Campbell of the Borough to Winchester in County of Frederick [to] John Kean Esq. of the same place ... Consideration of three hundred pounds ... a certain half Lott or parcel of Land situate lying and being on the Western side of Loudoun Street in said Borough between a certain half Lott on the said Street purchased by Col. Joseph Holmes of Capt. William Eskridge and Elizabeth his wife and a Lott the property of Edward McGuire Esq. on which he now lives ... three and one quarter Acres of Land ...
Wit: Edward Smith   Wm Campbell
    Robert White, Jun.
    J. Peyton
Recorded: 2 March 1785

Bk 20, p. 341 - 17 Feb. 1785
    Between Jeremiah Lehew and Milly his wife of County of Frederick [to] Robert Haines of County aforesaid ... consideration of Ten pounds ... a certain Tract or Lot of Land lying and being in County aforesaid ... on the East Bank of Happy Creek ... Corner to Allen Wily ... Containing five acres & 24 perches ... It being part of a greater Tract Granted to William Russell Esq. by Paton the 17th Dec. 1735 ... the said Russell conveyed four hundred acres thereof to Christopher Marr ... the said Marr conveyed 200 acres thereof to Peter Lehew by his Deed the 2nd Feb. 1754 ... The said Peter Lehew by his last Will and Testament did bequeath 33 acres thereof to said Jeremiah Lehew ...
Wit: Charles Peyton   Jeremiah (+) Lehew
    Francis Lehew   Milley (+) Lehew
    Lennor Lehew
Recorded: 2 March 1785

Bk 20, p. 343 - 27 Feb. 1785
    Between Francis Lehew and ___ his wife of County of Frederick [to] Robert Haines of County aforesaid ... consideration of Ten pounds ... a certain Tract or Lot of Land lying and being in County aforesaid ... nearly opposite the lower corner of Francis Lehew's cabbin ... Solomon Vanmeters corner ... Containing two acres and fifteen perches it being part of a greater Tract Granted to William Russell Esq. by paton the 17th Dec. 1735 ... the said Russell convaid (sic) four hundred acres thereof to Christopher Marr by his Deed ... said Marr convaid 200 acres thereof to Peter Lehew by his last Will & Testament did bequeath 33 acres to the above said Francis Lehew ...
Wit: Charles Payton   Francis (+) Lehew
    W. Millo   Lenner Lehew
    Jeremiah Lehew

Recorded: 2 March 1785

Bk 20, p. 344 - 26 Feb. 1785

    Between David Lehew and Elizabeth his wife of County of Frederick [to] Robert Haines of County aforesaid ... consideration of Ten pounds paid by Nathan Nickles ... Two small Lotts of Land lying and being in County aforesaid ... Corner to Allen Wiley ... Containing one acre and a half & 38 perches ... the other Lot ... in Solomon Vanmeters Line ... Corner to George Cheak ... Containing half an acre and seven perches of Land ... the two Lots containing two acres one quarter and five perches of Land it being part of a Greater Tract Granted to William Russell Esq. by Paton the 17th Dec. 1735 ... The said Russell conveyed 400 acres thereof to Christopher Marr by his Deed ... the said Marr convaid (sic) 200 acres thereof to Peter Lehew by his Deed the 2nd Feb. 1754 ... said Peter Lehew by his last Will and Testament did give and bequeath 33 acres thereof to his son the said David Lehew.

Wit: Mason Jones   David (X) Lehew
    Charles Peyton   Elizabeth (+) Lehew
    William Mulliken

Recorded: 2 March 1785

Bk 20, p. 346 - 20 Feb. 1785

    Between Francis Lehew and Leanah his wife of County of Frederick [to] John Rumgay of County aforesaid ... consideration of Five pounds ... a certain Tract of Lot of land lying and being in County aforesaid ... Containing one acre of Land it being part of a greater tract Granted to William Russell Esq. by Patton the 17th Dec. 1735 ... the said Russell conveyed 400 acres thereof to Christopher Marr by his Deed ... the said Marr conveyed 200 acres thereof to Peter Lehew by his last Will and Testament did give and bequeath thirty three acres to said Francis Lehew ...

Wit: Mason Jones   Francis Lehew
    Charles Peyton   Leanner Lehew
    William Mullikin

Recorded: 2 March 1785

Bk 20, p. 348 - 25 Feb. 1785

    Between Francis Lehew and Leanner his wife of County of Frederick [to] James Miller of Shannandoah County ... Consideration of five pounds ... a certain Tract or Lot of Land lying and being in County aforesaid ... At William Miller's corner ... in Bailes Ashbys line ... Containing one acre and twenty one perches ... it being part of a greater Tract Granted to William Russell Esq. by patton the 17th Dec. 1735 ... the said Russell conveyed 400 acres thereof to Christopher Marr ... the said Marr conveyed 200 acres thereof to Peter Lehew by his deed the 2nd Feb. 1754 ... Peter Lehew by his last Will and Testament did give and bequeath thirty three acres to said Francis Lehew ...

Wit: Charles Peyton   Francis Lehew
    William Mulliken   Leanner Lehew

Mason Jones
Recorded: 2 March 1785

Bk 20, p. 350 - 15 Jan. 1785
    Between Francis Lehew and Leannah his wife of County of Frederick [to] Solomon Vanmeter of County aforesaid ... consideration of 2 pounds ... a certain Tract or Lot of Land lying and being in County aforesaid ... at George Cheeks corner ... Containing one acre of Land it being part of a Greater Tract Granted to William Russell Esq. (by) Patton the 17th Dec. 1735 ... said Russell conveyed 400 acres thereof to Christopher Marr by his Deed ... said Marr conveyed 200 acres thereof to Peter Lehew did give and Bequeath thirty three acres to said Francis Lehew ...

Wit: Mason Jones   Francis Lehew
    Charles Peyton   Leanner Lehew
    William Mulliken
Recorded: 2 March 1785

Bk 20, p. 352 - 25 Feb. 1785
    Between David Lehew and Elizabeth his wife of County of Frederick [to] Mason Jones of County aforesaid ... consideration of Thirty pounds ... a certain Tract or Lot of land lying and being in County aforesaid ... in Alen Wileys line ... in William Clouds line ... Containing five acres & a half and seven perches it being part of a greater Tract Granted to William Russell Esq. by Patton the 17th Dec. 1735 ... said Russell conveyed 400 acres thereof to Christopher Marr ... said Marr conveyed 200 acres thereof to Peter Lehew by his deed the 2nd Feb. 1754 ... said Peter Lehew by his last Will and Testament did give and bequeath 33 acres thereof to said David Lehew ...

Wit: Charles Payton   David (+) Lehew
    William Mulliken   Elizabeth (X) Lehew
    Jos. Robinson
Recorded: 2 March 1785

Bk 20, p. 353 - 21 Feb. 1785
    Between David Lehew and Elizabeth his wife of County of Frederick [to] George Cheek Sen of County aforesaid ... consideration of Five pounds ... a certain Tract or Lot of Land lying and being in County aforesaid ... at Barnard Myers Corner ... Containing acres & twenty one perches it being part of a Greater Tract Granted to William Russell Esq. by Patton the 17th Dec. 1735 ... said Russell conveyed 400 acres thereof to Christopher Marr ... said Marr being so possessed with said Land conveyed two Hundred acres thereof to Peter Lehew by his Deed the 2nd Feb. 1754 ... said Peter Lehew by his last Will and Testament did bequeath thirty three acres thereof to said David Lehew ...

Wit: Charles Payton   David (X) Lehew
    Mason Jones   Elizabeth (X) Lehew
    William Mulliken

Recorded: 2 March 1785

Bk 20, p. 355 - 21 Feb. 1785
    Between David Lehew and Elizabeth his wife of County of Frederick [to] George Cheek of County aforesaid ... consideration of five pounds ... a certain Tract or Lot of Land lying and being in County aforesaid ... in Allen Wilys line ... in Solomon Vanmeters line ... Containing one acre and a half & 17 perches it being part of a Greater Tract Granted to William Russell Esq. by paton the 17th Dec. 1735 ... the said Russell convaid (sic) 400 acres thereof to Christopher Marr by his Deed ... said Marr convaid 200 acres thereof to Peter Lehew by his Deed the 2nd Feb. 1754 ... said Peter Lehew by his last Will and Testament did bequeath 33 acres thereof to said David Lehew ...

Wit: Charles Peyton	David (X) Lehew
William Mulliken	Elizabeth (X) Lehew
Mason Jones	

Recorded: 2 March 1785

Bk 20, p. 357 - 17 Jan. 1785
    Between David Lehew and Elizabeth his wife of County of Frederick [to] Joseph Robinson of County aforesaid ... consideration of three pounds ... a certain Tract or Lot of Land lying and being in County aforesaid ... George Cheeks corner ... Containing one quarter & 8 perches (of an acre) of Land it being part of a Greater Tract Granted to William Russell Esq. by Patton the 17th Dec. 1735 ... the said Russell conveyed 400 acres thereof to Christopher Marr by his Deed ... said Marr conveyed 200 acres thereof to Peter Lehew by his deed the 2nd Feb. 1754 ... said Peter Lehew by his last Will and Testament did give and bequeath 33 acres to the aforesaid David Lehew ...

Wit: Charles Payton	David (X) Lehew
William Mulliken	Elizabeth (X) Lehew
Mason Jones	

Recorded: 2 March 1785

Bk 20, p. 359 - 28 Feb. 1785
    Between David Lehew and Elizabeth his wife of County of Frederick [to] Joseph Robinson of County aforesaid ... consideration of Twelve pounds ... a certain Tract or Lot of Land lying and being in County aforesaid ... Corner to George Cheek Sen. ... in Allen Wileys line ... Mason Jones corner ... Containing one acre a half and Seven perches it being part of a greater Tract Granted to William Russell Esquire by patton the 17th Dec. 1735 ... said Russell conveyed 400 acres thereof to Christopher Marr ... said Marr conveyed Two hundred acres to Peter Lehew by his Deed 2nd Feb. 1754 ... said Peter Lehew by his last Will and Testament did bequeath thirty three acres thereof to said David Lehew ...

Wit: Charles Payton	David (X) Lehew
William Mulliken	Elizabeth (X) Lehew

Mason Jones
Recorded: 2 March 1785

Bk 20, p. 361 - 16 Feb. 1785
    Between David Lehew and Elizabeth his wife of County of Frederick [to] William Cloud of Shannandoah County ... consideration of 20 pounds ... a certain Tract or Lot of Land lying and being in County of Frederick ... Corner to Joseph Robinson and Barnard Mier ... Corner to James Millers Lott ... in Solomon Vanmeters line ... Containing 8 Acres of Land ... It being part of a greater Tract granted to William Russell Esq. by Patton the 17th Dec. 1735 ... said Russell conveyed 400 acres thereof to Christopher Marr by his deed ... said Marr being so possessed with said Land conveyed 200 acres thereof to Peter Lehew by his deed the 2nd Feb. 1754 ... said Peter Lehew by his last Will and Testament did give and bequeath thirty three acres to aforesaid David Lehew ...

Wit: Mason Jones   David (X) Lehew
     Charles Peyton   Elizabeth (X) Lehew
     William Mulliken
Recorded: 2 March 1785

Bk 20, p. 363 - __ day of __ 1785
    Between David Lehew and Elizabeth his wife of County of Frederick [to] George Featheringill of County aforesaid ... consideration of Three pounds ... a certain Tract or Lot of Land lying and being in County aforesaid ... in Solomon Vanmeters line ... Corner to Cheak ... Containing one Acre ... It being part of a greater Tract of Land granted to William Russell Esq. by Patton the 17th Dec. 1735 ... said Russell conveyed 400 acres thereof to Christopher Marr ... said Marr conveyed 200 acres thereof to Peter Lehew by his Deed the 2nd Feb. 1754 ... said Peter Lehew by his last Will and Testament did give and bequeath Thirty three acres to the aforesaid David Lehew ...

Wit: Charles Payton   David (X) Lehew
     Mason Jones   Elizabeth (X) Lehew
     William Mulliken
Recorded: 2 March 1785

Bk 20, p. 364 - 20 Feb. 1785
    Between Francis Lehew and Leannah his wife of County of Frederick [to] Mason Jones of County aforesaid ... consideration of Thirty pounds ... a certain Tract or Lot of Land lying & being in County of Frederick ... corner to John Rumgay ... near Balis Ashbys corner ... Containing 12 Acres and 25 perches of Land it being part of a greater Tract Granted to William Russell Esq. by Patton the 17th Dec. 1735 ... the said Russell conveyed 400 acres thereof to Christopher Marr by his Deed ... said Marr conveyed 200 acres thereof to Peter Lehew by his deed the 2nd Feb. 1754 ... said Peter Lehew by his last Will and Testament did give and bequeath 33 acres to said Francis Lehew ...

Wit: Charles Peyton
   William Mulliken
   Jos. Robinson
Recorded: 2 March 1785

Francis Lehew
Leanner Lehew

Bk 20, p. 366 - 17 Jan. 1785
    Between Francis Lehew and Leannah his wife of County of Frederick [to] William Millar of County of Shannandoe ... consideration of Thirty pounds ... a certain Tract or Lot of Land lying and being in County of Frederick commonly called Franks Meadow ... a small distance above said Francis Lehews house ... in Balis Ashbys line ... Containing 4 acres 3 quarters 27 perches it being part of a greater Tract Granted to William Russell Esq. by Paton the 17th Dec. 1735 ... said Russell conveyed 400 acres thereof to Christopher Marr by his Deed ... said Marr being so possessed with said Land conveyed 200 acres thereof to Peter Lehew by his Deed the 2nd Feb. 1754 ... said Peter Lehew by his last Will and Testament did bequeath 33 acres thereof to said Francis Lehew ...
Wit: Charles Payton
   Jeremiah Lehew
   Robert Haines
Recorded: 2 March 1785

Francis Lehew
Leanner Lehew

Bk 20, p. 368 - 15 Nov. 1784
    Between George Beeler Adm. of the goods and Chattles & Credits of William Vestal dec'd. who was Exor. of the last Will and Testament of John Vestall dec'd. who was Adm. of the goods and Chattles & Credits of Thomas Speaks of County of Berkeley [to] Christopher Fry of Frederick County ... WHEREAS William Green of County of Frederick being indebted unto said Thomas Speaks in sum of twenty pounds ... and for better Securing the payment whereof said William Green by Indenture the 9th March 1765 made between William Green & Elizabeth his wife [to] said Thomas Speaks ... did grant and sell unto him said Thomas Speaks one certain Lot of Land situate on Cameron Street in Winchester being the same which said William Green obtained a patent for from Lord Fairfax ... which said Lot he the said William Green hath since sold and conveyed unto said Christopher Fry ... said George Beeler on behalf of the estate of said Thomas Speaks and the aforesaid William Green three remains a balance of two pounds Seven Shillings & nine pence said Christopher Fry hath paid unto him the said George Beeler ... NOW THIS INDENTURE in consideration of Two pounds Seven Shillings & nine pence paid by said Christopher Fry ... said George Beeler doth Surrender unto him said Christopher Fry all the right title and Interest in trust property of said George Beeler which said Thomas Speak, John Vestall & William Vestall might enjoy in parcel thereof ...
Wit: Meredith Helm
   George Calmes
   Wm McPherson

G. Beeler

Andrew Kiger
Recorded: 3 March 1785

Bk 20, p. 370 - 3 March 1785
    Between Jacob Sowers & John Sowers of County of Frederick Exors. of Jacob Sowers dec'd. [to] Daniel Sowers of the same County ... consideration of two hundred & fifty pounds ... one full equal moiety or half part of a certain lot or half acre of land situate in the Borough of Winchester known by No. 17 being the southernmost half thereof fronting Loudoun Street ... together with a certain Lot or Tract of five acres and Nineteen perches of land situate in the Common of the sd Borough being that part of Lot No. 42 which lies between the Potowmack and Cumberland roads the same being part of the lots which the Right Honorable Thomas Lord Fairfax by his Patent the 15th May 1753 Granted to Jacob Sowers who by his last Will & Testament devised that the same should be sold by his Executors ...
Wit: none
Recorded: 3 March 1785
                          Jacob Sowers
                          John Sowers

Bk 20, p. 372 - 16 Oct. 1784
    Between Frederick Conrad and Robert Craigan of Winchester in County of Frederick [to] Thomas Cochran of the same place ... WHEREAS said Philip Woolwine in and by a certain Indenture the 1st March 1774 did sell unto said Frederick Conrad and Robert Craigan a certain Quarter or part of a Lot of land on Loudoun Street in Winchester aforesaid known by No. 15 the same being one half of the half Lot which had conveyed to said Philip Woolwine with a proportional part of the out Lot No. 22 ... for and during the term of five hundred years ... WHEREAS said Philip Woolwine hath since fully paid his said Bond with the said Frederick Conrad and Robert Craigan to Meshack Sexton and hath sold and conveyed the said part of Lotts to said Thomas Cochran ... NOW THIS INDENTURE in further consideration of Five Shillings ... doth grant bargain and sell (above mentioned Lotts) ...
Wit: J. Peyton   Frederick Conrad
  George Kiger   Robert Craigan
  Geo. Sommerville
Recorded: 4 March 1785

Bk 20, p. 374 - 16 Oct. 1784
    Between Philip Woolwine late of the Borough of Winchester but now of the Town of Stanton in Augusta County [to] Thomas Cochran of Winchester aforesaid in County of Frederick ... WHEREAS said Thomas Cochran being indebted unto said Philip Woolwine in the sum of one hundred pounds ... and for better Securing the payment whereof said Thomas Cochran & Phebe his wife by their Indenture the 2nd Sept. 1783 ... did bargain and sell unto him said Philip Woolwine a part of Lot No. 15 situate on the east side of Loudoun Street in the said Borough of Winchester ... together with two acres and a half of Land in the Common of sd Borough being one

full equal moiety of Lot No. 22 ... NOW THIS INDENTURE for and in consideration of one hundred pounds ... all the right title and Interest in the said premises ...
Wit: J. Peyton   Philip Woolwine
    Frederick Conrad
    George Kiger
    Robert Craigan
Recorded: 4 March 1785

Bk 20, p. 376 - 21 Oct. 1784
    KNOW all Men by these presents that I Bryan Bruin of the Borough of Winchester County of Frederick ... for and in consideration of One hundred pounds paid by Mr. Edward McGuire of said Borough & County ... have bargain and sold unto said Edward McGuire ... One clock, bowles and dishes, Plates, Candle Sticks, Glasses, Waiters, Pictures, One blue painted cupboard, etc ... etc ... etc ...
Wit: Eliz.th Jane Kayser   Bryan Bruin
Recorded: 4 March 1785

Bk 20, p. 377 - 15 Feb. 1785
    [Lease] Between Samuel May of Frederick County [to] Samuel Pleasant of the City of Philadelphia and State of Pennsylvania ... consideration of One Thousand pounds ... a certain Tract of Land lying and being in County aforesaid Containing three hundred and fifty three acres ... which said Tract of Land Robert Wilson Sen. by his Deeds of L & R the 2nd & 3rd March 1761 conveyed to Robert Wilson Jun. and from Robert Wilson Jun. to Samuel May ... Yielding and paying rent of one pepper corn on Lady day next ...
Wit: Michael Deadwick   Samuel May
    John Deadwick
    Alex. White
Recorded: 5 March 1785

Bk 20, p. 379 - 16 Feb. 1785
    [Release] Between Samuel May & Rosannah his wife of County of Frederick [to] Samuel Pleasants of the City of Philadelphia and State of Pennsylvania ... for and in consideration of One thousand Pounds ... 353 Acres (same as above) ...
Wit: same as above   Samuel May
Recorded: 5 March 1785   Rosannah May

Bk 20, p. 381 - 7 March 1785
    Between John Haymaker of the Town of Winchester of County of Frederick & Motlena his wife [to] Martin Riley of the said Town and County ... consideration of Fifty pounds ... One full equal Moiety or half part of that proportion or part of Lot No. 30 situate in the Borough of Winchester whereon the said John Haymaker now lives being the Southern most half thereof and which was conveyed unto said John Haymaker by Deed from Philip Bush ... Together with a proportionate part of the

Out lot No. 69 situate in the Commons of the said Town ...
Wit: David Deadwick
  Joseph Neill
  Absalom Hammond
Recorded: 6 April 1785

John Haymaker
Salley (+) Haymaker

Bk 20, p. 383 - 5 April 1785
    WHEREAS Charles Smith late of the County of Frederick died Seized of and in two Tracts of Land situate lying and being upon Penningtons Marsh in said County of Frederick containing Seven Hundred & Eighty Six acres ... And WHEREAS said Charles Smith before he departed this life made & published his last Will and Testament appointed his dearly beloved wife Rebecca Smith, Col. John Hite, John Hite Jun. & Captain Francis Peyton his Exors. to either sell or divide his whole Estate and make an equal division among his children, John Smith, Elizabeth Hite Smith, Charles Smith & Sarah Smith ... And WHEREAS said Rebecca Smith widow & relict of said Charles Smith hath since departed this life & said John Hite & John Hite Jun. have taken upon them the Executing of the Will of Charles Smith ... NOW THIS INDENTURE made Partition of the Real Estate of said Charles Smith dec'd. in manner and form following - that said John Smith shall have ... all that portion from Snickers to Winchester ... containing One hundred & Sixty Seven Acres ... that the said Elizabeth Hite Smith now Morton shall have hold & enjoy ... all that portion on the No. side of Penningtons Marsh ... crossing the Road from Buckskin to Battletown ... Containing one Hundred and fifty seven acres ... the said Charles Smith shall have hold & enjoy ... all that portion below the road leading from Battletown to Cunninghams Chappel ... Containing two hundred and ten Acres ... that the said Sarah Smith now Easton shall have hold & enjoy ... all that portion on the north side of Penningtons Marsh ... corner with said Mortons line ... in Stephen Johnstons line ... Containing Two hundred and fifty two acres ...
Wit: none
Recorded: 6 April 1785

Jno. Hite
Jno. Hite Jr.

Bk 20, p. 386 - 5 April 1785
    KNOW all Men by these presents that WHEREAS Charles Smith late of the County of Frederick did before he departed this life make & publish his last Will and Testament thereof appointed his wife Rebecca Smith, Colonel John Hite, John Hite, Jun. & Captain Francis Peyton Exors. and Whereas said Rebecca Smith is since dead & the said Francis Peyton has refused to Act as Exor. ... the said John Hite & John Hite Jun. have taken upon our Selves as Records of County Court may Appear ... NOW KNOW YE that we the said John Hite & John Hite Jun. Both of County aforesaid have ordained authorised & appointed Charles Smith of the said County our True and lawful Attorney for us and in our name and for our use as Exors. of the said Charles Smith dec'd. ...
Wit: none
Recorded: 6 April 1785

Jno. Hite
Jno. Hite Jr.

Bk 20, p. 387 - 1 April 1785

[Lease] Between Evan Thomas of County of Frederick [to] Richard Ridgway of the County of Berkeley ... consideration of five Shillings ... Part of a Tract of Land lying and being on the drains of Opecon Creek and is part of a larger Tract which was Granted to Evan Thomas Sen. by Patent the 12th Nov. 1735 and by said Evan Thomas Sen. conveyed to Evan Thomas Jun. by Deeds of L & R the 3rd & 4th March 1745 ... Containing twenty five Acres ... Yielding and paying rent of one pepper corn on Lady day next ...

Wit: John Steed
   John Washington
   Joseph Day
Recorded: 6 April 1785

Evan (E) Thomas

Bk 20, p. 388 - 2 April 1785

[Release] Between Evan Thomas & Margaret his wife of County of Frederick [to] Richard Ridgway of County of Berkley ... consideration of Sixty eight pounds fifteen Shillings ... 25 Acres (same as above) ...

Wit: same as above
Recorded: 6 April 1785

Evan (E) Thomas
Margaret (M) Thomas

Bk 20, p. 390 - 9 Sept. 1784

Between Isaac Southerland and Sarah his wife of Frederick County [to] Henry Whiteman, John Williams and John Hite of the same place and Benjamin Boylston, John Hite, Joseph Hite and Thomas Boylston of Berkley County Trustees for the Christian Society called Methodists ... consideration of Twenty Shillings ... all that Lot of Ground Containing one Acre and a half of Land situate lying and being near the North side of the North Mountain near the Gap leading to Winchester in the said County of Frederick ... part of a Tract of Land containing two Hundred and fifteen Acres granted to said Isaac Southerland by Deed under the Hand and Seal of the Right Honorable Thomas Lord Fairfax the 2nd July 1777 ... beginning with the new erected Preachers House ... Provided that said persons preach no other Doctrin that is contained in the Rev. Mr. John Wesleys Notes ...

Wit: Clement Shimm
   Edward Whiteman
   John Thompson
Recorded: 6 April 1785

Isaac (I) Southerland
Sarah (X) Southerland

Bk 20, p. 392 - 4 April 1785

[Lease] Between Jacob Sowers and John Sowers Exors. of Jacob Sowers late of Winchester in County of Frederick [to] William Pyles of the same place ... consideration of Five Shillings ... one full equal Moiety or half part of a certain Lot of half an acre of Land situate in the Borough of Winchester known by No. 17 being the Northernmost half thereof fronting Loudoun Street on the West ... Together with the residue or remainder of out Lot No. 42 in the Common of said Borough which lies

on the East side of Cumberland road and contains four Acres & thirty five perches ... the same being part of the lotts which were granted by patent from the Right Honorable Thomas Lord Fairfax the 15th May (1753) to the said Jacob Sowers dec'd. who by his last Will and Testament directed that the same should be sold ... Yielding and paying rent of one Pepper Corn on Lady day next ...
Wit: none   Jacob Sowers
Recorded: 7 April 1785   John Sowers

Bk 20, p. 393 - 5 April 1785
   [Release] Between Jacob Sowers and John Sowers Exors. of Jacob Sowers late of Winchester in County of Frederick dec'd. [to] William Pyles of the Borough & County aforesaid ... consideration of Two hundred and fifty pounds ... part of Lotts No. 17 & 42 (same as above) ...
Wit: none   Jacob Sowers
Recorded: 7 April 1785   John Sowers

Bk 20, p. 395 - 6 April 1785
   [Lease] Between William Pyles of Winchester in County of Frederick [to] Jacob Sowers of the same place ... consideration of Five Shillings ... all his equal moiety or half part of a certain Lot or half an Acre of Land situate in the said Borough of Winchester known by No. 17 being the northernmost half thereof fronting on Loudoun Street on the West ... Together with the residue and remainder of the Out Lott No. 42 situate in the Common of the said Borough ... containing four Acres and thirty five perches the same being part of the Lotts which the Right Honorable Thomas Lord Fairfax by his Patent the 15 May 1753 Granted unto Jacob Sowers dec'd. and by Jacob Sowers and John Sowers Exors. of Jacob Sowers dec'd. conveyed unto said William Pyles by Deeds of L & R the 4th & 5th April 1785 ... Yielding and paying rent of one pepper corn on Lady day next ...
Wit: none   William Pyles
Recorded: 7 April 1785

Bk 20, p. 397 - 7 April 1785
   [Release] Between William Pyles and Ann his wife of Winchester in County of Frederick [to] Jacob Sowers of the same place ... consideration of Two hundred and fifty pounds ... part of two Lots No. 17 & 42 (same as above) ...
Wit: none   William Pyles
Recorded: 7 April 1785   Ann (X) Pyles

Bk 20, p. 399 - 1 Dec. 1784
   [Lease] Between John Shultz of the Borough of Winchester in Frederick County [to] Samuel Calvert of the same County ... consideration of five Shillings ... proportion of a certain parcel of Land which Mrs. Mary Wood Relict and Devisee of James Wood Gent. late of Frederick County dec'd. conveyed to Thomas Rutherford and which the said Rutherford conveyed to said Shultz situate or adjoining to the said

Borough of Winchester ... in the line of Braddock Street ... in the Line of Thomas Rutherford ... in the line of Robert Rutherford ... in the line of John Shultz ... Yielding and paying rent of one Pepper Corn on Lady day next ...
Wit: J. Peyton Jr.   John Shultz
Recorded: 9 April 1785

Bk 20, p. 400 - 2 Dec. 1784
    [Release] Between John Shultz of the Borough of Winchester in Frederick County [to] Samuel Calvert of the County aforesaid ... consideration of Eighteen Pounds ... parcel of Land in the addition to the Borough of Winchester (same as above) ...
Wit: same as above   John Shultz
Recorded: 9 April 1785

Bk 20, p. 402 - 9 Dec. 1784
    [Lease] Between Samuel Calvert of Frederick County [to] John Brady of the Borough of Winchester in County aforesaid ... consideration of five shillings ... Tract of Land situate in the said County of Frederick containing Ten Acres ... corner to William Glover ... being part of a Tract which the said Samuel Calvert purchased from Isaiah Calvert ... Yielding and paying rent of one Pepper Corn on Lady day next.
Wit: none   Samuel Calvert
Recorded: 9 April 1785

Bk 20, p. 403 - 10 Dec. 1784
    [Release] Between Samuel Calvert and Milley his wife of Frederick County [to] John Brady of Winchester in County aforesaid ... consideration of Thirty pounds ... 10 Acres (same as above) ...
Wit: none   Samuel Calvert
Recorded: 9 April 1785

Bk 20, p. 405 - 3 May 1785
    Between Alexander White surviving Executor of the last Will and Testament of John Greenfield late of the Town of Winchester in County of Frederick [to] Edward McGuire of the same Town ... Consideration of thirteen Pounds ... a certain Lot in the Town of Winchester known by No. 69 with the Lot in the Common No. 3.
Wit: none   Alex. White
Recorded: 3 May 1785

Bk 20, p. 406 - 31 Jan. 1785
    [Lease] Between Thomas Martin of County of Frederick [to] Undril Barton of the same place ... consideration of five Shillings ... all that Tract of Land containing Two hundred and Sixty One Acres ... It being part of a Tract Granted to said Thomas Martin under the Hand and Seal of the Right Honorable Thomas Lord Fairfax by deed the 8th Aug. 1760 ... Corner to Ulrick Ruble (now George Ruble) ... in Nicholas

Henchers line (now William Henchers) ... Yielding and paying yearly rent of one pepper corn on the feast day of St. Michael the Arch Angel ...
Wit: Wm Crumly   Thomas (T) Martin
   George Ruble
   Jesse Ruble
Recorded: 3 May 1785

Bk 20, p. 407 - 1 Feb. 1785
   [Release] Between Thomas Martin of County of Frederick [to] Undril Barton of the same place ... consideration of Four hundred and thirty one pounds ... 261 Acres (same as above) ...
Wit: same as above   Thomas (T) Martin
Recorded: 3 May 1785   Albenah (X) Martin

Bk 20, p. 409 - 27 Feb. 1785
   [Lease] Between Asa Clevinger of County of Frederick [to] Lewis Walker of the County aforesaid ... consideration of five shillings ... part of a Tract of Land in Said County of Frederick and is the same which was conveyed to Asa Clevinger by Thomas Wright by Deeds of L & R the 23rd & 24th July 1780 ... corner to division between Thomas Wright & Jonathan Wright ... Corner to Robert Haines ... Containing Seventy one Acres ... Yielding and paying rent of one pepper corn on Lady day next ...
Wit: Amos Jolliffe   Asa Cleavinger
   Jas. Bruce
   Jos. Day
Recorded: 3 May 1785

Bk 20, p. 411 - 28 Feb. 1785
   [Release] Between Asa Cleavinger and Hannah his wife of County of Frederick [to] Lewis Walker of County aforesaid ... consideration of one Hundred & Forty two pounds ... 71 Acres (same as above) ...
Wit: same as above   Asa Cleavinger
Recorded: 3 May 1785   Hannah Cleavinger

Bk 20, p. 413 - 2 May 1785
   Between Henry Lewis and Mary his wife of Frederick County [to] Eve House of County aforesaid ... consideration of Six pounds ... a certain Lot or half acre of Land situate in the Town of Stephensburg ... Known by No. 62 ...
Wit: Wm Glascock   Henry Lewis
   Haz. Williams   Mary (+) Lewis
   Elizabeth Glascock
Recorded: 3 May 1785

Bk 20, p. 414 - 3 May 1785
> Between Thomas Allen Esq. and Abigail his wife of County of Shanandoah [to] Captain James Wilson of County of Frederick ... consideration of Six pounds one Shillings ... a certain Lot of Land containing five Acres situate in the suburbs of Stephensburg in the Lands commonly called out Lots ... known by No. 104 ... which lot of five acres was conveyed to said Thomas Allen by Deed in fee Simple ...
Wit: none   Thomas Allen
Recorded: 3 May 1785

Bk 20, p. 416 - 3 May 1785
> Between Thomas Allen Esq. and Abigill his wife of County of Shanandoah [to] Col. John Nicewanger of County of Frederick ... consideration of Six pounds Seven Shillings ... a certain Lot or five acres of Land in the suburbs of Stephensburg Commonly called an out Lot ... known by No. 47 ... which said Lot of five acres of Land was conveyed to said Thomas Allen by Deed in fee Simple ...
Wit: none   Thomas Allen
Recorded: 3 May 1785

Bk 20, p. 417 - 3 May 1785
> Between Thomas Allen Esq. of County of Shanandoah [to] Vance Bush and Cassimore Plumb Trustees of the German Presbyterian Meeting house of the County of Frederick ... consideration of Five pounds ... a certain Lot or half acre of Land situate in the Town of Stephensburg distinguished by No. 69 ... on the East side of Mulberry Street ...
Wit: none   Thomas Allen
Recorded: 3 May 1785

Bk 20, p. 418 - 10 Jan. 1785
> KNOW all men by these presents that I William Kees of County of Frederick for the consideration of thirty pounds paid unto Samuel May by said William Kees ... Jacob Hotsinpeller of said County is Security ... the said William Kees hath sold unto sd Jacob Hotsinpiller three Horses, three head Cattle, three sheep etc ... etc ...
Wit: Thomas White   William (O) Kees
   Stephen Hotsinpiller   David (X) Garllians
Recorded: 3 May 1785

Bk 20, p. 418 - 1 March 1785
> KNOW all Men by these presents that I William Kees of County of Frederick for the consideration of thirty pounds paid by Jacob Hotsinpiller ... hath granted and sold unto said Jacob Hotsinpiller 1 Desk & Bookcase, one cas Drawers, Two Beds and every other Article the said Kees has now in his possession ...
Wit: Stephen Hotsinpiller   William (O) Kees
   Thos. Cochran
Recorded: 3 May 1785

Bk 20, p. 419 - 3 May 1785

[Lease] Between Philip Eastin of Frederick County [to] William Taylor of the said County ... consideration of five Shillings ... a certain Tract of Land situate on Buck or Penningtons Marsh in aforesaid County ... in line of Elizabeth Hite Smith now Mortons land ... in Stephen Johnsons line ... Containing two hundred & fifty two acres which said Tract of Land is part of two Tracts which were Granted by two separate Patents to Isaac Pennington one the 3rd Oct. 1734 & the other 2 April 1754 ... the former under the Crown and the latter the proprietor of Northern Neck and by said Pennington conveyed to John Hite and Gabriel Jones by Deeds of L & R the 30th Sept and 1st Oct. 1754 and the said Gabriel Jones conveyed his part unto said John Hite by Deeds of L & R the 13th & 14th May (year not given) and by said John Hite the same was conveyed to Charles Smith by Deeds of L & R the 7th & 8th May 1765 who by his last Will and Testament dated the 10th March 1774 directed his Exors. therein named to either sell or divide the same among his children at the death of his wife Rebecca and by Deed of Partition the 5th April 1785 executed by John Hite and John Hite, Jun. the surviving Exors. in the said Will mentioned part thereof allotted to Sarah daughter of said Charles Smith dec'd. with whom the said Philip Eastin hath intermarried ... Yielding and paying one pepper corn on Lady day next ...

Wit: none   Phil Eastin
Recorded: 4 May 1785

Bk 20, p. 421 - 4 May 1785

[Release] Between Philip Eastin and Sarah his wife late Sarah Smith of Frederick County [to] William Taylor of the said County ... consideration of Seven hundred and fifty six pounds ... 252 Acres (same as above) ...

Wit: Thos. Throckmorton   Phil Eastin
    William Helm   Sarah Eastin
    Chas. Smith
Recorded: 4 May 1785

Bk 20, p. 423 - 4 May 1785

Between Stephen Pritchard and Margaret his wife of Frederick County [to] Christian Carman of the same place ... consideration of Forty pounds ... a certain parcel or Lot of Land situate in the said County ... near the Winchester road leading to Stephensburg ... Containing four acres and three quarters of an acre the same being part of a Tract of land whereon said Stephen Pritchard now lives ...

Wit: none   Stephen Pritchard
Recorded: 4 May 1785   Peggy Pritchard

Bk 20, p. 425 - 4 May 1785

Between Stephen Pritchard and Margaret his wife of Frederick County [to] Charles Neill of the same place ... consideration of Twenty pounds ... a certain Parcel or Lot of Land situate in the said County ... corner to Stephen Pritchard and Adam

Kerns Land on the south side of Hogs Run ... Containing Sixty four square Poles the same being part of the tract whereon said Stephen Pritchard now lives ...
Wit: none
Recorded: 4 May 1785

Stephen Pritchard
Peggy Pritchard

Bk 20, p. 427 - 15 May 1784
    Between Henry Dearing and Barbara his wife of Shannandoah County [to] James Walker of Winchester in County of Frederick ... consideration of two hundred & fifty pounds ... one equal half part of Lot No. 51 of half an acre situate in the said Borough of Winchester being the S. half together with the Out Lot of five Acres in the Common of said Borough known by No. 62 which said Lots were granted to Lewis Stephens by Lord Fairfax and from said Stephens conveyed to Everheart Dearing Dec'd. father of said Henry ...
Wit: J. Peyton
  Jas. Anderson
  Jacob Sperry
Recorded: 4 May 1785

Henry Dearing

Bk 20, p. 429 - 22 July 1784
    Barbara the wife of the within mentioned Henry Dearing released Dower right to above land ...

John Anderson
Joseph Pugh

Bk 20, p. 429 - __ day of __ 1785
    [Lease] Between Edward Snickers of Frederick County [to] Thomas Shepherd of County aforesaid ... consideration of five Shillings ... Tract of Land situate in said County ... Thomas Shepherd's corner ... Cornelius Anderson's corner ... containing Eighty seven acres one Rood and thirty eight poles which said Tract of Land Bartholomew Anderson dec'd. by his last Will and Testament devised to his son Abraham Anderson who conveyed the same to Edward Snickers ... Yielding and paying rent of one pepper corn on Lady day next ...
Wit: none
Recorded: 4 May 1785

E. Snickers

Bk 20, p. 430 - __ day of __ 1785
    [Release] Between Edward Snickers of Frederick County [to] Thomas Shepherd of the County aforesaid ... consideration of Two hundred pounds ... 87 Acres 1 Rood & 38 poles (same as above) ...
Wit: none
Recorded: 4 May 1785

Ed. Snickers

Bk 20, p. 432 - 5 May 1785
    Between Benjamin Davis and Sarah his wife of Frederick County [to] Charles Johnston of County aforesaid ... consideration of Sixty pounds ... a certain undivided

eighth part of two Tracts of Land conveyed to William Chambers dec'd. by the Right Honorable Thos. Lord Fairfax dec'd. the 4th and 8th days Nov. 1754 ...
Wit: none
Recorded: 4 May 1785
Benjamin (X) Davis
Sarah (X) Davis

Bk 20, p. 434 - __ day of __ 1785
    Between Gabriel Jones of County of Rockingham [to] Strother Jones of the County of Frederick ... consideration of One thousand pounds ... Tract of Land situate on waters of Cedar Creek containing Seven hundred and Seventy five Acres ... on the East side of the Run division between Joseph McDowell and James Colvill ... line of Thomas Ashby ... Corner to Lawrence Stephens ... which tract of Land is part of three several Tracts one is the remainder of Six hundred Acres granted or conveyed form Jost Hite to Charles McDowell and by said Charles McDowell to Casper Measner and by him to the said Joseph McDowell another is a part of two hundred & Seventy two Acres Granted by Deed from the Proprietors Office the 20th Sept. 1750 ... the other or third Tract is one of two hundred & fifty Acres granted by Deed from the same Proprietors Office to said Joseph McDowell the 20th June 1754 which said Tract of Seven hundred & Seventy five acres of Land was conveyed by Isaac Zane to the above Gabriel Jones by Deed ...
Wit: none
Recorded: 6 May 1785
Gabriel Jones

Bk 20, p. 437 - 6 May 1785
    Between John Smith and Sarah his wife of County of Culpepper [to] Charles Smith of County of Frederick ... Consideration of Eighty pounds ... a certain Tract lying and being in County of Frederick which said Charles Smith is now in actual possession of containing two Acres one Rood and twenty poles ... in the line of William Morton and line of sd John Smith ...
Wit: none
Recorded: 6 May 1785
John Smith

Bk 20, p. 438 - 6 May 1785
    Between Alexander White of Frederick County and Sarah his wife [to] William Richardson of the Town of Winchester in County aforesaid ... consideration of Eighty pounds ... two Lotts in the Town of Winchester ly(ing) adjacent to each other on the Eastern side of Braddock Street known by number 4 and 5 ...
Wit: J. Peyton
  Wm. Taylor
  Joseph Sommerville
Recorded: 7 May 1785
Alex. White
Sarah White

Bk 20, p. 440 - 7 May 1785
    KNOW all Men by these presents that we Joseph Holmes Sheriff of Frederick County, Edward Smith, John Milton & William Taylor are held and firmly Bound

unto Jacquilin Amble Treasurer of Virginia in the just and full sum of Ten Thousand pounds ... The Condition of the above Obligation is such that the above Joseph Holmes is appointed Collector of the several Taxes in this County ...
Wit: none   Joseph Holmes
                                                                                             Edward Smith
Recorded: 7 May 1785   John Milton

Bk 20, p. 441 - 6 June 1785

Between John Lehew and Elizabeth his wife of County of Frederick [to] Allen Wily of County aforesaid ... consideration of fifty Pounds ... Tract of Land lying and being in County aforesaid and on the great Hapy (sic) Creek joining a village called Front Royal ... corner to Robert Hariness Lot ... corner of Solomon Vanmeters Tan yard ... corner to David Lehew ... in Henry Clouds line ... corner to George Cheeks Taveren Lot ... containing fifty three acres and three quarters ... it being part of a greater Tract granted to William Russell Esq. by paton the 17th Dec. 1735 ... the said Russell convaid (sic) 400 acres thereof to Christopher Marr by his Deed ... said Marr convaid 200 acres thereof to Peter Lehew by his deed the 2nd Dec. 1754 ... said Peter Lehew convaid the said Premises to John Lehew ...
Wit: none   John Lehew
Recorded: 7 June 1785   Elizabeth (X) Lehew

Bk 20, p. 442 - 20 March 1785

Between Allen Wiley and Eve his wife of County of Frederick [to] John Lehew of County aforesaid ... consideration of Fifty Pounds ... Tract of Land lying and being in County aforesaid ... corner to Nathan Smith ... Contains Eighty four acres of Land it being part of a Tract of 416 acres granted to Thomas Chester by Deed ... said Chester by his last Will and Testament did appoint Charles Buck & James McKay his Exors. to convey 416 acres thereof to Thomas Smith, David Smith, Edward Smith, Martin Smith and Nathan conveyed Eighty four acres to William Harrell by Deeds the 14th & 15th March 1777 ... the same hereby conveyed to said John Lehew ...
Wit: David Smith   Allin Wiley
    Nathan Harrel   Eve Wiley
    William Cox
Recorded: 7 June 1785

Bk 20, p. 444 - 6 June 1785

[Lease] Between Roger Barton of County of Frederick [to] Phillip Shearer of the same place ... consideration of Five Shillings ... full equal moiety or half part of a certain Lot of half an acre of Land situate in the Borough of Winchester and known by No. 161 in that part called Lord Fairfax's addition ... containing one fourth part of an acre of Land which said Lot of Land was granted to Jacob Fortney by deed from Lord Fairfax the 25th May 1753 ... and said Fortney conveyed to Alexander Dromgoole who divided the same and conveyed the above mentioned part thereof to said Roger Barton ... Yielding and paying rent of one pepper corn on Lady day

next ...
Wit: none   Roger Barton
Recorded: 7 June 1785

Bk 20, p. 445 - 7 June 1785
   [Release] Between Roger Barton and Margaret his wife of Frederick County [to] Phillip Shearer of County aforesaid ... consideration of twenty Pounds ... one half of Lot No. 161 (same as above) ...
Wit: none   Roger Barton
Recorded: 7 June 1785   Margaret (X) Barton

Bk 20, p. 447 - 22 May 1785
   [Lease] Between Thomas Smith of the Borough of Winchester in County of Frederick [to] William Holliday of the same place ... consideration of Five Shillings ... a certain Lott of Land situate in said County & the Common of the said Borough and contains ten acres the same being part of a greater Tract of Three Hundred and Twenty acres of Land which was granted to Robert Rutherford by Deed from the Right Honorable Thomas Lord Fairfax the 15th June 1754 ... corner to Henry Bakers Lott ... in the line of John Smith (now Edward) ... which said Lot is (known by) No. 8 and being the same which said Robert Rutherford by his deeds of L & R conveyed unto said Thomas Smith ... Yielding and paying rent of one pepper corn on Lady day next ...
Wit: Jacob Kiger   Thomas Smith
   Adam Hiskill
   Thos. Welsh
Recorded: 7 June 1785

Bk 20, p. 449 - 23 May 1785
   [Release] Between Thomas Smith of the Borough of Winchester in County of Frederick [to] William Holliday of the same place ... consideration of Thirty pounds ... 10 Acres (same as above) ...
Wit: same as above   Thomas Smith
Recorded: 7 June 1785

Bk 20, p. 451 - 4 June 1785
   Between Edward Rogers and Elisabeth his wife of County of Frederick [to] John Brownly of the County aforesaid ... consideration of one hundred pounds ... Tract of Land situate in County of Frederick containing twenty four Acres being part of a Tract of eight hundred Acres vested in Edward Rogers father of the said Edward Rogers by virtue of a Patent and being part of the Tract whereon said Edward Rogers now lives ... line of Moses Walton dec'd. ... line of said John Brownly ...
Wit: John Cordell   Edward Rogers
   Saml. Earle   Elizabeth Rogers
   Esa. Earle

Recorded: 7 June 1785

Bk 20, p. 453 - 7 June 1785
    Between Jacob Klyne of County of Frederick [to] George Worth of the County aforesaid ... consideration of one hundred pounds ... Tract of Land said George Worth Mortgaged to me the 15th June 1784 ... I do relinquish all right title Interest and claim I have unto the above mentioned premises ...
Wit: George Worth   Jacob Klyne
    Alexander Hite
Recorded: 7 June 1785

Bk 20, p. 454 - 23 June 1782
    I have received of Elizabeth Miller wife of William Miller twenty eight Silver Dollars for to take up Land at Kentucky for the above consideration ... I do bind myself or assign in the penal Sum of Two hundred pounds to be paid in Gold or Silver to convey with a Good Deed One thousand Acres of Good Land ... the said Land to lay in Kentucky in Jefferson County to the above mentioned Elizabeth Miller ...
Wit: Thomas Smith   Jacob Myers
    Duncan McLean
Recorded: 7 June 1785
    The above Land is Located on the Beach fork of the Salt River at the mouth of Chaplins fork ...

Bk 20, p. 454 - 25 May 1785
    [Lease] Between William Morton of Frederick County [to] John Milton of the same place ... consideration of Five Shillings ... Tract of Land situate in the said County on Bucks or Penningtons Marsh ... in the lane leading from Battletown to the dwelling house of him the said Morton ... Containing one hundred and fifty seven Acres which said tract of land is part of two tracts which were granted to Isaac Pennington one of which under the Crown the 3rd Oct. 1734 and the other from Lord Fairfax the 2nd April 1754 and by said Pennington conveyed to John Hite and Gabriel Jones by deeds of L & R the 30th Sept. & 1st Oct. 1754 ... the said Gabriel Jones conveyed his part thereof unto said John Hite by deeds of L & R the 6th & 7th Sept. 1756 ... and by said John Hite conveyed unto Charles Smith by deeds of L & R the 7th & 8th May 1765 who by his last Will and Testament the 10th March 1774 directed his Exors. to Sell or divide the same among his children at the death of his wife Rebeccah and by a deed of Partition the 5th April 1785 executed by John Hite and John Hite Jun. the surviving Acting Exors. mentioned in said Will ... assigned to said Elizabeth Hite daughter and devisee of said Charles Smith dec'd. with whom the said William Morton hath intermarried ... Yielding and paying rent of one pepper corn on Lady day is same shall be demanded ...
Wit: Robt. Mackey   William Morton
    David Kennedy
    Chas. Smith

Frederick Conrad
Recorded: 7 June 1785

Bk 20, p. 456 - 26 May 1785
[Release] Between William Morton and Elizabeth Hite his wife of County of Frederick [to] John Milton of the same place ... consideration of One thousand Pounds ... 157 Acres (same as above) ...
Wit: same as above
Recorded: 7 June 1785
William Morton
Elizabeth H. Morton

Bk 20, p. 459 - 7 June 1785
Between Thomas Edmondson of Winchester in County of Frederick [to] Adam Albert of the same place ... consideration of Fifty Pounds ... a certain Lot or half acre of Land situate in that addition of five Acres which Thomas Edmondson aforesaid Obtained An Act of Assembly for annexing to the said Borough of Winchester known by No. 2 ... the same lying & adjoining to the Lot of Isaac Sidler on the west side ...
Wit: none
Recorded: 7 June 1785
Thomas Edmondson

Bk 20, p. 460 - 6 June 1785
[Lease] Between Adam Albert of the Borough of Winchester in the County of Frederick [to] Adam Kiger of the Borough aforesaid ... consideration of five Shillings ... a certain part of Lot No. 2 situate in the addition made to the said Borough of Winchester by Thomas Edmondson ... on the East side of Potowmack Road ... which said Lot was conveyed to said Adam Albert by deed bearing date with these presents form said Thomas Edmondson ... Yielding and paying rent of one pepper corn on Lady day next ...
Wit: none
Recorded: 7 June 1785
Adam Albert

Bk 20, p. 461 - 7 June 1785
[Release] Between Adam Albert and Elizabeth his wife of Borough of Winchester in County of Frederick [to] Adam Kiger of the Borough & County aforesaid ... consideration of Nine pounds ... part of Lot No. 2 (same as above).
Wit: none
Recorded: 7 June 1785
Adam Albert
Elizabeth (X) Albert

Bk 20, p. 463 - 6 June 1785
[Lease] Between Adam Albert of Winchester in County of Frederick [to] Adam Young ... consideration of five Shillings ... One full equal moiety or half part of Lot No. 98 situate in Lord Fairfax addition to the Town of Winchester being the westward part ... contains one fourth part of an Acre of Land ... the said Lot being Granted by patent from Lord Fairfax the 15th ___ 1753 to Daniel Shively Jun. and by said Shively conveyed unto said Adam Albert by deed the 2nd Nov. 1779 ... Yielding

and paying rent of one Pepper Corn on Lady day next ...
Wit: none   Adam Albert
Recorded: 7 June 1785

Bk 20, p. 464 - 7 June 1785
   [Release] Between Adam Albert and Elizabeth his wife of Winchester in County of Frederick [to] Adam Young of the other part ... consideration of Fifty pounds ... half part of Lot No. 98 (same as above) ...
Wit: none   Adam Albert
Recorded: 7 June 1785   Elizabeth (X) Albert

THE END

DEED BOOK 20 [1783 -1785]

FREDERICK COUNTY, VIRGINIA

INDEX

ABERNATHY, Anne 30
  James 14,29,30
ABRILL, John 27
ADAMS, Henry 65
  John 100
AIRHEART, Nicholas 13
ALBERT,
  Adam 52,121,142,143
  Elizabeth 142,143
ALBIN, William 61
ALDER, Martha 89
ALDRED,
  Christopher 38,39
  Henry 38-40
  Margaret 38,39
ALDRIDGE, Robert 10,48
  William 115
ALEXANDER, William 39
ALLEN, Abigail 135
  John 12
  Reuben, Sen. 81
  Robert 12,25,38
  Thomas 27,94,98,135
ALLISON, Patrick 51
AMBLE, Jacquilin 139
ANDERSON,
  Abraham 32,137
  Adam 49,50
  Bartholomew 32,56,137
  Christina 41
  Cornelius 137
  Daniel 2
  Henry 38-40
  Jacob 41
  James 137
  John 137
  Margaret 38-40
ARMISTEAD, Henry 98,106
ASHBY,
  Baylis 108,123,126,127
  David 45,110
  George 102
  Jane 110
  John 36,79,121
  Lewis 36,79
  Martin 45,88,89
  Miriam 88
  Nathaniel 78,79,92
  Nimrod 45,88

ASHBY, Robert 36
  Thomas 87,138
ASPINAL, William 113
BABB, Hannah 103,104
  Joseph 103,104
  Mary 103
  Philip 65,103
  Sampson 103
  Thomas 103
BACHELOR, John 69
BAILEY, Abraham 1
  John 17
BAKER, Elizabeth 30
  Henry 32,49,50,77,140
  Henry, Sen. 25,26
  Jacob 12
  Joshua 110,111
  Martin 30
  Samuel 73,118
BALDWIN, Cornelius 105
  Francis 55
  Innocent 55
  Jean 56
  Thomas 55,56
  William 55,56
BALL, Jesper 30
BALMAIN, Alexander 74
BARNELL, James 18
BARNETT, James 78
  John 77,78
BARR, John 45
BARRATT, BARRETT,
  Richard 114
  Thomas 114
  William 106,107
BARROW, John 22,48
  Lydia 48
  William 48
BARTON, Margaret 140
  Roger 46,59,139,140
  Undril 61,62,133
BAYLIS, John 4,35,42
  William 4,58,85
BEALE, Tavener 95
BEAMER, George 19
BEAN, BEANE, Judith 50
  Mordicai 50,51
BEARD, John Lewis 3
BEASLY, William 29

BEATTY, Henry 55
BECKET, BICKET,
  Jane 25
  John 25,97,98
  Robert 25,97,98
  Samuel 25,98
BEELER, George 127
  Joseph 82,83
  Margaret 82
BELL, John 79,121
BENDLES, William 13
BENEZET, Daniel 81
  Elizabeth 81
BENGLE, Henry 67
BERRY, Benjamin 34,56,81
  Francis 87,88
  Joseph 36,77,87,88,225
  Moley 87,88
  Thomas 52,77,118,119
BISHOP, Samuel 19
  Solomon 19
BIXTER, Jacob 20
BLACK, Edward 91
BLACKBURN,
  Benjamin 73,74
  Margaret 108
  Robert 107,108
  Samuel 73
BLACKFORD, Benjamin 84
  John 84
  Peter 15
BLY, Philip 50
BOND, George 15
BOOTH,
  William 46,61,66,78
BORDEN, Benjamin 43
BOROMAN, George 91
BOSHER, John 55
BOWEN, Henry 20
BOWER, Dorothy 4
  Henry 4
  Philip 93,49
BOWMAN, Abraham 26
  George 31
  George, Jun. 26
  George, Sen. 26
  Joseph 95,121
BOYD, John 85
  Samuel 90

145

BOYERS, Leonard 37
BOYLSTON, Benjamin 131
  Thomas 131
BOYS, James 15,16
  Mary 15,16
BRADLEY, Andrew 82
BRADY, John 37,39,112,133
BRANSON, Abraham 43
  John 18,108
BRIDGES, Joseph 67
BRINGHURST, John 28
BRINKER,
  George 26,86,87,101
  Henry 86
  Rebeccah 87
BRISCOE, Gerald 64
  John 113
BROWN, Daniel 43
  David 24,44,59,60
  Samuel 82
  Timothy 43
BROWNING, James 73
BROWNLEY, BROWNLY,
  John 43,44,140
BRUCE, Charles 63
  George 37
  James 134
BRUIN, Bryan 10,11,28,31,
      33,37,52,55,
      68,95,104,129
BRYAN, Morgan 43
BRYLEY, Thomas 79
BUCHANAN, Elizabeth 84
  John 84
BUCK,
  Charles 11,84,85,102,139
  Lettice 84
  Mary 84,85
  Thomas 32,84
BULGER, James 46,47
BULLIT, BULLITT,
  Cuthbert 29,30
BURDEN, Benjamin 7
BURKET, George 62
BURRELL, Nathaniel 47
BUSH, Catharine 86
  Daniel 41
  Dennis 7,8,54,71,119
  Philip 34,40,41,44,45,
      76,86,129
  Thomas 27
  Vance, Vane 71,81,100,135

BUTLER, John 50
CABBAGE, Catharine 81
  George 81
CALDWELL,
  Andrew 96,116,117
CALMES, George 127
  Marquis 42,52,105
  Miriam 42,106
  Mrs. 61
  William 42,105
CALVERT, Isaiah 13,133
  John 13,17
  Margaret 13
  Mary 13
  Milley 133
  Robert 13
  Samuel 13,16,132,133
CAMPBELL, Ens. 23
  John 47
  Thomas 30,117,120
  William 19,52,122
CAMPLE, John 45
CANON, John 44
CAPPER, John 79
CARLYLE, John 65,74
CARMAN, Christian 136
CARTER, Ann 17
  Benjamin 28,29
  Charles 79
  George 54,79,120,121
  James 17
  John 78,79
  Joseph 28,29,37,113
  Rachel 78,79
  Richard 29,116
  Robert 7
CARTHRAE, William 18
CARTMILL, Edward 27
  Nathaniel 25,97
CARVER, Henry 119
  Henry W. 119
CASTLEMAN, David 45
  Jacob 17,99,110
CATLETT, Charles 85,102
  Peter 42,48
  Robert 43
CHAMBERS, Mary 64
  Susannah 78,79
  William 64,78,138
CHANDLER,
  Goldsmith 106
CHEAK, George 123

CHEEK, George 80,108,
      124,125,139
  George, Sen. 124
  James 109
CHENOWETH, John 55
  William 55
CHESTER, CHESTOR,
  Thomas 11,102,139
CHRISMAN, Jacob 77
  Mary 37
CHURCHMAN,
  Thomas 14,47
CIRDEN, Edward 27
CLARE, Edmond 114,115
CLEVINGER, Hannah 134
  Asa 13,22,134
CLOPTON, George 113
CLOUD, Henry 12,139
  William 124,126
COCHRAN, Isabella 90
  James 90,94,115
  John 94,115
  Phebe 77,128
  Robert 90,94,115
  Sarah 115
  Thomas 77,120,128,135
  William 6,51,52,104
COE, John 79
COLVERT, Mr. 105
COLVILL, James 39,138
CONNARD, Joseph 40
CONRAD, Frederick 57,68,
      128,129,142
CONWAY,
  Miles Withers 87,88
COOKE, John 107,115
COOPER, Jeremiah 24
COPENHAVER, Michael 94
CORDELL, John 43,140
COTTRALL, Elizabeth 70
  John 70
COWDON, James 20
COWGILL, John 107,108
COX, William 139
CRAIG, John 51
CRAIGAN,
  Robert 83,128,129
  Robert, Jun. 83
  Robert, Sen. 83
  Susanna 83
CRAIK, James 57,58
  Marianne 57,58

CRIDER, Peter 106
CROCKWELL,
  John Collin 83
CROFF, John 106
CROMLY, John 113
CROUDSON, John 18,40,52
CRUM, Christian 37,38
CRUMLY, William 134
CUNNINGHAM, George 20
  John 3
CUNS, John 94
CURLET, CURLETT,
  John 19
  William 59
DALTON, John 65
DARLINGTON, David 79
  Gabriel 79
  John 79
  Joseph 79
  Margaret 79
  Meridith 79
  William 79
DARNALL, Jeremiah 36
DAVIS, Benjamin 137,138
  David 79
  John 79,87
  Sarah 137,138
  William 78,85
DAY, Catharine 117
  Joseph 7,12-15,25,26,29,
    30,56,61-63,72,
    101,102,108,112,
    117,118,131,134
DEADWICK, David 5,33,53,
    75,82,91,94,98,
    105,112,120,130
  John 129
  Michael 105,129
DEANEY, Barbara 112
  Henry 112
DEARING, Barbara 137
  Everheart 137
  Henry 137
DELANY, Joseph 17
DENNY, Rachel 35
  Robert 35,65
  Samuel 35
DENT, James 88
DEVAULT, DEVOLT,
  Elizabeth 51
  Nicholas 7,51
DILLON, Daniel 63

DILLON, James 97
  John 113,114
  Luke 113
  Lydia 63
  William 97,113
DODD, Edward 72
DONALDSON, John 6,31,
    33,62,101,104,
    107,111,112,118
DOUGHERTY, John 55
DOUGLAS, DOUGLASS,
  William 52
  William, Jun. 40
DOWDALL, Ham.t 42
  James Gaml. 3,52
DOWS, John Carey 24
DRAPER, Thomas 60
DREW, Hannah 48,49
  J. 97
  William 48,49,86
DRIVER, Eleanor 69
  John 7-9
  John W. 90
  John Windsor 66,67,69
DRUMGOOLE, Alexander
    3,35,41,42,46,48,
    57,59,94,105,106,139
  Margaret Elizabeth 41,42,
    46,59,105,106
DUCKWORTH, John 26
DUFFIELD,
  John 1,2,25,26,83
DUKES, John 50
DUNCAN, William 63
EARLE, Esa. 140
  Samuel 140
EASTON, EASTIN,
  Philip 136
  Richard 34,52
  Sarah Smith 130,136
EDMONDSON, John 100
  Thomas 68,69,74,75,
    102,107,118,142
  William 68
EDWARDS, John 113
  Samuel 113
ELEY, Henry 89
ELLIS, Daniel 91
ELLISON, Henry 96
EMETT, EMIT, EMMET,
  John 7,8,9,10,64
  Mary 8,64

ENDERS, Christianna 62
  Earnest 62,66
ENGLAND, Isaac 24
ERKSTINE, Leonard 95
ESKRIDGE, Elizabeth 122
  William 122
EVANS, Dorothy 103
  William 21,103,121
EWING, John 45
  Robert 45
  Samuel 45
  Thomas 45,82
  William 45
FAIRFAX, George W. 30
  Lord 31,33,46,52,59,
    93,94,99,105,109,
    110,112,127,137,
    139,141,142
  Thomas Lord 5,6,12,13,15,
    20,21,26,27,29,30,35,
    39,41,42,49,51,55,57,
    60-62,64,65,67,72,88,
    92,97,101,102,104,106,
    108,111,113,114,128,
    131-133,138,140
FAWCET, FAWCETT,
  Joseph 18,108
  Thomas 76
FEATHERINGAL,
  George 126
  John 11,12
FERGISON, Hugh 30
FERREE, Abraham 17,18
  Elizabeth 18
FERREL, Thomas 2
FINK, Henry 25,26,33,54
FIRES, Abraham 108
FISHER, Barrack 100
  Mires 28
FITZPATRICK, Bryan 52
FLUE, John 41
FOGLESONG,
  Christian 119
FOLEY, Elizabeth 102
  James Mann 102
  Rachel 12
  Richard 102
  Richard, Jun. 102
  Selby 102
  Thomas 12
FOOSE, Frederick 3
FOREMAN, Peter 55

FORTNEY,
  Jacob 35,46,59,94,139
FOSTER, Achillis 100
  Isaac 10,100
  Margaret 10
FOULKS, Palser 65
FRAER, William George 47
FRAKER, Michael 72
FROMAN, FROWMAN,
  Paul 18,108
FROST, William 15,30,52
FRY, FRYE,
  Benjamin 18,40,108
  Christopher 1,2,127
  Jacob 18
  John 50
  Mary 2
FULKES, George 79
GADDIS, John 20
  Priscilla 20
  William 20
GAMBLE, Elizabeth 77
  Robert 10,73,77
GARDINER, GARDNER,
  Michael 20,101,110
GARISON, Nehemiah 30
GENNINGS, Mary 98
GIBSON, Jacob 31,76
GILKESON, John 16,25,
      73,77,90,97,98
  Margaret 16
  Samuel 18,19,25,34,38,
      78,90,97,98,115
  Susannah 34,98
  William 16
  William, Sen. 97,98
GILKEY, David 37
GILLASPY, John 85,86
GILLIAM, William 113
GLASCOCK,
  Elizabeth 7,8,35,36,41,
      53,54,98,106,134
  William 7-9,22,35-37,41,
      48,53,54,64,134
  William, Jun. 21,22,80,
      98,99,106,114
GLASS, David 38,90
  Joseph 38,90
  Robert 19,21,38,115
  Samuel 25,38,90,98
  Sarah 21
GLOVER, John 52,53,63,64

GLOVER, Sophia 63
  William 13,133
GOINEY, William 12
GOOCH, William 42
GOODYKUNT, George 121
GOOS, George 20
  Mary 20
GOWDY, Magdalena 10
  William 10,77
GRAY, John H. 89
GRAYHAM, William 109
GRAYSON, GRASON,
  Benjamin 7,51,57
  Elenora 57
  William 57
GREEN, Elizabeth 127
  William 127
GREENFIELD,
  John 40,110,133
GREGG, Robert 58
GRIFFITH, Mary 120
  Samuel 120
GRIMM, Jacob 49,111,112
  Mary 111,112
GRINNING, James 76
GROVE, GROVES,
  John 36,54,71,80,90
GUDEHUNST,
  George 95,96
HACKNEY, Jacob 106
  William 106
HAGGIN, James 72,73
  John 72,73
HAINES, Benjamin 84
  Levi 84
  Richard 13
  Robert 76,84,122,123,
      127,134
  Simeon 13
HALL, James 120
  Richard 120
  Sarah Ann 120
  Thomas 120
  William 120
HAMILTON, John 24,35
HAMMOND,
  Absalom 50,130
HAMPTON, Thomas 2
HANES, William 87
HANKINS, Jane 14
  William 14
HANNAH, Bryce 59

HARDEN, HARDIN,
  Ann 94
  George 46,51,53,59,93,94
  John 82
HARDING, George 89
HARINESS, Robert 139
HARMAN, HARMEN,
  Jacob 27,41
HARRELL, HARREL,
  David 11,12
  John 11,12
  Nathan 139
  Susannah 11,12
  William 11,12,139
HARRISON,
  Benjamin 44,59
HAVELY, Jacob 69
HAWKINS, Ann 47,48
  Joseph 47
  William 47
HAWLINGS,
  Thomas P. 90,91
HAYES, HAYS,
  John 85
  John, Jun. 85,86
HAYHURST,
  Cuthbert 43,95
HAYMAKER, Adam 59
  John 32,77,129,130
  Motlena 129
  Salley 130
HAYWORTH, Absolum 67
  James 106,113
HEATON, David 5,109
HEDGMAN, Peter 79
HEISKILL, Godlove 96
HELM, George 5,41
  Joseph 86
  Meredith 3,7,28-30,86,
      101,127
  Meridith, Sen. 74
  Sarah 74
  Thomas 29,49,86
  William 44,57,74,77,97,
      115,136
H E L P H E N S T I N E ,
  Catharine 5
  Peter 5,109
  Philip 1,5,54,55
  Rebecca 5,55
HENCHER, Nicholas 134
  William 134

HENDERSON,
  Alexander 79
HENING, HENNING,
  James 56,71,116,119
HENSHAW, Nicholas 20
  William 20
HETH, Agnes 65,78,96
  Henry 65,78,96
  John 120
  William 78
HETHERLING,
  Christopher 39
HEWLINGS, Abraham 91
HICKMAN,
  William, Jun. 34,59
HIGGERS, Mary 89
HINGLE, Leanard 11
HISKILL, Adam 140
HITE, Alexander 91,
    101,110,141
  G. 97,107
  George 82
  Isaac 24,95,121
  Isaac, Jun. 66
  Isaac, Sen. 66
  Jacob 65,82,83
  John 22,41,42,53,71,119,
    130,131,136,141
  John, Jun. 69-72,114,130,
    136,141
  John, Sen. 99
  Joseph 131
  Jost 7,24,25,39,40,71,
    98,100
  Sarah 42
  Susanna 71,72,114
  Thomas 83
  Yost 77
HOBSON, George 20
HODGEN,
  Robert 46,114,115
  Sarah 115
HODGSON, Elizabeth 70
  Hannah 70
  John 70
  Robert 24
HOFF, Lewis 68
HOG, HOGE, HOGG,
  Agnes 66
  James 1,27,66,95
  James, Jun. 1
  Solomon 117

HOLDING, Elias 1,99
HOLLIDAY, James 76
  William 4,40,57,140
HOLLINGSWORTH,
  Abram 51
  George 17
  Isaac 17,75
  Jonah 103,104
  Robert 46
HOLMES, Col. 31
  Joseph 17,25,33,48,68,76,
    86,87,98,105,
    108,111,112,118,
    122,138,139
HOOVER, Henry 89
  Philip 31
HORBERT, Thomas 84
HORNER, Joseph 28,113
  Margary 113
HOTSINPILLER, Jacob 135
  Stephen 16,135
HOUSE, Eve 134
  William 100
HOUSEMAN, David 6,7,51
  George 6,7,14
  Martin 6,7
  Mary 7,51
HOWARD, John 111
HUFF, John 58
HUGHES, HUGHS,
  John 51,103
  Mary 119
  Micajah 22,106,119
HULLET, Hulda 88
HUMPHREYS, John 31,33
  Ralph 31,33
HUNGERFORD, Cha. 23
HUNTER, Ann 101
  David 87,111,112
  Henry 64,101
HUNTSBURRY, Conrad 66
  Elizabeth 66
  Henry 62,66
  Jacob 61,62,65,66
HURBOUGH, Katharine 69
  Peter 50,69
HUSTON, John H. 28
HUTT, George 14
HUVER, Henry 99
ISAACS, Godfrey 110
  Samuel 110
JACK, Andrew 90

JACKSON, Eleanor 19
  James 19
  Josiah 79
JAMISON, Robert 108
JENIFER, Daniel 57,58
  W. H. 57,58
JOHNSON, JOHNSTON,
  Abigail 22,23
  Ann 32
  Bartholomew 22,23
  Charles 78,79,137
  Daniel 32
  David 56
  George 56
  Stephen 45,77,130,136
JOLLIFFE, JOLIFFE,
  Amos 134
  Elizabeth 84
  James 55
  John 92
  Mary 117
  William 55,56
JONES, Ann 109
  Gabriel 39,40,65,89,
    136,138,141
  John 79
  Joseph 1,64
  Mary 108,109
  Mason 80,108,109,123-126
  Stephen 28
  Strother 138
  Thomas 109,112
JULIAN, George 9
  John 9
KAIN, John 86
KAY, John 34
KAYSER,
  Elizabeth Jane 129
KEAN, John 4,48,122
KEELER, David 96
KEES, William 135
KEITH, James 5,6,82
KELLAR, KELLER,
  George 31,76,77
  Margarad 77
KEMPTON, Moses 91
KENDERICK, KENDRICK,
  Abraham 12,94,98
  Benjamin 27,94
  Jacob 27,94,95
  Mary 27
KENNEDY, David 13,17,23,

KENNEDY, David (con't.)
  42,74,86,87,102,
  104,108,118,141
KEPPELE, Henry, Sen. 86
KERCHIVAL,
  John 35,56,78,86,
    114,117,118
  Samuel 115
KERN, KERNS,
  Adam 89,99,137
  Esther 89,90
  Hester 99
KEYES, KEYS, F. 65
  William 24,59
KEYGER, Jacob 75
KEYZER, John 87
  Sally 87
KIGER, Adam 142
  Andrew 128
  George 78,128,129
  Jacob 32,75,107,116,
    118,140
  Mary 107
KING, Joseph 94
KINKEAD, Will 1,51
KITE, Robert 90
  Sarah 90
KLINE, Anthony 36,119
KLYNE, Jacob 141
KRISER, Christopher 101
KULEE, Phillip 29
KUNHALL, James 3
  John 3
KURTZ, Frederick 39
KYGER, Andrew 99
LAMBERT,
  Christopher 49,105,112
LANGLEY, Benjamin 101
LA REU, John 78
LARRICK, Casper 50
  George 27
LA RUE, Jacob 77
LAWISON, John 109
LAWRENCE, John 2,31
LAWSON, Gavan 117
LEADEY, Benedick 21
LEE, Alice 90,91
  John 32,90,91,95
  Michael 66
LEGETT, William 121
LEHEW, David 123-126,139
  Elizabeth 64,65,123-126,139

LEHEW, Frances 65,80,81
  Francis 80,102,109,122-124,
    126,127
  Jeremiah 64,65,117,118,
    122,127
  John 80,117,139
  Leannah 80,122-124,126,127
  Milly 117,118,122
  Peter 65,80,117,122-127,139
  William 64,117
LEHUE, Spencer 73
LEITH, John 89
LEMLY, Catharine 39
  John 39
LENTZ, John 121
LEONARD, LENARD,
  Jacob 35,36,41,80
LEVERISON, John 5
LEWIS, Fielding 50,120
  Fielding, Jun. 50
  George 50
  Hannah 27,28
  Henry 53,64,83,134
  John 61
  Mary 134
  Mordicai 27,28
  Samuel 9
LIKINS, Jonas 102
LIMRALL, James 74
LINDSEY, LINDSAY,
  Edmund, Sen. 46,47
  Elijah 46,47
  Elizabeth 115
  Hezekiah 114
  Jacob 46,47,114,115
  James 115
  John 114
  John, Sen. 46
  Thomas 46,47
LITTLE, William 73
LITTLER, LITLER,
  Isaac 68,118
  John 4,56,64,101,108,
    111,113,117
  Mary 37,120
  Nathan 92,93,116
  Rosannah 56
LIVINGSTON, Corn. 7,8,10
LOCK, John 30
LOCKART, Robert 2
LOFTON, Thomas, Sen. 30
LONG, Armistead 99

LONG, Ben 51
  Rosman 51
LONGACRE, John 67,68
  Joseph 11,41,64,69,100
  Richard 67,68
LOVELL, William 96
LOWNES, James 32
LUCAS, Fielding 96
LUKE, Elizabeth 29,30
  Peter 29,30,51
LUNSFORD, Swanson 2
LUPTON, John 23,24,79,95
  Jona 106
  Jonathan 24
  Joseph 103
  Sarah 24
LYLE, Hugh 85
  John 85
  Robert 85
MACHEN, Thomas 59
MACKEY, MACKY,
  Robert 78,118,141
MACKINTOSH, La 99
MADDIN, John 109
MAGILL, A. 52
  Archibald 96
  John 38,42,90,112
MAGSON, Marmaduk 94
MARBURGER,
  John 100,119
MARKER, Ann 9
  George 8,9
  Jacob 119,121
MARNEY, Robert 91
MARPLE, David 60
  Enoch, Jun. 60
MARR, Christopher 65,80,
  117,122-127,139
MARTIN, Albenah 134
  Thomas 133,134
  Thomas Bryan 43,59,60
MAUCK, Mary 28
  Michael 29
MAUK, Matthias 62
MAURICE, Benjamin 78
  Samuel 78
MAUZEY, MAUZY,
  John 3,34
MAY, Cassamar 73
  Rosannah 109,110,129
  Samuel 5,33,34,49,104,105,
    109,110,129,135

MAZEY, John 97
MC BEAN, Robert 66
MC CALL, George 71
MC CAN, Daniel 121
MC CARTY, Thads. 114
MC CLOUD, William 36,41
MC CLUM, MC CLUN,
  Thomas 64,101
MC COOL, James 34
  John 9
MC CORMICK,
  Francis 46,47,73,74
MC CREA, Robert 23
MC DONALD, Allen 28
  Angus 5,68
  Archibald 16
  Columbus 3,19
  John 5,89,112
MC DOUGAL, MC DUGAL
  Alexander 110
  Thomas 78
MC DOWELL,
  Charles 39,40,77,138
  Joseph 39,40,138
  Margaret 40
  Rachael 39
MC GINNIS,
  Edmond 66,119
  Elizabeth 45,119
  J. 57
  John 43,45,48,66,100,119
MC GUIRE,
  Edward 3,11,13,19,23,32,
    76,86,98,101,
    105,122,129,133
  William 19,105,120
MC KAY, James 11,102
  John 139
  Parson 60
MC KEAN, Thomas 24
MC KEMIE, Robert 63
MC KENSEY, Franklin 79
MC KEWN, Michael 49
MC LEAN, Duncan 141
MC LEED, William 90
MC LEOD, MC LEODE,
  William 54,57
MC LEOR, William 35
MC MACHEN, John 37
  William 6
MC MAHEN, William 96
MC PHERSON, Daniel 82

MC PHERSON, Nathan 102
  William 61,127
MEADE, Garrett 24
  George 24
  Henrietta Constantia 24
  Richard K. 121
  Richard Kidder 54
MEASE, Robert 23
MEASNER, MESMORE,
  Casper 39,138
  Nicholas 68,69,111
MEDE, Richard 79
MERCER, Aaron 65,67,68
MERRYFIELD, Samuel 24
MESSEMER, C. 81
MICHLENBURG, Peter 96
MIER, MIERS, Barnard 126
  Jacob 21,35,53
  Stephen 21,27,35,66
MILBOURN, MILLBURN,
  Andrew 64,101
  John 111,115,116
  Mary 116
  Robert 101
  William 116
MILLER, MILLAR
  Daniel 110
  Elizabeth 141
  James 102,123,126
  Michael 39,41
  Peter 110
  Rebekah 98
  Susannah 36
  William 123,127,141
MILLO, W. 122
MILTON, J. 34,56,86,95
  John 1,47,89,110,138,
    139,141,142
MIRE, MIRES,
  Casper 26,31,48
  George 91
MOCK, George 101,110
MOFFETT, Walter 15
MOONEY, Joseph 63,100
MOORE, MOOR,
  Anthony 76
  Cato. 107
  Henry 111
  Peter 21
MORGAN,
  Daniel 47,86,88,89
MORRISON, James 85

MORTON,
  Elizabeth Hite 142
  Elizabeth H. Smith 130,136
  John Hatley 47
  William 138,141,142
MOUSER, John 108
MOXLEY, Ann 22,23
  John 22,23
MOYERS, Jacob 53
  Widow 33
MULLIKEN,
  William 123-127
MULLIN, Mary 100
MUSE, Battaile 118
MYERS, Barnard 124
  Elizabeth 21,25,26,54,55
  Jacob 36,141
  Leonard 20,21
  Stephen/Steven 20,21,36
MYLINGER, Daniel 80
NEALL, NEIL, NEILL,
  Abraham 3,28,95
  Charles 136
  John 9,29,41,55,95,112
  John, Jun. 9
  Joseph 45,84,95,130
  Lewis 3,28,29,56,84,95,112
  Lydia 9,112
  Thomas 84
NICHOLAS, NICKLES,
  James B. 24
  Nathan 70,123
NISEWANGER,
  Abraham 71
  Barbara 6
  Christian 6
  David 27,73,77,103
  Jacob 100
  John 12,27,37,57,100,
    116,135
  Margaret 100
  Mary 6
NOBLE, George 18,23,52,81
  Thomas 81
NOLL, Martin 81
NORTON, D. 103,120
  John Hatley 120
  (see Morton)
NUT, John 2
OBANION, Fra. 89
ODELL, James 9
ONAN, ORAN, Dennis 5,109

ONION, Hannah 76
  Stephen 76
  Zachius 76
OVERACRE, George 78
PAINTER, John 76
PALSER, Peter 111
PANCOAST, David 34
PARKINS, PERKINS,
  Isaac 52,84,104
PARREL, Joseph 58
PATON, PAYTON,
  Charles 65,118
PEACHEY, Winifred 98
PEARIS, Robert 38
PEARSON, Enoch 75
PENDLETON,
  Philip 90,106,107
PENNINGTON, Isaac 141
  Jacob 82
PERRILL, Hugh 61
PERRY, Ignatious 54,112
PETERSON, Peter 28
PEYTON,
  Charles 109,117,122-127
  Francis 130
  J. 95,99,103,105,110,118,
    120,122,128,129,137,138
  J., Jun. 1,2,5,13,17,19,23,
    32,33,38,39,45,52,53,59,
    68,75,78,82,86,107,133
  John 97-99
  John, Jun. 94
  Thomas 68,75,82
PHILIPS, Solomon 26
PICKERING, William 100
PIERCE, George 73
  Michael 51
PITMAN, Andrew 43
PITNEY, Nathaniel 29,56
PLANK, John 32
PLEASANT, Samuel 129
PLUM, PLUMB,
  Cassimore/Kassamer
    100,135
POILES, Joshua 17
POKER, John 114
  Michael 69
POLLARD, Challen D. 2
  Elisha 2
  Frances 2
  Joseph 2
  Nanny 2

POLLARD, William 2
POOSE, Henry 80
PORTER, Nicholas 115
POSTGATE, Mary 84
  Thomas 84
POWELL, Robert 15,16
POYLES, William 57
PRICE, Samuel 85
  Thomas 96
PRINCE, Henry 41,75
PRITCHARD, Margaret 136
  Peggy 137
  Stephen 136,137
PROVINCE, Thomas 5
PUGH, Azariah 15,113,114
  Jesse 100
  Joseph 137
PYLE, PYLES, Ann 132
  Joshua 99,110
  Sarah 99,110
  William 41,131,132
QUINN, Ann 47,48
  Patrick 14,47,48
REA, Robert 76
REAGLEY, Adam 103
REAGON, Reason 108
REARLY, Philip 3
REDD, Aggatha 121
  Andrew 21
  Mordicai 120,121
  Nathaniel 37
REDMAN, Henry 16,17
  Sarah 16,17
REED, Edward 121
  Elizabeth 53
REES, Henry 92
  John 102,112
  Lydia 102
  Margaret 101
  Robert 100
  Solomon 100
  Thomas 100,101
REESE, Joel 67
RENO, Lewis 59
REW, William 50
REYNOLDS, REYNOLL,
  John 27,32,55,74
RICE, John 73,114
RICHARDS, Henry 90,91
  John 90
  Jonathan 90
  Mary 90,91

RICHARDS, Peter 90,91
RICHARDSON,
  Joseph 18,25,26
  William 138
RIDGWAY, Josiah 63
  Margaret 93
  Richard 43,92,93,131
RIGG, Richard 13,18
RILEY, REILLEY,
  Martin 32,74,75,77,129
RINKER, Casper 9,10
  Jacob 9
RITTER, John 5
ROBINSON, Joseph 124-127
ROBISON, Alexander 76
RODMAN, Thomas 91
ROGERS, Edward 43,44,140
  Elizabeth 140
  Evan 84
  Jacob 72,73
  John 100
ROMINE, Samuel 17
ROOTES, Thomas 19
ROSS, David 43,72,92,93
  George 117
  James 12,14
  Jonathan 72
  Stephen 117
ROWZIE, Reuben 32
RUBLE, George 3,133,134
  Jesse 134
  Peter 63
  Ulrick 133
  Woolrey 113
RUMGAY, John 123,126
RUSSELL, RUSSEL,
  Moses 50
  William 65,117,122-127,139
RUTHERFORD,
  Archibald 111
  Benjamin 18,28
  Drusilla 107
  Mary 27,53,75,87
  R. 53
  Robert 27,34,52,53,63,
    72,75,87,133,140
  Thomas 20,78,95,107,
    132,133
RYAN, George 98
SAMPLE, Samuel 19,33,54
SCHNEPP, Lawrence 69
SCOTT, George 106

SEABERT, Jacob 3,41,42
  Mary 42
  Mary Ann 2
SEABORN, George 17
SELF, Abigail 34,35,65
  Joseph 34,35,65
SENSENIG, Peter 121
SEOWICK, Benjamin 18
SEXTON,
  Meshack 77,96,116,128
SEYEANT, John 12,14
  Rachael/Rachel 12,14
SHANNON,
  Patrick 7-9,35,36
SHARPE, John 14
SHEARER, Philip 139,140
SHEAVER, George 76,77
SHEIP, George 116
SHEPHERD, Thomas 137
SHERMAN, Jacob 67
SHIMM, Clement 131
SHIP, George 115
SHIPLER, John 61,62
  Magdalen 62
SHIVELY, Daniel, Jun. 142
SHLOSSER, Frederick 101
SHORT, Thomas 63
SHREVE, Benjamin 32,77
  Hannah 32
SHULTZ, John 107,132,133
SHUTER, William 46,47
SIDLER, SITLER,
  Barbara 116
  Benjamin 49,105,112
  Catharine 49
  Isaac 49,76,91,96,
    116,117,142
  Mathias 49,105,112
SIDWELL, Hannah 58
  James 58
SIERE, Widow 108
SIMS, Henry 9
SINVALL, James 25
SLAUGHTER,
  William 101,102
SLUSHER,
  Ann Galihar 79,80
  Frederick 79,80,110
SMALLZEHAFFIN,
  Lewis 31,32,76
SMITH, Bartholomew 114
  Benjamin 38

SMITH, Charles 24,130,136
    138,141
  Daniel 121
  David 11,12,102,139
  Edward 11,12,28,48,75,86,
    87,107,118
    122,138-140
  Elizabeth Hite 130,141
  John 18,20,29,34,75,97,108,
    130,138,140
  Mahlon 106
  Martin 11,12,139
  Nathan 11,12,139
  Rebecca 130,136,141
  Sarah 130,136,138
  Thomas 11,12,30,62,139-141
  William 36,91
  William, Jun. 44,45
  William, Sen. 44,45
SNAPP, John 25,67,69
  Lawrence 67
  Lorone 80
SNICKER, SNICKERS,
  Edward 30,47,54,56,88,
    110,115,137
SNIPE, Christian 71
SOMMERVILLE,
  George 83,94,98,104,128
  James 97
  Joseph 138
SOUTHERLAND, Isaac 131
  Sarah 114,131
SOVAIN,
  Abraham 1,5,58,59,94
  Lydia 1,59,94
SOWERS, Daniel 51,128
SPEAKS, Thomas 127
SPERRY,
  Catharine 62,63,91,92
  Elizabeth 31,121,122
  Jacob 31,32,121,137
  John 31,32,116,121
  Nicholas 96,106
  Nicholas, Jun. 27,31,91,95,
    96,121,122
  Nicholas, Sen. 31,91,95
  Philip 35
  Thomas 61-63, 91,121
  Thomas, Sen. 95
STAFFORD, Richard 70,71
STEARLEY, STEARLY,
  Jacob 28,29,95

STEARLEY, STEARLY,
  Mary 29
  Mary Magdilen 95
STEED, John 131
STEER, Grace 76,96
  James 97
  Joseph 76,116,117
  Joseph, Jun. 79,96
  Joseph, Sen. 96
STEIP, George 64
STEPHENS, George W. 71
  Henry 6,116
  Isaac 8,9
  Lawrence 31,39,91,138
  Lewis 3,6,10,22,37,40,
    43,44,50,56,57,
    67-69-72,80,119,137
  Lewis, Jun. 27,44,116
  Lewis, Sen. 116
  Mary 37,40,43,56,67,69,
    70,71,80,116,119
  Peter 4,6,37,43,69,71,80
  Peter, 3rd 70
STEPHENSON,
  Lawrence 81
STEVENS, Joseph 90
STEWART, Catharine 95
  Joseph 111
  Robert 29,95,113,120
STITLER, John 67,68
STONEBRIDGE, John 9,10
  Mary 10
STOVER, Christian 58,94
  Joseph 91
STRIBLING, STRIPLING,
  F. 33
  Francis 110,111,115
  Taliaferro 47,88,89
STRITCH, Thomas 24
STROEBEL, J. C. 95
STULTZ, Philip 7
  Wilson 7
SUELL, David 120
  John 120
SUTHERLAND,
  Isaac 14,114
  Ruth 14
  Sarah 14
SWORDS, William 78,99,110
SYDNOR, William 114
TAYLOR, Abram 108
  Arg. 102

153

TAYLOR,
  Edmund 32,43,50,56,97
  Harrison 2
  John 37,43,46,53,90,116
  Jonathan 111
  Sarah 32
  Simeon 102
  William 23,42,59,136,138
THARP, Andrew 21
  John 21
  Priscilla 21,22
  Zebulon 21
THOMAS, Ellis 51
  Else 42,43
  Enos 92
  Evan 42,43,92,93,120,131
  Evan, Sen. 131
  Isaac 63
  John 13,19,42,43,45,51,
         55,57,75,88,
         89,92,93,108
  Lydia 51
  Margaret 92,93,131
  Robert 99
THORNTON, John 31
THROCKMORTON,
  Gabriel 23
  Gabriel, Jun. 118
  Robert 17,23,24,38
  Thomas 23,38,61,118,
         119,136
  William 23,24,38
THRUSTON, C. M. 97
  Charles Mynn 7,16,47
TRAVILIAN, Thomas 31
TREMBLE,
  John 92,93,108,113
TRIECE, Martin 114
TROUT, Jacob 36,37,77
  Philip 36,37,119
TROUTWICK, George J. 15
TROWBRIDGE,
  Joseph 5,109
TUCKER, Elizabeth 51
  James 51
TYGART, Francis 17,99,110
UPP, OP, Peter 81,90,100
UTTERBACK, Jacob 73
VANCE, David 16,24,44
  James 16
  Sarah 24,44
  William 25,66,73,77

VANMETER, VANMETRE,
  Isaac 7
  John 7
  Solomon 80,122-126,139
VARLEY, VARLY,
  Catharine 3
  Jacob 3,37
  John 3
  Susanna 3
VESTAL, VESTALL,
  John 127
  William 127
VOLK, George 101,110
WAGGONER, A. 100
WALKER, Abel 43,84,92,93
  James 40,74,116,137
  Lewis 106,117,134
  Martha 43
  Mordicai 15,93,106
WALTON, Moses 140
WARE, James 52
WARNER, John 61
WASHINGTON,
  George 120
  Hannah 60
  John 61,131
  Warner 47,60,61
  Warner, Jun. 60
  Warner, Sen. 30
WATSON, Joseph 5,24,109
WAYMAN, Anne 56
  John 32,56,90
WEAKS, WEEKS, Ann 58
  Rachel 58
  Samuel 69
WEEKLEY, Elizabeth 50
  Thomas 50
WELSH, Thomas 140
WESANT, Joseph 69
WESLEY, John 131
WEST, Hugh 78
WETZELL, WITSEL,
  Christopher 39,112
WHITE, A. 7
  Agnes 67
  Alexander 2-4,19,65,81,96,
         117,129,133,138
  Ann 60
  Edward 3,47
  Elizabeth 2,60,81
  J. 48
  Jacob 67,68

WHITE, John 60,110
  Jost 3,28
  Major 60
  Michael 67,68
  Mordicai 4
  Robert 2,3,23,52,60,64
  Sarah 138
  Thomas 135
  Warmal 48
  William 67
WHITEHEAD, Edward 6,77
WHITEMAN, Edward 131
  Henry 131
WHITEMORE, David 108
WICKERSHAM,
  Samuel 114
WILEY, WILY,
  Allen 11,12,117,118,122,
         123,124,125,139
  Eve 139
WILKENSON, Joseph 2
  Mary 2,3
WILKES, WILKE,
  Isaac 49,57,58,76,105
  Jean 105
WILL, Lewis 12
WILLIAMS, Barnett 109,120
  Benjamin 4,18
  Elisha 23,25,27,41,52,
         100,118
  George 113
  Haz. 134
  James 120,121
  John 131
  John Swearingen 121
  Mary 120,121
  Roger 113
WILLIAMSON, Thomas 92
WILLIS, Richard, Jun. 61
WILLS, Lewis 14
WILSON, Galnala 16
  James 16,19,20,27,37,135
  Margery 16
  Mary 13,105
  Robert 13,16,129
  Robert, Jun. 104,105,129
  Robert, Sen. 105
  Thomas 21
WHITMAN, Andrew 37
WODROW, Andrew 65
WOLF, Lewis 35,105
WOLFE, Elizabeth 7

WOLFE, John 7
 Peter 7,16
WOMACK, William 4
WOOD, Col. 39,107
 Elizabeth 81
 James 1,4,34,38,40,58,81,
  112,120,132
 James, Jun. 110
 Joseph 87
 Mary 1,4,34,38,81,99,
  107,112,120,132
 Robert 4,18,32,81,120
 Thomas 1,16,99
 Zepheniah 22
WOODCOCK,
 John S. 42,52,112,118
WOOLVERTON,
 Andrew 37,38
 Sarah 38
WOOLWINE,
 Elizabeth 26,34,40,41
 Philip 1,25,26,32-34,40,
  41,54,77,128,129
WORTH, George 27,45,141
 John 45
WRIGHT, George 21
 James 36
 Jonathan 13,134
 Thomas 13,134
YARNALL, Mordicai 2
 Phebe 2
YATES, Charles 96
YEALY, Richard 44
YOUNG, Adam 142,143
 Edwin 102
 James 112
ZANE, Isaac 4,10,18,19,39,
  40,50,51,77,138
ZUBER, Daniel 67

THE END

Other Heritage Books by Amelia C. Gilreath:

Frederick County, Virginia Deed Book Series, Volume 1, Deed Books 1, 2, 3, 4: 1743-1758

Frederick County, Virginia Deed Book Series, Volume 2, Deed Books 5, 6, 7, 8: 1757-1763

Frederick County, Virginia Deed Book Series, Volume 3, Deed Books 9, 10, 11: 1763-1767

Frederick County, Virginia Deed Book Series, Volume 4, Deed Books 12, 13, 14: 1767-1771

Frederick County, Virginia Deed Book Series, Volume 5, Deed Books 15 and 16: 1771-1775

Frederick County, Virginia Deed Book Series, Volume 6, Deed Books 17 and 18: 1775-1780 Plus Early Troop Records 1755-1761

Frederick County, Virginia Deed Book Series, Volume 7, Deed Books 19 and 20: 1780-1785

Frederick County, Virginia Deed Book Series, Volume 8, Deed Book 21: 1785-1789

Frederick County, Virginia Deed Book Series, Volume 9, Deed Books 22 and 23: 1789-1793

Frederick County, Virginia Deed Book Series, Volume 10, Deed Books 24A and 24B: 1793-1796

Frederick County, Virginia Deed Book Series, Volume 11, Deed Books 25 and 26: 1796-1800

Page County, Virginia Will Books A, B, C and Deed Book A, 1831-1848

Shenandoah County, Virginia Abstracts of Wills, 1772-1850

Shenandoah County, Virginia Deed Book Series, Volume 1, Deed Books A, B, C, D: 1772-1784

Shenandoah County, Virginia Deed Book Series, Volume 2, Deed Books E, F, G, H: 1784-1792

Shenandoah County, Virginia Deed Book Series, Volume 3, Deed Books I, K, L: 1792-1799

Shenandoah County, Virginia Deed Book Series, Volume 4, Combination Minute Book 1774-1780 and Deed Books M and N: 1784-1792

Shenandoah County, Virginia Deed Book Series, Volume 5, Deed Books O, P, Q: 1804-1809

Shenandoah County, Virginia Deed Book Series, Volume 6, Deed Books R, S, T: 1809-1813

Shenandoah County, Virginia Deed Book Series, Volume 7, Deed Books U and V: 1813-1815

Shenandoah County, Virginia Deed Book Series, Volume 8, Deed Books W and X: 1815-1817

Shenandoah County, Virginia Deed Book Series, Volume 9, Deed Books Y and Z: 1817-1820

www.ingramcontent.com/pod-product-compliance
Lightning Source LLC
Chambersburg PA
CBHW081234170426
43198CB00017B/2755